The Adv

Living a   al media

Copyright © 2024 by Anna Alcott

All rights reserved. No part of this publication may be reproduced, stored or transmitted in any form or by any means, electronic, mechanical, photocopying, recording, scanning, or otherwise without written permission from the publisher. It is illegal to copy this book, post it to a website, or distribute it by any other means without permission.

First edition

Cover art by SelfPubBookCovers.com/ litberry

This book was professionally typeset on Reedsy. Find out more at reedsy.com

Contents

	Foreword	vi
1	The big move (1968)	1
2	Mrs Rostova	6
3	Tom & Gwen Carson	12
4	A Russian mystery	18
5	Holly	23
6	Italy	32
7	Franco	39
8	Venice	45
9	Beirut	51
10	Khalid	58
11	Adib	62
12	A Special Event	69
13	London	73
14	Alfredo	80
15	Amsterdam & Caracas	88
16	Rivisondoli Ski Resort	94
17	Newbury	102
18	Spain	107
19	The Bus Crash	113
20	An actor's life	118
21	Katherine	123
22	The Escort Service	128
23	Saudi Arabia	134

24	Ramadan, Hajj & Bedouins	139
25	Party time	145
26	Edmond	149
27	Arabian Nights	156
28	The Cairo Affair	163
29	Montreal	170
30	Ottawa	174
31	The Break up	180
32	Marilyn	185
33	The Travel Agent	191
34	Budapest	197
35	The Bahamas & Jamaica	202
36	The Countess	208
37	Toronto	213
38	Romance and Poetry	219
39	The yacht	226
40	The Crew	232
41	Life on the High Seas	238
42	Dry land at last	244
43	Captain Brian	249
44	Some Like it Hot	254
45	Richard	259
46	House sitting in Florida	266
47	Finally Legal	272
48	The Entertainment Industry	277
49	Human Trafficking	282
50	The Oscars	288
51	Hollywood	294
52	East Berlin	299
53	A Documentary	306
54	9/11 (2001)	310

55	Arizona	316
56	About the Author	321

Foreword

"We all have a Zoe Hunter in us, whether we realise it or not."

I had a strange déjà vu feeling after reading the book you are now holding in your hands, or viewing on a screen: Zoe, Ms Alcott's protagonist, strongly reminded me of Julia Roberts starring in *Eat, Pray, Love* – the 2010 film based on the homonym memoir written by Elizabeth Gilbert. Both narratives resonate deeply with the audience because they serve as accounts of the bravery it takes to break down a life that isn't fulfilling, and then reconstruct it, piece by piece, with honesty and self-exploration as the foundation. The young women's journeys are both deeply personal and profoundly relatable. They also try to find answers to fundamental questions: What happens when you lose your way? How do you rediscover yourself? And is it possible to truly find happiness?

The fifty-five adventures (and chapters) are not simple tales of escapism or brief voguish fads: *The Adventures of Zoe Hunter* is about the hard work required for self-awareness, the vulnerability of embracing new experiences, and the life-changing impact of engaging with diverse cultures. Infused with humor and deep insights, Ms Alcott's book serves as a kind reminder that self-discovery is a journey rather than a destination, and that very often, the most delicious and fulfilling life is rooted not in our possessions, but in our personal development; or, to paraphrase C.S. Lewis in his *The Four Loves:* "Do not let your happiness depend on something you may lose."

Do not expect to find a definitive guide to happiness within this book. Conversely, it contains something far more valuable: an invitation. An invitation to examine your own life with unwavering honesty, to listen to your heartbeats' jargon and translate their subtle whispers into intelligible idioms, and to boldly follow a path that resonates better with your authentic self. Zoe's journey is a reminder that this therapy works, that joy can be found even in the most unexpected places, and that sometimes, the most significant adventure lies in simply embracing the unknown.

I have always believed that a well-considered foreword should avoid revealing crucial details, significant plot twists, or spoilers of the book. For that reason, I tend to emphasize the significance of the book and bits of the author's background, rather than robbing the readers of the authentic pleasure and experience of discovering the story naturally, as its creator intended it. Therefore, although it may sound somewhat unorthodox, here we are today:

The book
Living a Life Before Social Media – this is certainly a thoughtfully selected subtitle for the book. Is Anna Alcott a nostalgic author? By no means, I would say. Making sense of the past doesn't mean rejecting the present but rather celebrating something uncontaminated, and it is important to better

understand the present and avoid making the same mistakes in the future. Nowadays, we inhabit an era where human lives are meticulously curated and shared through social media. *The Adventures of Zoe Hunter* transports us to a time when spontaneity and real-life experiences shaped the essence of one's life journey through a world unfiltered by digital means, and where decisions were taken with intuition rather than algorithms. If you like, you can consider the book as an ode to a generation that experienced the world without the safety net of instant communication. It is a celebration of self-reliance, human connection, and the courage to forge one's path. As you turn the pages, allow yourself to be immersed in the genuine essence of Zoe's world – a place where every experience is deeply felt, fully lived, and vividly remembered. Prepare yourselves to be moved, challenged, and inspired to embark on your own journey of self-exploration. Whether you are a seasoned adventurer, an aspiring artist, or someone simply longing for a taste of an unfiltered recent history, this book offers an invigorating and uplifting experience. Let lovely Zoe Hunter be your guide to a world where adventure is not merely documented, but actively experienced. Fasten your seatbelts and enjoy this unforgettable ride.

The author

Based on what I have read about Ms Alcott, it is clear to me that the story provides insights into her own life. Generally, novels originating from the author's personal past experiences can be particularly engaging due to their genuine authenticity, which helps make the settings and characters feel more real and occasionally even relatable. A well-known fact about Anna Alcott is that she had always had a fervent desire to travel, explore new places, and experience different cultures: after living in Blackpool and London, she relocated, lived, and worked in Italy, Spain, Lebanon, Saudi Arabia, the Bahamas, Jamaica, Canada, the US, then back to Cornwall, followed by Greece, and (for now) Portugal. There are no doubts left regarding the autobiographical elements in the book, when Zoe Hunter travels through thirteen different countries, which largely mirror the same places Anna Alcott did visit in her life. To a much greater extent, there is a *Zoe Hunter* in each of us, whether we realise it or not.

In 2020, Ms Alcott settled in Algarve (Portugal) and, since then, she has dedicated much of her time to writing, studying Portuguese, taking walks, socializing with friends, or simply keeping Pumpkin – her cat – company.

Has Zoe matured through her experiences? I sense a positive reflection mood in *Arizona*, the 55th (and last) chapter. And the book's closing line *"In the end, the greatest adventure often lies not in what we accomplish, but in recognizing when it's time to rest and start anew"* seems quite open-ended; at least for me it is obvious that the book does not wrap up with a firm conclusion but rather leaves Zoe facing future challenges. Is it possible that Ms Alcott is preparing a follow-up and trying to bring Zoe Hunter to the Algarve? I have a strong feeling that we shall hear about her again shortly.

Dan Costinas, the 11th of February 2025

(Former diplomat, Dan Costinas is a contemporary writer, essayist, aphorist, journalist, reviewer, and poet who has already authored, co-authored, translated, or edited several dozen books.)

1

The big move (1968)

Zoe Hunter sat in the train carriage, her heart racing with a blend of anticipation and nervousness. Travelling from the small northern town she had always called home; she was on her way to the bustling metropolis of London. Would she enjoy it? She was certain she would—life in Newlyn had grown dull. She would miss her brother, but tensions with her mother made leaving feel more like an escape than a sacrifice.

Inside the carriage, passengers were reading or sleeping while others stared out the window as the landscape unfurled like a cinematic panorama. As the train journeyed on, a sudden squeal of brakes pierced the air, jolting passengers from their various activities. The train slowed to a halt, but to Zoe's surprise, it wasn't at a scheduled station. Confusion rippled through the carriage as passengers exchanged puzzled glances. Then, over the crackling intercom, came the reassuring voice of the conductor, explaining there would be a slight delay. Zoe glanced away from the window, catching the flicker of unease in the passenger seated across from her. A crease deepened between her brows, and her fingers drummed nervously against the armrest as she looked at Zoe and asked, 'I didn't understand the announcement, did they say it was a signal malfunction or track maintenance?'

Zoe noticed the faint hint of a foreign accent and was curious of her origin, but too polite to ask. 'No, but I'm sure it's not serious,' replied Zoe in a reassuring tone. Despite her limited travel experience and less-than-ideal family life, she possessed a natural talent for comforting others.

The lady smiled warmly and expressed her gratitude. 'Thank you, my name is Natalya,' she said, her voice tinged with a hint of weariness.

'Pleased to meet you, my name is Zoe.'

'I'm feeling a bit tired. I've been on the train since seven this morning, all the way from Edinburgh, Scotland.'

Zoe nodded sympathetically, 'Heading to London, then?'

'Yes,' said Natalya, 'I'm going there to reunite with my family. I haven't seen them for over a year.'

'Well, I'm glad you're able to see them again, family is important' said Zoe sympathetically. A pang of guilt tugged at her for having left her mother and brother behind.

'Thank you for your kind words.'

'Would you like me to get you a tea or a coffee?' said Zoe.

'Thank you, but please excuse me, I need to take a nap.'

Zoe moved her 5'8" frame to a more comfortable position and swept back her long straight, dark chestnut hair. She glanced around the carriage. Amidst the hum of voices, she wondered about the stories that lay hidden behind the mask of polite conversation.

She relaxed and took the quiet time to ponder about what had brought her to this point in her life. She had spent the last twenty-two weeks of the summer working as a waitress and bartender at Pontins Holiday camp, in Blackpool. The city was livelier than her hometown and it had offered her a reprieve from the drudgery of the eighteen months office job she had endured after leaving school.

One of the drawbacks at Pontins had been her two roommates, Teresa and Mary.

'Well, who do we have here?' asked Mary, a short blonde girl with a heavy Scottish accent.

'My name is Zoe.'

Teresa joined them. Also, blonde but a little overweight. 'Who the fuck are you?' she squeaked.

At that moment Zoe felt like Cinderella and these two were her ugly sisters who would be her companions for the next 22 weeks. It was the start of an unhappy relationship. However, Zoe was a survivor, and these girls were not going to drag her down to their sad and sorry world. The word *fuck* was an essential part of their vocabulary. It was an adverb, an adjective, a verb, a noun and a ... well anything else you can use a grunt for.

Swearing and clothes shopping were the hallmarks of these rough and tumble ladies. They loved trying on dresses. Swearing wasn't in Zoe's DNA, but she gave in to their calls to shop. 'Come on shy Zoe, we're going shopping, are you fucking coming, or no?'

Zoe wanted to save every penny she earned, so she'd wander around while they did all the trying on and buying.

'This is fuck'n gorgeous, isn't it? It looks good on me.' said Mary.

'Really lovely,' said Zoe, crossing her fingers behind her back.

Back at the Pontins cabin, Zoe sat outside for some fresh air when she heard raucous laughter, so went inside to see what was so funny. Two dresses lay on the bed.

'I thought you decided not to buy anything,' said Zoe.

Hearty laughter once again. 'We didn't!'

Zoe then realised they had stolen them. Despite her light-fingered roommates, Zoe managed to stay on the straight and narrow, but their antics did toughen her up and teach her some street smarts.

However, even though Pontins was a whirlwind of hard work that had left her exhausted, there was one day in particular that stood out in Zoe's memory. It was the day she watched the dancers perform. In that moment, Zoe felt something shift inside her—a stirring of longing and inspiration that she couldn't ignore. It was then that she made the decision, to pursue her passion for dancing and turn it into a career. Hence her move to London.

With a sudden jerk, the train commenced on its journey. Zoe walked to the buffet bar for some refreshments, where she met two young men. From their conversation, she guessed they were Russian so spoke the only word she knew as they made way for her. 'Spasiba'

'Ah, you speak Russian? My name is Alexander.' Standing tall and slender, he possessed an air of quiet confidence that commanded attention. His piercing blue eyes, like shards of sapphire, pierced through her. His blonde hair framed his face with casual elegance.

'No. I only know how to say thank you.' said Zoe.

The other boy introduced himself as Nikolai. 'Okay, we speak English with you. We need learn.' Despite being slightly shorter in stature, he was more muscular and exuded a vitality. Like his counterpart, his eyes held the same mesmerizing shade of blue, and his hair, a darker hue of blonde was several inches longer.

'We need to learn,' corrected Zoe.

'You see, English lessons already,' said Nikolai.

They laughed and shared bacon sandwiches and British rail, tasteless tea all the way to London. To Zoe's delight, they offered her a sofa to crash on until she found a place of her own. This suggestion did not pose any problems for her as they were both not interested in women. She had just gained two brothers. They were originally from St. Petersburg and were in the UK studying acting. They said they lived in a cramped apartment in Notting Hill Gate, but they were still willing to help Zoe. One stop before reaching London Victoria Station, they returned to their seats.

Zoe thought about her own brother Jonathan. She felt a little guilty as he had to deal with Mother, who was not the easiest person to get along with. Jonathan was still a teenager but very mature for his fourteen years. Since Mother had divorced Father, life had been tough both mentally and financially for her.

2

Mrs Rostova

157 Bayswater Avenue was an old Victorian townhouse that the elderly owner, Mrs Rostova, kept from being repossessed by renting rooms out to young people, especially students. Zoe recognised the name from Natasha Rostova, a character portrayed in Leo Tolstoy's War and Peace novel, and she wondered if it were a common name? The house was decorated with classic Victorian furniture that had seen better days. As Alexander entertained Mrs. Rostova, Nikolai sneaked Zoe up to their room. Zoe's keen sense of smell never failed and the musty odour that greeted her as she had entered the house was no exception. It hung heavy in the air. But amidst the mustiness, she smelled a curious blend of exotic spices wafting from the old lady's kitchen. Nickolai commented in a whisper, 'She likes to cook old Russian recipes. She owned a restaurant before she arrive in UK.'

There were strict house rules and one of them was NO VISITORS. Old lady Rosto, as her new friends called her, was a bristly old aristocrat and kept a close eye on her tenants. Spot checks under plausibly, innocent enquiries were frequent and whenever she came knocking on the door, Zoe was obliged to dive into the wardrobe. She was slim and flexible so easily squeezed herself between the suitcases and winter coats. 'Allo,' Mrs. Rostova, would shout through the door. 'I thought I heard a women's voice!'

'No, don't be silly,' said Nikolai. 'We rehearse our show, you know, *Life's a Drag.*'

They all stifled their laughter until it brought tears to their eyes.

Coming and going was a real cloak and dagger event so after two weeks of avoiding the landlady, Zoe was grateful at finding a job in a pub. Thankful for those hard-working nights she had spent working in the pub at Pontins Holiday Camp.

The boys were sorry to see her leave and gave her a present. 'Open, when you get to new place,' said Nikolai, 'Now please wait here, we check where Old Lady is.'

Zoe put the gift in her suitcase that held her few belongings, then looked in a drawer for a plastic bag to carry a few snacks. Underneath some papers were two passports. She was curious to see how their pictures looked, and it also reminded her that she needed to apply for one, as a lot of the dance contracts were abroad. She peeked inside and gasped as both passports had different names to what they had given her. She quickly shoved them back in the drawer, grabbed her suitcase and opened the door. Nikolai had his fingers to his lips, 'Wait. Old lady go in kitchen.' Alexander went down and distracted Mrs Rostovo. With a subtle wave of his hand behind his back, Zoe quietly crept down the stairs to her waiting taxi. She turned and waved goodbye to the boys as the taxi pulled away.

As they drove by Hyde Park, Zoe marvelled at the tranquillity that enveloped the bustling city of London on a lazy Sunday afternoon. The traffic, typically a cacophony of noise and chaos, had quieted to a mere whisper. Londoners dotted the grassy expanse of the parks, basking in the rare moments of sunshine that graced their city, a respite from the hustle and bustle of urban life.

The taxi pulled up outside the Old Vic pub. It was a popular local, right next to the Old Vic Theatre. Zoe heard the distant chimes of Big Ben strike ten times. The owners, Mr and Mrs Hayley, had wanted her to arrive before opening to show her around the premises.

Entering a typical English pub in the late 1970s was like stepping into a time capsule of tradition. The interior had a cozy, lived-in charm, with wooden beams overhead and polished brass fixtures gleaming in the soft glow of dim lighting. The air was thick with the mingling scents of ale and tobacco smoke, which made Zoe cough slightly. Behind the bar, rows of beer pumps offered a selection of local ales and brews on tap, some of which Zoe had never heard of. Bottles of spirits lined the shelves, their colourful labels adding a splash of vibrancy to the rustic surroundings. Zoe wondered if she would ever learn to make all the different cocktails.

Mrs Hayley, the landlady met her and saw her worried look. 'Don't worry love, most of our customers drink beer and spirits, very few ask for fancy cocktails. They are usually served to the few tourists that stumble into our pub.'

'You have a lovely establishment, Mrs Hayley.'

'Thank you. We're not formal people so just call me Sonia.'

Zoe admired the crackling fire in one corner, which cast a warm, inviting glow.

'That corner is very popular on a damp evening in London,' said Sonia.

Wooden tables and chairs were arranged in clusters throughout the room, their surfaces worn smooth with years of use. Zoe stopped to read a huge poster on one wall advertising the upcoming shows at the theatre next door.

'We get a lot of the theatregoers, some very artsy fartsy,' said Sonia.

Zoe laughed at the typical English term as Sonia showed her to her room. She set down her belongings and looked around. The room was small and sparsely decorated, but she knew she wouldn't be spending much time there.

An hour later, Sonia asked Zoe if she could start work immediately. They unlocked the large wooden door and the already waiting patrons filed in. It was a pub for people who appreciated the simple pleasures of good company, good conversation, and a pint of ale in a quintessentially English setting.

On her first day, Zoe stood behind the bar and took her first order. 'Allo, you're new here, aren't you?' said a man with a thick head of brown wavy hair and dark framed glasses.

'Yes, I'm Zoe. I guess you must be a regular. What can I get you?'

'I'm Eddie. I'm here two or three times a week. Today is my wife's birthday so we're celebrating early.'

Early was true, thought Zoe. It´s not even noon.

'I'll have two pints, two gin and tonics, two vodka lime and six bags of crisps.'

'Will you be ordering lunch?' said Zoe.

'This is lunch,' said Eddie.

Zoe smiled and added up the order. Thank goodness she was good at mental arithmetic as there was no calculator available. The days that followed were punctuated by bursts of laughter and the clinking of glasses and slowly Zoe got to know all the regulars. Her favourite customer was Theodore, but he preferred to be called Ted. He was about seventy, smoked like a trooper and had a great sense of humour, his yellow teeth flashing when he laughed. He would sit in his usual seat and tease Zoe, while the other customers found it entertaining.

'I'll have a pint of your finest, please.' said Ted.

'Finest? You're in a pub, not Buckingham Palace. How about a pint of our 'won't knock you out till the third round' ale?' said Zoe.

'Sounds perfect. I'll take anything that doesn't taste like it was brewed in a bathtub.'

'Well, you're in luck. We save the bathtub brew for special occasions. Today you get the, *brewed in a slightly cleaner barrel*, special.'

'As long as it comes with a side of your charming service, I'll take it.'

'Flattery gets you everywhere, but it won't get you a discount. Here's your pint. Cheers!'

'Cheers! If my girlfriend comes in, I'll be ordering another round, if I survive this one.'

Zoe always wanted the last word as she said, 'I'll have the paramedics on standby!'

Nikolai and Alexander had visited the pub once but felt out of place. She also felt a little awkward as she thought about their passports but didn't know how to approach the subject. In her room she had placed their present, which was a cuddly Russian bear, on her bed among the decorative cushions.

The pay from the pub was ridiculous but she got food and lodgings and even got tips, just enough to pay for her dance classes. Though she may not have seen herself as conventionally stunning, the compliments from the customers flowed freely. She possessed a certain charm—a sweetness. Her hair was long and straight, never teased up like the popular style of the 60s. Her makeup consisted of black eyeliner and pale glossy lipstick. She had been compared to Joan Baez a couple of times, a compliment in her mind.

Her slight Northern accent made her a novelty in the bar, which drew a lot of attention to her and made her popular among the regulars. They always asked, 'So, you're not a Londoner, where are you from?'

'I'm from Newbury, a small town up north, a few miles from Newcastle.' And the response was usually the same. 'Great football team up there.' *Why were the Brits so enamoured with football? There was so much more to see up north, so much history.*

Mr. Arthur Hayley, the pub landlord, had a reputation for being overly friendly with the young female patrons. Balding and overweight, he gave Zoe the creeps. His unwanted advances soon targeted Zoe, attracting the attention of both the patrons and, more critically, his wife. After two months, a jealous Sonia unjustly fired Zoe.

Once again, Zoe found herself jobless, staring into an uncertain future. But inside, she was still young, energetic, and determined to succeed in life.

3

Tom & Gwen Carson

Zoe stayed in a cheap motel, armed with her hard-earned savings from her time at Pontins, a sum that felt substantial in those days. She wasn't comfortable calling her Russian friends. She wasn't sure what to think. Were they criminals or refugees? Until she had more time to talk with them, she would stay out of their way.

All week she scoured the newspapers and after looking at several unsuitable bedsits, finally found a room in a lovely house in Finsbury Park. The room was bigger than she had been given at the pub. The bed was comfortable, and there was a nightstand and an actual dressing table with a lighted mirror. Another big plus was the public phone booth nearby.

Zoe found herself enveloped in a warm and welcoming atmosphere, which made her feel like part of a family. The house was owned by a young couple, the Carsons. Tom Carson was a local lad, sporting a ragged red beard, who had married Gwen, a bubbly blonde girl from Wales. They had two adorable children, Curt and Becky, both of whom had red hair and as much energy as a pair of Duracell-powered bunnies. She now needed a job as her savings were going down fast. Each morning as Zoe left, the children would cry out, 'Goodbye Zooey. See you.' It put a huge smile on Zoe's face as she made her way out the door. The location was ideal, with easy access to the Dance Centre via a short tube ride. Three days later, she secured an office job just a short bus ride and two tube stops away from her bedsit. The work was mundane — mostly printing and copying files for the senior staff. The most frustrating part was changing the ink, which often left Zoe's hands and clothes stained, so she requested a company overall to protect her clothing. Despite the job's tedium, it provided the financial stability she needed to continue her dance lessons.

She sent postcards to her mother, her long-time childhood friend Dot and her two Russian friends, letting them know her new address.

Despite the distance from her mother, Zoe sent part of her salary back home out of a sense of duty. Their relationship was often fraught with tension, leading to many arguments. Yet beneath the surface, Zoe understood her mother's bitterness; she felt abandoned when her father had died from alcohol poisoning. Zoe was ten and her brother Jonathan was six. Though obviously not a perfect husband, he had provided enough for them to have clothes on their backs and food on the table. So, Zoe assumed her mother married her stepfather for security, as he was neither handsome nor wealthy. However, as time went on, her mother realized she had made a mistake. The marriage only lasted four years as her stepfather was mentally abusive to Zoe's mother and never spent time with Zoe or her brother.

Over the course of six months, Zoe went to dance classes four times a week – Ballet, jazz and tap. Zoe's bubbly personality often led her to engage in lively conversation, sometimes perhaps even talking a bit too much. However, despite her warmth and sociability, Zoe couldn't shake the feeling of isolation when her dance colleagues never extended invitations to socialize outside of class. This left her feeling somewhat overlooked and lonely. She was able to make a weekly phone call to her school friend Dot, just to chat. Dot always made her laugh.

One day, after a ballet class, Zoe met James McDonald. He was black, a brilliant tap dancer and Scottish. He came over to Zoe and said, 'Hello, would you like to join us for a drink?' He had class and a refined accent.

'Thanks. That would be lovely,' said Zoe surprised. She didn't have much money left over after her bills but spending 25 pence on a pint of beer and 7 pence on a bag of crisps was worth it. Most of the dancers were broke as dance lessons proved to be expensive. Eventually, Zoe and James became good friends and with his focused attention, her tap dancing improved immensely. Zoe loved the music and the rhythm. It gave her much more pleasure than ballet, or was it just a little easier?

Their favourite hangout was the Dance Centre in South London. It was held in a huge warehouse type of building and always felt cold until they finished a strenuous class. Afterwards, they would sit and drink hot coffee and smoke a cigarette. Ah, the seventies, even dancers smoked, and Zoe wanted to fit in so she would have an occasional cigarette but never inhaled deeply. Not only was it cool, but the story had it that Dame Margot Fonteyn, the legendary ballerina and possibly the greatest dancer of her generation, was a heavy smoker and she was still performing in her 50s.

On her day off, James suggested they tour London together. He was from Scotland and had not done the tourist thing as he didn't want to explore the city alone.

The morning sunbathed the streets of London in a golden glow as Zoe and James stepped off the number nine bus. First stop breakfast. They wandered over to Borough Market, a bustling haven of food stalls and fresh produce. Normally there would be the aroma of freshly baked bread and pastries, but the nation's bakers had decided to switch off their ovens and join the picket lines in search of a 66 per cent rise in pay. Slightly disappointed, they each ordered a steaming cup of tea and buttered toast.

'Where to next?' James asked, as he wiped his mouth with a napkin.

'How about the Tower of London?' Zoe suggested, her eyes twinkling with excitement.

A short tube ride later, they arrived at the historic fortress. The ancient stone walls loomed above them, whispering tales of the past. They joined a guided tour, led by a charismatic Beefeater who regaled them with stories of treachery and intrigue.

Zoe whispered to James, 'Do you know where the name Beefeater originated?'

'No, but I'm sure you're going to tell me.' He knew what a curious mind Zoe had and was constantly looking up words in the dictionary or an encyclopedia.

'It literally means, a well-fed servant, usually the ones that served the kings.'

After the tour, they strolled along the River Thames, enjoying the view of the iconic Tower Bridge. The sun had risen higher, casting a shimmering reflection on the water. James had a camera, so they paused to take a few photos.

Next, they headed towards the heart of the city. A leisurely walk brought them to Covent Garden, a vibrant district filled with street performers, boutique shops, and charming cafes. Zoe's attention was caught by a small antique shop. She pulled James inside, where they spent a half-hour browsing through an eclectic collection of vintage jewellery, old books, and quirky trinkets. Zoe purchased a delicate silver necklace, which she couldn't afford but wanted a memento of their adventure. They passed a local cinema where "Blazing Saddles" was playing. 'Next trip, I will treat to a film. Hope that one is still playing as it's supposed to be hilarious.' said James.

'I have only seen "The Sound of Music", in a cinema, said Zoe.

'Also,' added James, 'there's a new place opened I'd like to check out. I think it's called McDonalds, but I don't think it's from Scotland- probably America.'

'Talking of food, I'm ready for a quick lunch.' Zoe admitted with a grin.

They enjoyed a leisurely lunch of spaghetti and wine and sat back to relax.

'My feet are starting to hurt,' said Zoe, 'I think it's time to call it a day. I've had so much fun today James, thank you.'

'Me too.' he said, 'We must do it again soon.'

As Zoe's dancing skills improved, her confidence as a person grew. However, going on auditions was still scary, but in time she realised she was nearly as good as anyone else there and would improve over time. To earn more money, Zoe started

Gogo dancing at various pubs and clubs. Her friend Eileen from her day job was born and bred in London so knew her way around. She was a witty and bubbly girl, and they enjoyed many laughs together. Eileen would be with Zoe on every gig. She would go check out the venue, and on some would say, 'You're not dancing in there. It's a real dive.'

Many times, on their tube rides home, they would encounter strange people. When they were confronted by men exposing themselves, Zoe and Eileen would point to the man's penis and burst out laughing. That trick always worked.

Zoe applied for a passport, but they needed a full copy of her birth certificate, which she didn't have or had ever seen. She wrote to the General registry office up north and received a copy within five days. She studied it. She was only ten when her father had died, so didn't have a lot of fond memories of him. Zoe wondered if he had any siblings. Maybe she had an aunt or an uncle somewhere? Maybe one day she would find out how to research long lost families. Now she was ready to complete her application for her passport.

.

4

A Russian mystery

Zoe flopped on her bed, nestling against two pillows that propped her up comfortably. She flipped open her latest Agatha Christie novel. She loved to read and immerse herself into a good story, especially mysteries. She knew one day she would write a book, maybe two, as writing had been her passion since her school days.

A knock on the brought her back to reality. It was Tom. 'You have a visitor,' he said, 'A bit strange looking. A foreigner, I think.'

Zoe thought it must be Alexander or Nikolai. She walked to the front door and out to the garden gate. A burly man stood in front of her. He looked around and then said hello.

'Hello,' she said warily as she didn't recognise him. 'Who are you?'

'I am a friend of Alexander. I went to the old lady's house, but she said she didn't know where he was.'

'So, how did you find me?'

The man looked at Zoe, 'I found a card with your address on it.'

'But if Alexander wasn't there, who let you in his room?' asked a worried Zoe.

'Look lady, I don't have time for this. Where is he, and his friend?' he said, grabbing Zoe's arm.

'Let go of me,' she screamed. At which point Tom came running down the path. 'I think you'd better be going,' he growled.

The man turned and took off. 'Shall I call the police,' asked Tom.

'No. I just don't know who he is or what he wanted with my friends.'

'Come inside. Gwen's just made a pot of tea.'

As they sat sipping the hot brew, Zoe mentioned how her friend's names differed from their passports. 'I don't know if they are criminals or illegal immigrants, but in either case, I am worried. I think I should go see if they have returned home.'

'I'll drive you there,' said Tom.

The evening air was chilly, so Zoe reached for her coat and scarf before slipping into Tom's 1965 VW Beetle. The vintage car, resplendent in a soft shade of blue, was well maintained inside and out, despite the demands of his two children.

Zoe knocked on the door of the boarding house while Tom waited in the car. The door was slightly ajar, which was unusual as Mrs Rostova always kept it locked. Zoe beckoned Tom to join her, and they walked quietly inside. She called out, 'Mrs Rostova. Are you there?'

They walked to the kitchen and gasped when they saw her lying on the floor. Zoe's heart was beating too fast as she felt the old lady's pulse. 'I think she's just unconscious, call an ambulance please,' she told Tom.

Tom looked around for the phone and quickly dialled 999. While they waited, Zoe ran upstairs but the boys had gone – so had their belongings.

Tom and Zoe followed the ambulance to St Ann's hospital. Zoe gave the only information she had to the nurse and then joined Tom in the waiting room. Why were the waiting rooms in hospitals so stark with uncomfortable seats and bright fluorescent lights? Zoe asked herself. Thirty minutes passed before the doctor came over and said that Mrs Rostova was conscious, but they were keeping her overnight in case she had concussion. He asked Zoe if she knew what had happened.

'No, sorry Doctor. I went to visit a couple of her tenants.'

'Is it possible to talk to them?' asked the Doctor.

'No. I'm afraid they had already left. I will come back tomorrow and escort Mrs Rostova home, if that's okay. I don't think she has any relatives here.'

Zoe and Tom drove home in silence, each in their own thoughts.

The following day Tom kindly drove Zoe back to the hospital. As they entered Mrs Rostova's room, she was sitting on the bed with a small bandage on her forehead. She looked up and said, 'Who are you? What do you want?'

Zoe walked over to her and said, 'I am a friend of Alexander and Nikolai. I went to see them yesterday and that's when I found you. But they were gone. Do you know where they went and why?'

'No, big man come looking for those two bad boys and then he hit me.'

Zoe and Tom looked at each other. 'Maybe it's the same man

who paid you a visit yesterday,' whispered Tom.

Zoe nodded her head, her face shadowed with concern. They drove Mrs Rostova home. When they helped her inside, Zoe asked if she could look in the boy's room.

'Why not? Please lock up after.' She gave her a key and Zoe ran up the stairs, but the key wasn't needed. The door had been forced open. She scanned the room but didn't see anything until she caught a glimpse of an envelope on the dresser. She picked it up. To her surprise, the envelope bore her name, already neatly addressed and adorned with a stamp. She tucked it in the back pocket of her jeans, locked the door and went back downstairs.

'I am sorry Mrs Rostova, but the door has been damaged. Here is the key.'

'Another expense,' said Mrs Rostova, and then something in Russian, which sounded a bit like swearing from the tone of her voice.

'Can I get you anything Mrs Rostova?'

'No,' she replied, 'You very kind.'

'Okay,' said Zoe, 'Please call me if you need anything and handed her a piece of paper with Tom's phone number.'

Obviously, the boys had no idea what had happened to their landlady. As Tom drove her back to the house, Zoe discreetly read the letter:

Dear Zoe,

Someone we didn't want to see come looking for us. He is my uncle and works for KGB. He forced my father to tell him where we were. Please do not worry, we not criminals. My uncle does not like I am gay. Homosexual acts were decriminalized but being openly gay is still not widely accepted. My uncle wants me to return so he can straighten me out. (Excuse the pun.) We leave today to go

California. We hope to see you again. We write you.
p.s. Hope you like gift.
Love Alex and Nick.

She assumed they meant the toy bear they had given her. It was an adorable gift and reminded her of them. Zoe regretted that she hadn't reached out to her friends to enquire about their well-being. Perhaps if she had, she could have offered support or assistance in whatever they were facing. However, Zoe recognized her own reticence when it came to sharing her personal problems, which might have inadvertently discouraged them from confiding in her. She read the letter again and smiled to herself. She couldn't help but notice the remarkable improvement in their English skills after only a few lessons.

At home, Zoe gathered around the crackling fire with the family, the warm glow casting a comforting embrace over the room. They drank hot tea and devoured a packet of chocolate digestives biscuits. Zoe shared the contents of her letter.

'Russia isn't the only place that stigmatizes gays,' Tom remarked with a tinge of sadness in his voice. 'I have a few homosexual friends, and they've shared some truly awful stories about their experiences.'

'In my dance classes, there are a few individuals, and they're some of the most vibrant and fun-loving people I know,' Zoe interjected, her voice filled with empathy.

5

Holly

Zoe stood at the bar and tried to get the bartender's attention away from the radio. The football results were coming in and he, and probably along with thousands of others listened to see if they had won the football pools. It was early afternoon, so not many customers had arrived. She tapped on the bar to get his attention. 'I need a double scotch, please.'

He looked at her in surprise. 'You look more like a wine drinker.'

She rolled her eyes, 'I am, but I'm going to a dance audition, and a strong drink will help calm my nerves.'

'Coming right up,' he said pouring what looked more like a triple.

She knocked it back in two gulps, then walked into the intimidating building where the audition was being held. Stepping into the room adjacent to the stage of the Old Vic Theatre, Zoe couldn't help but feel a sense of awe. The walls seemed to whisper tales of performances past. The ceilings soared high above her, casting a shadowy veil over the room, while the sound of her footsteps echoed in the cavernous expanse. In the dressing room, anticipation hung in the air as ten hopeful young women stood, each one eager for the opportunity that lay ahead. They exchanged nervous smiles as they changed into their dance wear. Zoe couldn't help but notice the conspicuous displays of wealth among some of the other girls, their expensive outfits and accessories standing in stark contrast to her own modest attire. It was evident that some had invested more money in their dance clothes than Zoe likely earned in an entire week. Despite this observation, she remained undeterred, her focus unwavering as she prepared to showcase her talent.

Standing before the panel of judges, Zoe felt a surge of nervous energy course through her veins. 'Okay, ladies, please state your names,' ordered the choreographer.

With a steady breath, Zoe announced her name, alongside the other hopefuls. They awaited instructions from the choreographer, who stood poised to lead them through their audition. As the music began to play the choreographer demonstrated the steps. Zoe's mind sprang into action. Though she may not have been the most formally trained dancer, her extraordinary memory served as her greatest asset, allowing her to absorb and recall each movement with remarkable precision. The choreographer restarted the music and yelled, 'five, six, seven, eight'

Zoe threw herself into the routine. This was a chance to prove herself. The ten-minute dance felt like an eternity. The music ended and the choreographer said, 'Well done ladies.'

They all exited and gathered in the changing room; the air thick with tension. With trembling hands, they hastily shed their dance attire and dressed back into everyday clothes as they awaited the verdict. The head judge came out and read aloud. Emotions ran high among the dancers, with tears of joy and disappointment mingling in the air. Zoe didn't get accepted. Seated on the bench, her heart heavy with disappointment, she processed the sting of rejection. She couldn't help but steal glances at the other girls who shared in her disappointment, their faces exhibiting the sense of defeat.

Would she ever be good enough? Could she truly make her dreams a reality, or were they destined to remain out of reach forever. As she brushed away her tears and lifted her head high, Zoe vowed to herself not to give up, determined to prove to the world that no setback could extinguish her dreams.

'Hi.'

A tall thin girl with brown eyes and blonde hair, an unusual combination, stood beside her. 'Hi,' replied Zoe.

'My name is Holly. I didn't get accepted either. Do you feel like going for a drink?'

'Sure,' said Zoe, surprised that someone actually came over to talk to her. She had noticed the girl earlier, as she was a bit of a loner, and she had watched her dance. She was very good, so Zoe was surprised that she hadn't been chosen. They grabbed their belongings and on Zoe's suggestion went to the Old Vic Pub. 'I used to work there, so I'm sure there will be a couple of regulars willing to buy us a drink.'

'Now that would make my day, because I'm broke right now. My parents won't let me touch my trust fund unless I give up dancing and get a real job.' Holly said, making quotation marks with her fingers.

Despite Holly's comment, Zoe couldn't help but admire her appearance—her expensive jeans and stylish top spoke volumes about her taste and upbringing. Coupled with her refined accent, reminiscent of the halls of Oxford or Cambridge

University, she presented an image of sophistication and privilege. Normally a posh accent intimidated Zoe a little. She didn't have a strong northern accent but enough for her to stand out in a crowd. However, Holly made her feel at ease. Toting their dance gear, they walked over to the pub. They sat at the bar and immediately drinks were sent over to them. Two gin and tonics. Zoe turned and raised her glass in a silent toast to the one regular she recognised, Ted. He was looking a little more tired than she remembered.

'Hey, Ted, thanks. How are you doing?'

'Well, look who it is! If it isn't my favourite troublemaker,' he replied.

'Me? Never! I leave all the mischief to you.' Zoe took a big gulp of the gin and continued, 'Ted, did you always have that many grey hairs or are they new?'

'Oh, these? They're wisdom highlights, Zoe. You'll get them too, someday.'

'I'll stick to my highlights from a bottle, thanks. By the way, this is my friend Holly.'

'You actually got a friend?'

'We've been friends for years,' said Holly, holding back her laughter at this banter.

Ted laughed and turned back to his friends.

'You used to work here?' said Holly.

'Yes, when I first moved to London.'

'It must have been a lot of fun, especially with customers like him. Why did you leave?'

Zoe looked around and said, 'You see that bald headed gent over there?'

Holly turned to look and said, 'You mean that creep who's flirting with that young girl?'

'That's the one. He's the landlord and he has a very jealous wife. He got a little overly friendly with me, and his wife didn't like it, so fired me.'

'Jeez,' said Holly laughing, 'If I was married to that, I'd be glad he was keeping his hands off me.'

Zoe almost spluttered her drink as she laughed out loud.

She thought back to her childhood. She had been a nervous, shy child, but she discovered that she had a sense of humour, which she used to mask her insecurities. Being with Holly inspired her, and once again, Zoe's own humour resurfaced.

As the night wore on and the drinks flowed freely, Holly's reserved demeanour melted away, revealing a sharp wit and a tongue as quick as lightning. The two of them were like a circus act or maybe like Morecombe and Wise. With each sip of their cocktails, their sarcasm became more pronounced. The patrons couldn't help but be entertained as they effortlessly turned even the most mundane topics into comedy gold. Holly's sensuality emanated effortlessly, as if woven into the very fabric of her being. As the evening progressed, Holly's wit sharpened, proving that alcohol didn't dull her senses; it merely uncorked her comedic genius. They heard someone singing happy birthday, so Holly looked over and saw a cake covered in candles and quipped, 'You know you're getting old when the candles cost more than the cake.'

As time went by, the alcoholic drinks kept on coming, which helped erase their disappointment from the rejection of the audition. Despite their different backgrounds and circumstances, Zoe found a kindred spirit in Holly. Zoe's tummy rumbled, 'Let's order some food. I'm starving.'

'What do you suggest?' said Holly, perusing the menu.

They both decided on fish and chips. The portion was huge,

but they devoured every morsel. They said goodbye to their new and old friends and stood by the door waiting for their taxis home, which neither of them could afford, but it was the only way, as neither of them could stand up straight. Before the taxis arrived, Zoe asked Holly, 'By the way my last name is Hunter. What's yours?'

'Hollywood,' stammered Holly.

'Hol, Hollywood," exclaimed Zoe, 'Holly Hollywood? What were your parents thinking?'

Holly laughed. 'No, my name is Victoria Siobhan Hollywood. I don't like Victoria, and no one can pronounce my middle name, so I go by Holly.'

In Zoe's half drunken state, she looked at Holly and said, 'I've never heard that last name before.'

'Most people haven't,' continued Holly, 'It's an old Irish name. My great, grandfather emigrated from Ireland to the US, and no one could pronounce his last name, so as he worked in the film industry, he changed it to Hollywood. My mother never liked the US, so she emigrated to England when she married my father.'

The taxis arrived. 'You must tell me more sometime,' said Zoe.

'Sure, here's my phone number of where I'm staying,' she said, handing a piece of paper to Zoe.

'You have a phone?'

'Oh, no. It's a public phone in the hallway that all the tenants share.'

Zoe woke up at 6 a.m, her head throbbing and her dry mouth clamouring for refreshment. As she downed a huge glass of tap water, she noticed a note under her door. It was from her landlord Tom. *Was it bad news?* She opened it slowly. It was from the company she had auditioned for yesterday. As Zoe read it, a broad smile stretched across her face. Was she still interested in the position? *Hell yeah!* The company had decided on six dancers instead of four. She dressed quickly, grabbed the piece of paper with Holly's number on it and went to the phone booth. 'Damn, it's bloody broken,' she mumbled to herself. She went back in the house and asked Tom if she could use his phone. She called Holly. No answer.

An hour later, still trembling with excitement and disbelief, Zoe held a pen in her shaking hand, poised over the Equity contract spread before her. For Zoe, this was not just a job—it was an opportunity to spread her wings and soar, to dance across the stages of Europe - well at least Italy. The dance troupe paid fifty pounds a week – a healthy salary in the seventies – and included accommodation. On her way out, she bumped into Holly. 'Please tell me you also got accepted.'

'Yeah. Just glad we didn't have to do another audition as my bloody head hurts.'

'Mine too,' said Zoe, 'I'm excited that we will be together.'

'We'll see about that,' replied Holly, 'I can be a little obnoxious at times.'

'Okay, I gotta go. See you in rehearsals,' said Zoe hardly able to contain her excitement. As she was leaving, she saw Natalya, the lady that she had met on the train when she had travelled down from the north. 'Hello, Natalya,' said Zoe.

Natalya turned and said, 'Hello, how are you?'

'I'm very excited as I was accepted for the contract in Italy.'

'Good. Don´t let me down,' she said and continued on her way.

Zoe wondered what she had meant by that. The choreographer who was standing close by said to Zoe, 'That goes for me too.'

'I'm sorry,' said Zoe confused, 'Who was that?'

'That lady is one of the best dance teachers in town and she put in a good word for you.'

Zoe gasped and thought that kind words did pay off after all. She smiled and leaned against the wall as she waited for the public phone to be free. The first person she called was Eileen, who had covered for her at the office.

'That's great news,' said Eileen, 'But I am going to miss you – a lot.'

'It's only for six months. I'm coming in to work so I can hand in my notice as rehearsals begin next week.'

The last day of work Eileen and Zoe went out for a farewell drink. She would miss Eileen too, but reminded her, 'You have a boyfriend now, so that should keep you busy.' Eileen gave a sheepish smile and lifted her left hand. 'Oh my God,' said Zoe, 'You're engaged. Congrats!' Zoe ordered two glasses of champagne to celebrate.

Two strenuous weeks were spent rehearsing alongside Holly and four other girls. Hazel, Michelle, Suzi and Andrea, each with their own distinct personalities and quirks. Hazel, with her radiant blonde hair and bubbly demeanour, immediately struck a chord with Zoe and the two of them quickly became friends. Michelle with her striking beauty and confident presence, exuded an air of poise and grace that commanded attention and Andrea, sporting dark-rimmed glasses, carried herself with an air of quiet mystery and Suzi, pale skinned with long black hair, definitely stood out as the most intellectual of them all.

Gathered in the bustling lounge of Heathrow airport, they all stood among the throng of travellers, waving goodbye to their respective loved ones. Zoe had no-one and neither did Holly. Zoe had called her brother to let her mother know the good news. She watched the scene in front of her. It was just a six-month contract, but apparently her fellow dancers had never been apart from their families that long before. Personally, she wouldn't miss England. She had always felt more European.

6

Italy

Two hours and seventeen minutes later, the plane made a smooth landing at Fiumicino airport in Rome. It was late October but still pleasantly warm, accompanied by a slight breeze. They lugged their heavy suitcases from the baggage claim out to the door where they met up with the choreographer, a bald headed, muscular, black man called Ben Johnson. His slender, blonde wife Dana and her black poodle, Dulcinea, were with him. Dulcinea sniffed Zoe's hand, then licked it. Zoe fell in love with it instantly and the two of them stayed close for the rest of the time there.

Hazel and Zoe watched as Michelle and Andrea sought Ben´s attention, while Holly and Suzi dozed off. Ben's wife Dana seemed oblivious to the attention her husband was getting, or maybe she was used to it, and sat in the back of the company van, between Hazel and Zoe. It was about an hour and a half to the village, *Soriano Nel Cimino* so Dana amused them with her stories about the time she had been a ballerina in a professional American ballet company.

Once settled in their modest rooms at the *pensione,* Zoe was determined to learn the language. Her first Italian phrase was *svegliami alle otto* – please wake me up at 8am.

Zoe woke before her alarm call, with the smell of coffee coming from the kitchen. The others weren't up so she joined the *Senora* for a coffee, who insisted on talking to her in Italian. *Doesn't she realise I don't speak the lingo?* She said *grazie* and set off to explore the village. Through her wanderings she came across a small jewellery shop and walked inside. She was excited as she purchased a matching ring and bracelet. It was the first time she could afford such small luxuries. After a couple of hours walking up many hilly areas and enjoying a delicious lunch, she'd had enough, so returned to her room for a siesta before that night's show.

In the dressing room, the girls were getting ready without much enthusiasm.

'Where did you go today?' asked Holly.

'I took the time to explore the village and treated myself to some jewellery,' said Zoe showing off her newly acquired bracelet and ring.

'Let's go out after the show tonight, as I'm already feeling bored,' said Holly.

'Five minutes,' called the stage manager.

The first club was a bit of a shock. Dark and dingy, smelling of stale wine.

'What a dump. What have we got ourselves into?'

'Come on Holly, lighten up,' said Zoe.

'I will not,' said Holly, 'I have a good mind to jump on the next plane home.'

She stormed off to prepare for the first number. It was a lively jazz piece, and their attire consisted of sleek black jumpsuits with a daring split on one leg. Their vibrant red wigs, though uncomfortable due to being tightly pinned in place, added a striking flair to their ensemble. Despite the discomfort, Zoe and Holly embraced the routine with gusto, pouring their hearts into each step and movement. The second number featured a chain mail-like head dress that hinted a potential danger if they moved too abruptly. Afterwards Ben and Dana performed a beautiful duet. This evening the sparse and inattentive crowd prompted the troupe to cut their set short, performing only four numbers before calling it a night, glad they didn't have to perform the final number, which boasted a cumbersome headpiece

Afterwards, the troupe sat at a table relaxing and observing the customers. 'The patrons don't smell much better than the old carpets,' said Holly, 'They weren't even watching the performance. Why do we bother?'

Hazel and Zoe laughed. 'We did get a few whistles,' said Hazel. 'Let's celebrate just being in this wonderful country with a few glasses of cheap champagne.'

Ben came over smiling. 'Well done ladies. However, we will have to rehearse a new number tomorrow. This manager wants more skimpy costumes.'

'I guess, we'll have to go out another night as we need to rehearse the new bloody number tomorrow morning.' said Holly.

As they sat savouring their drinks, engrossed in lively conversation, their evening took an unexpected turn when a waitress approached, extending an invitation to join some other customers.

'Sorry, darling,' Holly replied with a wry smile. 'We're here strictly for the dancing, nothing more.' With a playful gesture, she said, 'Let those gentlemen know that we're not in the business of providing any extra services,' making quotation marks when she said gentlemen.

With that said, they swiftly finished their drinks and gracefully exited the club. It wasn't uncommon in certain establishments in Italy to blur the lines between dancers and escorts, but Zoe and her companions made it clear that they were not escorts.

A week passed by slowly. They gave the manager what he asked for. Skimpy costumes. Ben's wife had stitched dyed chicken feathers to bikinis and Ben gave them a simple routine to learn.

'There must be a lot of bald chickens running around,' said Holly.

After performing that particular number, it inevitably resulted in the stage looking like a back kitchen might, after ten chickens had been plucked for an evening meal.

'Well,' said Zoe looking at the pile of feathers, 'Maybe they can stuff some pillows, or something.'

'Oh, please, not another comedienne,' complained Andrea. 'It's bad enough having to listen to Holly's pathetic jokes.'

Zoe grabbed Holly before an argument ensued. 'Come on, let's get out of here. I need a drink badly.'

Their next venue was on the beach. The sun was shining but the temperature was bearable. It was a makeshift stage, and it didn't look safe at all. After their third number, Ben called them back as he could see the stage was about to collapse. Zoe was glad to be with Hazel and Holly. They saw the humour in it all, while the other girls constantly complained. They returned to the dressing room while Ben spoke to the crew in charge, then turned to the girls.

'Sorry ladies, that's it for now. Good news is you have some free time.'

It was early evening, so Zoe, Holly and Hazel started dancing in the sand for fun and were joined by the local children. After a quick swim they headed back to their *pensione*, happy that they had a free evening.

Zoe and Holly strolled through the quaint streets of the small Italian town, the cobblestones beneath their feet echoed with each step, they passed by charming cafes and colourful storefronts. The warm Mediterranean sun cast a golden glow over the picturesque scene. They spotted a cozy local bar, so pushed open the heavy wooden door and stepped inside. They were greeted by the lively chatter of locals and the inviting scent of freshly brewed coffee. They were welcomed with warm smiles from the *Barista* and fellow patrons. Zoe and Holly ordered two espressos, eager to indulge in the authentic Italian experience.

'Oh God,' said Zoe, 'I can't drink this. It's way too strong.' The barista laughed as she returned it to the counter and made her a *latte*, without charging her extra.

'Let´s find a wine bar. I want to try some local wine.' said Holly.

'Perfect idea,' agreed Zoe, adjusting her sunhat. 'This town is like a postcard come to life.'

As they turned a corner, they nearly bumped into two young men who were deep in conversation. The taller of the two, with curly dark hair and an infectious smile, immediately stepped back and apologized.

'*Mi dispiace, signorine,*' he said, switching to English with ease. 'We didn't see you.'

'No problem,' Holly replied, smiling back. 'We were just looking for a place to have a drink. Do you know a good spot?'

The shorter of the two, with striking blue eyes and an easy grin, stepped forward. 'Yes, we do! We were heading to our favourite *enoteca*. Would you like to join us?'

Zoe glanced at Holly, who gave a slight shrug and a nod. 'Sure, why not? We're always up for meeting new people.'

'Wonderful!' the taller one said. 'I'm Marco, and this is Alessandro.'

'I'm Holly and this is Zoe.'

'What's an *enoteca*?' said Zoe.

Marco smiled and explained. 'It refers to a special type of local or regional wine shop that allows visitors to taste and purchase wines at reasonable prices.'

'Sounds great,' said Zoe.

The *enoteca* they arrived at was quaint and inviting, with rustic wooden tables and shelves lined with bottles of local wine. Marco found them a table on the terrace, offering a breathtaking view of the sun setting over the vineyards. A waiter soon appeared, and Marco expertly ordered a selection of wines and antipasti for the table.

'So, what brings you to our beautiful country?' Alessandro asked, pouring the first glass of wine.

'We are . . .' started Zoe, but Holly interrupted.

'We are here on a short holiday.'

Zoe gave Holly a quizzical look.

'Where are the toilets, we must wash our hands,' asked Holly.

In the bathroom, Zoe asked, 'What was that about?'

'Well,' said Holly, 'We don't want them thinking we are escorts, and we can just give them a phony hotel name. You know, just to be safe.'

As the evening progressed, they enjoyed the delicious wine

and shared plates of bruschetta, olives, and cheeses. Marco and Alessandro were charming hosts, their lively stories and passionate descriptions of their homeland making the experience even more enchanting.

Eventually, the waiter brought the bill, and Marco insisted on treating them. 'It's our pleasure,' he said with a smile. 'We are happy to share our love for our town with you.'

'*Grazie mille*,' Zoe said sincerely. 'You've made our evening unforgettable.'

'Perhaps we can meet again before you leave?' Alessandro suggested. 'There is so much more to see and taste.'

'We'd love that,' Holly replied.

'Here is my number,' said Marco, '*Buona notte*, ladies.'

7

Franco

During the rest of the time in Italy, other inside venues sometimes had only three or four patrons, eyeing the group through their drunken stupor. But this was show-business and no matter what, the show went on. Despite the seedy venues and disappointing turnouts, the troupe put everything into their performance and imagined they were performing to a packed house in Milan's La Scala Opera Theatre.

They took advantage of any free time to hone their craft. Dana, a former professional ballerina was more than qualified to give lessons, so they practiced with her each morning. She was tough on them, but they learnt a lot.

On a free day, Hazel and Zoe explored the wonderful sights of a village called Vernazza, one of the beautiful Cinque Terre villages with colourful houses and a small harbour. They had invited Holly and her response was, 'Seen one village, seen them all.'

Zoe thought Holly must be depressed, especially with her excessive drinking, and was sure she went on stage a little drunk each night. She was worried. She asked Holly if something was wrong, but the answer was always the same: 'I'm bored.'

In this part of Italy, even the smallest villages had beautiful churches and buildings from another era, although many were crumbling from neglect. However, this town had been well looked after.

Zoe once again, the information gatherer held a brochure in her hand and said to Hazel, 'This town is a lot different to the ones we've seen. It is renowned for its vibrant, pastel-coloured houses, narrow streets and a small, charming harbour. Let's go to Doria Castle and then the harbour for some lunch.'

The visit to the castle gave them an amazing view of the coastline. After walking around the harbour, admiring the expensive boats they ate lunch which consisted of pasta with a creamy Pesto alla Genovese: Made with local basil, pine nuts, and olive oil.

On other visits to small towns, the locals were extremely helpful, friendly, yet curious, and many a time they invited Zoe and Hazel into their homes. This was Italy in the seventies, so when it happened, they sat and ate with the men, while their plump wives fussed around and served the meal. Zoe often wondered when they had time to eat, as they never seemed to sit down. Zoe found herself falling in love with Italy, so she practiced every moment she was with the locals, who graciously forgave her many mistakes.

The company arrived in a sleepy medieval town of Saluzzo, where pretty, red-tiled rooftops, bell towers, and ancient spires greeted them as they chugged up the last steep hill. The imposing snow-capped Cottian Alps rose above the town like sentinels. It was a beautiful sunny day, and they were in between shows. Hazel and Holly were recovering from a night of excellent wine, so Zoe decided to go on this adventure alone.

She walked past *La Castiglia*, a 14th century castle, promising herself to return when she had more time. The cobbled streets, high altitude, midday sun and her rumbling tummy convinced her to rejuvenate herself with a fresh pastry and a cappuccino. Across the town square was a delightful looking cafe, so she popped in and ordered. Not one woman in sight. She sat demurely at a small table by the window.

Most of the patrons were old enough to be drawing a pension, except for one man, probably in his early forties. His dark complexion and brown eyes made her sit up in anticipation as he walked towards her. 'May I join you?' he asked.

'Sure,' she responded.

He gazed at Zoe and asked, 'You're English, no?'

'Yes, I am,' she replied, surprised he had narrowed down her nationality so quickly, as she knew she looked more Mediterranean than the typical English rose.

'How are you enjoying our little town?' he asked pleasantly.

Zoe didn't usually feel shy, but this gentleman was so refined, almost intimidating.

His name was Franco and soon, Zoe felt more relaxed. They chatted comfortably for over an hour. He drank two espressos while Zoe only managed two cappuccinos. His English was excellent, and he spoke with a soft Italian accent. His few grey hairs gave him a look of sophistication along with his casual, but expensive outfit. Even though he had lived in this town all his life, his work as an actor had given him the opportunity to travel extensively.

'You seem so sophisticated for this small town. How come

you choose not to live in the city?' she asked.

He laughed, 'Because of my work in commercials, I have enough time to enjoy city life but come here to spend time with my mother. My father passed away three years ago – they were married for 45 years, so she misses his company.'

'And you have never married?'

'No, I was engaged once but it didn't work out.'

Zoe sensed he didn't want to talk about it.

'Would you like to see my town?' he offered, rising from his chair. He stretched out his hand and helped her up.

'Sure, that would be lovely.'

'Let's start with the cathedral.' He said goodbye in Italian as he waved to the owner who smiled as they left.

He told Zoe the cathedral had been built outside the walls of the village in 1491. The façade was of exposed brick, adorned by three portals surmounted by terracotta gables that housed statues of the apostles. It was beautiful and Zoe didn't want to leave, but when Franco saw her peeking at her watch, he said, 'I'm sorry, do you have to go?'

'Unfortunately, yes. I have a show to do.'

'Where? Can I come to watch?'

She hesitated. 'Well, it's at the Dolce Vita, not the fanciest place in town.'

'I know,' he smiled, 'I'll be there.'

He walked her to a taxi and handed the driver some Lira. The ride back to the hotel was a blur; Zoe was lost in a romantic dreamland.

She joined the others to walk to the theatre. 'What's up with you?' asked Hazel.

'Nothing,'

'Come on, tell us. You have this weird gaze in your eyes.'

insisted Holly.

'Well, if you must know, I just met this fantastic Italian man.' Before the two girls could grill her, it was time to get dressed and go on stage.

After the show, Zoe took a little extra time to look her best, removing every bit of stage makeup. That is one thing she disliked about being on stage. - too much makeup. She peeked out into the dark club and saw Franco sitting with Michelle. She checked herself in the mirror and walked over to his table. Franco stood up and kissed her cheek. Michelle looked annoyed. 'You know each other?'

'Yes,' Zoe replied. Michelle stormed off.

'Moody girl,' said Franco.

'You could say that.' She sat with him and drank champagne all evening.

'Franco, did you enjoy the show?'

'Yes, but I feel you girls are very talented and it's not being totally appreciated here.'

'We feel that way too. Some nights are better than others. We can't wait to get a contract back in London, or even in Los Angeles. However, there's a lot of competition out there.'

Franco took a sip of his drink. 'So does that mean, you will carry on dancing?'

Zoe knew where this conversation was heading. 'Let's not talk about me. When is your next commercial?'

Each night, as the curtains fell and the applause faded, Franco would linger, his eyes holding an unspoken invitation. After the third performance, he invited Zoe to join him at his apartment. As they entered his cozy abode, the air was thick with anticipation. With a shared understanding and a deepening affection, they surrendered to the tender embrace of their love, their bodies entwined in a dance of passion and intimacy.

In the soft glow of candlelight, each caress and whispered endearment gave Zoe a sensation she had never experienced before. In that moment, time seemed to stand still, their hearts beating as one. As they lay entangled in each other's arms, Zoe wondered how this relationship would end.

An hour's drive north, they worked a week in Turin, and then onto their final stop, Venice. Ben returned the rented minibus and handed out the train tickets. Franco was flying there to meet Zoe for a couple of days.

8

Venice

As they stepped out of the Santa Lucia train station, the water from the Grand Canal glistened under the light. The sight of gondolas gliding gracefully, *vaporettos* bustling with passengers, and centuries-old buildings rising directly from the water immediately captivated them. Zoe sighed and thought to herself, *Venice is not just a place you visit, it's a place you feel.*

'The first thing I'm doing is going on a Gondola,' said Holly.

'And I'm coming with you,' said Zoe.

'Not me,' said Hazel, 'I can't swim.'

Their luggage was taken to the hotel by a porter, but the girls decided to travel by vaporetto. Zoe's Italian was quite good now, so she handled the arrangements. A vaporetto can hold about 150 passengers, but there were barely 50 at this time in the evening. It was the time when most went out to eat. The architectural landscape of Venice remained much as it had been for centuries, with grand palazzos, churches, and bridges dominating the scene. The guide on the *vaporetto* talked about how preservation efforts were already underway, as concerns about the city's sinking foundations and the impact of water on its ancient buildings were becoming more prominent.

The cultural scene in Venice was vibrant, with the city hosting the Venice Biennale, which was an international art exhibition and the Venice Film Festival, which attracted filmmakers and film stars from around the world. The arts were deeply embedded in the city's identity, and there was a strong sense of tradition in music, opera, and visual arts. However, the social and economic changes caused a gradual decline in the city's population as younger generations moved away in search of better paying jobs.

One afternoon, the troupe gathered and made a trip to the famous St. Mark's Square. It wasn't too crowded, but the hotel receptionist warned them about pickpockets. 'If that's the only crime I have to worry about, maybe I'll live here one day,' said Holly.

'Holly, I know you are upset about something. You don't have to tell me, but you know I can be good sounding board. So, let's cheer you up and go for a gondola ride.'

'Thanks,' said Holly, 'The letter was from my cousin. He's like a brother to me. His parents threw him out because he told them he was a homosexual.'

'That's awful,' said Zoe, 'When will that generation start accepting the fact that homosexuals are part of everyone's life these days.'

It was a peaceful afternoon on the canals of Venice, so Zoe and Holly enjoyed their gondola ride, admiring the charming Venetian architecture. The gondolier, an older man named Marco, guided them along with his practiced strokes, singing Italian songs.

'Jeez, we certainly didn't get Pavarotti. I don't know if I can take this cat howling any longer,' said Holly.

Suddenly, Marco slumped forward, unconscious, causing the gondola to wobble slightly.

'Oh my God, Holly! You got your wish. Marco just—he just passed out!'

'What?! Are you sure? Marco? Marco, wake up!' said Holly shaking him.

'Marco! Marco, can you hear us?' said Zoe.

Holly started to panic, 'What do we do? We're in the middle of the canal!'

'Okay, okay, don't panic. We need to get this gondola back to the dock. We can do this.'

'Do what exactly? Neither of us knows how to steer a gondola!' said Holly.

Zoe grabbed the oar. 'I mean, how hard can it be? We've seen him do it a dozen times in the last half hour!'

Holly let out a nervous laugh. 'Zoe, that's like saying you can play the piano after watching a concert!'

'Well, we don't have a choice, do we? Just keep an eye on Marco and make sure he's breathing. I'll try to figure this out.'

Holly checked Marco's pulse. 'He's breathing, thank God, but he's completely out. What if he's having a heart attack? We need to get back fast!' She leaned over him, 'phew, he stinks of alcohol.'

'This is not as easy as it looks! It's all about balance, I think,' said Zoe struggling with the oar.

'Let me try!'

Awkwardly at first, Holly got the hang of it, steering the gondola towards the dock.

'I'm impressed,' said Zoe, 'We're actually moving in the

right direction! I can see the dock up ahead! Who knew you'd make such a good gondolier?'

'I can't believe this is happening. Only to us, Zoe. Only to us.'

As they approached the dock, Holly managed to bring the gondola to the dock, where a small crowd had gathered, alerted by the unusual sight of two women struggling with the boat.

Two gondoliers carried Marco out. *'E molto ubriaca,'* said one of them.

'Just as we thought, drunk,' said Zoe, 'He's going to have one heck of a story when he wakes up.'

'And so will we,' said Holly.

Venice was the last stop in Italy and frankly Zoe wasn't too sad it was over. The venues had not been up to their expectations and the routines were becoming boring, but Ben promised to give them new routines for the next contract which was going to be in Beirut, Lebanon. However, Zoe wasn't sure what she thought about leaving Franco. Deep down she wasn't ready for a serious relationship, and she wanted to keep dancing.

The final night, the girls were waiting in the wings of the stage as it was almost time to go on, when Michelle said, 'Where's Hazel?'

Holly looked around, then ran back to the dressing room. She returned, slightly flushed, 'She's nowhere to be seen.' Damn it! As lead dancer, she would have to be the one to switch sides. Although Zoe was good at memorizing the steps, she always found it hard to do that. Holly had no problem, but it wasn't fair to expect her to do it on a regular basis. As Zoe scanned backstage, her frustration grew when she realized Hazel was nowhere to be found. It wasn't the first time Hazel had been late, but this time felt different. With each passing moment, Zoe's apprehension mounted, and as the evening progressed, it became painfully clear that Hazel was not going to make an appearance. As the final curtain fell, Zoe couldn't shake the nagging worry for Hazel's well-being, and hoped she would eventually turn up safe and sound.

Ben joined the girls - His eyes narrowed, and his lips pressed into a thin line as his face flushed a deep shade of red. 'When she shows up, tell her to come and see me.'

Ben's strict policy on punctuality left little room for leniency, and Hazel's repeated tardiness had not gone unnoticed. Each late arrival incurred a fine, a consequence that Hazel had unfortunately become all too familiar with. Despite the financial penalty, Zoe couldn't help but worry about Hazel's underlying reasons for her consistent tardiness.

As Hazel finally stumbled in way past midnight, Zoe observed her friend with a mixture of concern and frustration but decided to hold off on addressing the issue until the morning.

At breakfast, Hazel joined the girls, a sheepish look on her face. 'What the hell happened,' said Holly, 'I am so sick at covering for you.'

'Please, don't shout,' said Hazel. 'My head hurts.'

'That wouldn't be the only thing that hurt if I had my way,' said Michelle.

'You are always complaining about your head. You shouldn't drink so much,' said Andrea.

Ben arrived and silence fell over the table. He stared at Hazel. 'I have a good mind to fire you and get someone to replace you for our next venue.'

Hazel looked up, red eyed, 'Please don't. I promise I will never be late again.'

'Okay, you promise?' said Ben. Hazel shook her head.

Zoe always had known that he had a soft spot for her. Ben stormed off and Zoe whispered, 'What happened?'

'I smoked some marijuana . . .'

'What?' interrupted Zoe. 'My God, if you ever . . .' Zoe was lost for words.

'I've been having these headaches, and someone told me that it would help. It just knocked me out.'

'Maybe you need to have your head examined,' said Zoe.

'You can say that again,' quipped Holly. They all laughed.

The following day the girls packed for their journey home and made their way to Milan airport.

Zoe's last day had been spent with Franco. As Zoe reflected on her time with him, memories of their shared experiences flooded her mind. He had not only introduced her to the culinary delights of Italy's finest restaurants, but also taught her valuable lessons in etiquette, paving the way for her to feel at ease in even the most upscale restaurants. Despite his tempting offer for her to stay in Italy with him, Zoe had to tell him that she wasn't yet ready to settle down. With a heavy heart, she bid farewell to him, tears welling up in her eyes. Promising to return, Zoe held onto the hope that their paths would cross again someday.

But would she? Had she made another mistake? This man was perfect. Would he wait for her? Did she want him to or did she want to pursue her dance career for a few more years? A dancer's life was short. With dance genres like contemporary, modern, or ballroom, some dancers may perform into their 40's or even 50's, as these styles can sometimes be less physically demanding than ballet. *Would that be her?*

9

Beirut

Zoe wasn't sure if she was sadder to leave Italy or Franco, but a new adventure was about to begin. Zoe hated goodbyes, but it seemed that was all she did these days.

The flight was almost four hours to Beirut, Lebanon, which was considered the Paris of the Middle East. Zoe turned to Holly, 'So, are you excited to go to Beirut?'

'I guess. While you were out with lover boy, I spent some time with that Moroccan waiter that worked at the hotel. So, now I know how to say hello, goodbye, how are you and one cup of tea please, in Arabic.'

'I'm impressed. You need to teach me,' said Zoe laughing.

When the taxi pulled up outside the St. George Hotel, they were certain there had been some mistake. They stood there, eyes wide and took in the beautiful gardens, the tall palm trees and the multi-tiered fountains - Even if it was a mistake, they were determined to enjoy the experience until they got transferred to Lebanon's version of a Travelodge.

Zoe approached reception. 'Hi, we're the Ben Johnson dance troupe.'

'We have your rooms ready; would you like your luggage sent up while you take some refreshment?'

Zoe was not sure what else the receptionist said as she was too distracted by the surroundings and the realisation that no mistake had been made. The hotel served gourmet food, delivered great service and offered a variety of water sports. They quickly changed into swimsuits and lounged by the pool for the next hour. Zoe could only handle one drink as she watched Holly down at least three.

Andrea looked over. She wasn't very fond of Holly and said, 'How can you dance after all that alcohol?'

Holly sat up, removed her sunglasses and glared at Andrea. 'Who do you think you are telling me what I can and cannot do?'

'Well, if you make any mistakes, Ben will notice and get mad.'

'Ignore her,' said Zoe, trying to keep the peace.

Andrea tried to get Michelle and Suzi involved but Michelle was too busy chatting up the man next to her. Michelle was the flirtatious one in the group. Suzi, looked up, rolled her eyes and carried on reading her book

Tucked away in the heart of the city's bustling nightlife scene, the club was a haven for Beirut's elite and jetsetters. Upon entering, guests were greeted by the soft glow of crystal chandeliers that cast a warm, light over the interior. Plush velvet drapes adorned the walls, and polished marble floors shone brightly. Zoe stopped to listen to the jazz music floating through the air. Holly and Michelle made a beeline for the bar, where impeccably dressed bartenders created cocktails, although most of the clientele seemed to prefer whiskey.

Later in their dressing room, which was not large, but well equipped with good lighting, racks for their costumes and complimentary water, they warmed up with simple exercises. Just before showtime, Zoe stared out from behind the curtain of the stage and was happy to see upscale clientele. At precisely 8 p.m., the show began. They performed all their numbers perfectly and the audience were attentive and even applauded.

Afterwards, Ben approached with a warm smile, 'Ladies, you were fantastic,' he began, then with a hint of hesitation, he said, 'Em, I hope you don't mind, but I've arranged for you to join some of the clientele for a brief chat over drinks. Nothing untoward, just a chance to mingle and enjoy a drink or two. I made it clear that you were not escorts, and they completely understood.'

Holly was poised to object, but Zoe intervened with a gentle nod of her head and a whispered reassurance. 'We'll stick together, Holly,' she murmured. 'We'll enter and leave as a group.'

Reluctantly, they emerged from their dressing room and settled at a table occupied by four Lebanese gentlemen. Despite the dancer's initial apprehension, they found themselves engaged in lively conversation. The gentlemen proved to be well-educated, polite, fluent in English, and considerably wealthy. The exchange of ideas was stimulating, and after a couple of drinks, the girls thanked them and made their way back to the hotel.

'Well, that wasn't too bad,' said a slightly inebriated Holly.

Although the club was modern and almost totally renovated, the lift was not. As they entered the old rickety lift, Holly said, 'Jeez, this lift is gonna break down one day, and I hope I won't be in it.'

Zoe laughed and when they reached the ground floor, she pulled up the iron gate and Andrea screamed. A young girl stretched out her arm in front of them crying "bakshish" which in Arabic literally meant, "Give me tip, bribe, or small monetary offering." It's a word the beggars used a lot.

'It's okay Andrea,' said Zoe softly as she handed some change to the girl.

'I know. She just took me by surprise,' said Andrea.

Unfortunately, some impoverished individuals resorted to desperate measures, such as intentionally maiming their children to evoke sympathy while begging on the streets. Another common ploy involved skillfully staging accidents—rolling in front of expensive cars and then claiming they wouldn't report the incident if the driver offered them money. Beirut was home to a significant number of wealthy individuals, but it was also a city where many were driven to such desperate tactics.

As if Holly had predicted the future, two days later the lift stopped in between floors with Zoe, Holly and two strangers.

'Oh crap,' said Holly. She looked at the two strangers and gave a weak smile, 'Sorry. Do you speak English?'

They nodded a yes. 'We are from Portugal and are here for a business conference. I am Alicia and this is Fernando.'

'Well, I'm sure it's just a glitch. I rang the emergency bell. We'll be out of here in no time.'

Fernando started **to** breathe heavily] 'Oh no... no, no, no. This can't be happening.'

'Are you okay? Try to take deep breaths. We'll be out soon,' said Alicia.

Pacing in the small space he said, 'No, you don't understand. I'm claustrophobic. I can't— *[gasping]* —I can't stay in here.'

Holly took his hand, 'It's not so bad. Look, we've got air. See the vent up there? We're not running out of oxygen.'

'It's not about the air! It's the walls closing in. I feel like I'm being crushed,' he said.

Zoe thought quickly, 'Fernando, listen. I've been stuck in worse places, like a crawlspace under a house. You'll be fine. Just sit down and focus on something else.'

'I don't know how you're all so calm. Don't you feel trapped?' he said as he slumped down into a corner.

' Try being stuck in an elevator with a goat. Construction site hazard. It chewed my briefcase,' said Alicia.

Holly looked at Zoe, her eyes wide, 'A goat? You're joking.'

'Nope. True story. Made it out fine, though. And so will we.'

Zoe tried to distract him.' What do you do for a living?'

'I... I'm a graphic designer. Mostly logos and marketing materials. Not very exciting.'

'That's amazing. And hey, by the time this elevator moves again, you'll have a captive audience for brainstorming your next project,' said Zoe.

Zoe and Holly kept him talking about his work when they heard a voice yell in Arabic. Holly quickly said, 'We speak English.'

'Hold on everyone!' said the man's voice.

Fernando relaxed slightly, 'Thanks, everyone. I guess I can handle this for a little while longer.

'There you go. One minute at a time. We'll be out of here soon,' said Holly.

The elevator jolted, and the lights stabilized. A voice came through the intercom announcing the repair crew was on their way.'

'See. Told you, no big deal,' said Zoe.

Fernando e*xhaled deeply.* 'Just remind me never to take an elevator again.'

'Especially this one,' said Holly. 'I'm taking the stairs from now on.'

The elevator began to move again, and the doors opened to freedom.

'That's enough excitement for one day. Thanks, everyone… for keeping me sane,' said Fernando and said a little prayer in Portuguese and making the sign of the cross.

They all stepped out, sharing a laugh as they went their separate ways.

'I need a drink,' said Holly.

Zoe decided to try out water skiing, much to the chagrin of Ben. She discovered she had a talent for it, so made it a daily routine. She flirted with the staff and they gave her a healthy discount. None of the other girls were inclined to join her.

One morning, she yelled to the driver of the boat, 'Go a little faster.'

'Okay lady,' he yelled back.

The sun was high in the sky, casting shimmering reflections across the sea as Zoe tightened her grip on the ski rope. Her muscles tensed in anticipation, heart pounding with excitement. The boat's engine roared to life, and she felt a sudden jolt as it surged forward, pulling her along. Zoe leaned back, letting the skis slice through the water. The spray from the saltwater felt cool against her sun-kissed skin. She adjusted her stance, finding her balance, and soon she was gliding effortlessly, the wind whipping through her hair. In the next instance, the boat turned, a little too quickly and flung Zoe across the water at an uncontrollable speed. She struggled to regain her balance, but the dock was suddenly rushing toward her. Boom! She tumbled off the skis, which crashed into the seawall, the world momentarily spinning before she surfaced. As she emerged, sputtering out seawater, she saw a man extending his arm to pull her out, 'Miss Zoe, are you okay?' he said nervously.

More embarrassed than hurt, she said, 'Shukran, I'm okay.'

He helped her hobble up the stairs to dry land and she sat down to regain her composure.

Arriving back at the club, Zoe couldn't shake the nagging discomfort from the sizable bruise on her leg. Despite her attempts to conceal it with a fistful of foundation, the discolouration peeked through. With each step, she felt the dull ache throbbing beneath the surface, but as she lost herself in the rhythm of the music, the pain of her bruised leg faded into the background and she managed to push through each dance number without any mistakes.

10

Khalid

After a week of working two shows a night, they were given a day off. Holly was in a bad mood, so Zoe accepted Hazel's invitation to join her and her boyfriend Khalid for lunch. Zoe gasped, 'Boyfriend? When on earth did you have time to find a boyfriend?'

Hazel laughed, 'I met him the first day we arrived.'

Zoe raised an eyebrow, surprised. 'Really?'

Hazel shrugged, 'You and I haven't hung out together very much lately, so we haven't had much time to chat. Plus, he's just a friend... for now.'

Zoe chuckled, 'Just a friend, huh? Sounds intriguing. Tell me more.'

Hazel leaned back, twirling a strand of hair around her finger. 'I met him the first day at the club bar after you lot left.'

'Why didn't you tell me sooner?' Zoe asked, genuinely curious.

'I guess I wanted to keep it to myself for a while,' Hazel admitted. 'But now that you know, maybe we can all hang out together. You'll love him, I'm sure.'

KHALID

Khalid was at least twenty years older than Hazel, but he was undeniably handsome—a man who had clearly taken care of himself. His salt-and-pepper hair and tailored linen suit spoke of elegance without effort. Over a sumptuous lunch of lamb kebabs, fresh tabbouleh, and warm, pillowy flatbreads, his charm flowed as freely as the mint tea.

When the plates were cleared, he leaned back, a playful smile dancing on his lips. 'Shall we explore the market? I know just the place for treasures.'

Hazel chuckled, brushing a strand of blonde hair behind her ear. 'Treasures? You do know how to tempt a woman, Khalid.'

Zoe, sipping the last of her tea, smirked. 'And I suspect you enjoy parading us around, too.'

Khalid's eyes twinkled. 'Guilty as charged. Two beautiful women on my arm—who wouldn't?'

Zoe smiled to herself. She had met quite a few Lebanese women and found them much more attractive than white women, but as the saying goes, "The grass is always greener..."

The market was a dazzling maze of colours, scents, and sounds—spices piled in pyramids, bolts of shimmering fabric swaying in the breeze, and the rhythmic clatter of copperware being hammered into shape. Khalid, ever the generous host, was quick to gesture toward a jewelry stall adorned with amazing items.

'Hazel,' he said smoothly, lifting a delicate gold bracelet, 'this would suit you perfectly.'

He turned to Zoe next, his smile widening. 'And you, my dear, choose anything you like. I insist.'

Zoe's gaze fell on a modest yet striking turquoise necklace. She picked it up, admiring its simple elegance.

Khalid frowned playfully, reaching for a more extravagant piece—a necklace dripping with diamonds. 'Why not take this one?' he said, holding it up so the gems caught the sunlight.

Zoe's eyes widened. 'Thank you,' she replied, her voice soft but firm, 'but I have simpler tastes. This one,' she said, brushing her fingers over the turquoise, 'feels more like me.'

Khalid clearly amused and impressed. 'A woman who knows her style—how refreshing.' He handed the merchant a roll of bills without another word.

Later that day, Khalid brought them to a private lounge where his friends had gathered—wealthy, confident men, their laughter ringing out over the low hum of music and clinking glasses. Zoe felt the familiar buzz of curiosity and excitement, always drawn to new faces and stories.

One man, however, drew her attention immediately. Adib. Tall, in his early thirties, with a lean, athletic build and an air of effortless confidence. His suit was sharp but understated, and his grooming immaculate. He had the easy charm of someone comfortable in any company. But what struck her most was his warmth—genuine, magnetic.

When Khalid introduced them, Adib's handshake was firm, his palm cool against hers. 'A pleasure, Zoe,' he said, his voice smooth, with just the faintest trace of an American accent.

'Your English is perfect,' she noted, curiosity in her voice.

He smiled. 'Thank you. I spent quite a bit of time in the States—business trips mostly. I'm with RC Cola. Vice President for the Middle East region.' He paused, a playful glint in his eye. 'The 'other' cola company. We're giving the giants a run for their money.'

'I don't really like any cola,' said Zoe. 'I prefer ginger ale.'

'Duly noted,' said Adib.

'And you speak French and Spanish too, I hear?' Zoe asked, intrigued.

He nodded. 'Yes. I picked up Spanish while living in Madrid for a year and French from my time in Paris. Business and pleasure, of course.'

Zoe raised an eyebrow. 'Impressive. A true cosmopolitan.'

His eyes sparkled with amusement. 'I try to keep life... interesting.'

There was an ease to their conversation that felt rare—fluid and effortless, without the pretense or posturing Zoe often encountered.

After Franco, her standards had sharpened. She had learned to spot charm without substance, allure without authenticity. Adib, however, felt different. There was confidence, certainly, but also a refreshing absence of arrogance.

As the evening wound down, Adib reached into his jacket and produced a sleek business card, holding it between two fingers.

'Call me the day after tomorrow?' he said, his eyes steady on hers.

Zoe accepted the card. 'I see you are a director with RC Cola.'

'Yes, that's why I travel a lot, especially to the US.'

'Didn't one of your truck turn over last week?'

'Unfortunately yes,'

Zoe laughed. 'I remember that well—on the sandy road, it looked like a river of cola.'

The timing was perfect. The show schedule had just been reduced to one performance per evening, freeing her afternoons, so she knew she would be seeing him again - soon.

11

Adib

In the next few weeks Adib took Zoe to expensive restaurants, paid for sessions at the beauty spa and let her drive his yellow Mustang, even though she didn't have a license. He was proud of his country and enjoyed showing her around. When he was away, his best friend Andre took care of her. Andre often hung out with them. He was an antique dealer and specialised in Russian Icons (religious paintings) Zoe was curious as she had read somewhere that it was illegal to take them out of Russia. He owned a place in Knightsbridge, London and offered Zoe a place to stay if she ever visited.

On one of her days off, she and Adib travelled to Baalbeck in North Lebanon. Baalbek was an ancient Phoenician city in the Beqaa Valley. In the centre of this city was a grand temple but now partially in ruins. Zoe felt very lucky as normally she hated being a tourist, but when one is shown the sights by a local, it is entirely different.

As they walked, Zoe turned to Adib, marvelling at the towering columns. 'I can't believe how majestic they are.'

Adib nodded, a proud smile on his face. 'Baalbek is one of

Lebanon's most treasured historical sites. The Romans built these temples to honour their gods. This temple here is the Temple of Jupiter.'

'It's incredible,' Zoe said, her eyes wide with wonder. 'The detail in the carvings... it must have taken years to complete.'

Adib chuckled. 'Indeed, it did. The construction of these temples began around 60 BC and continued for nearly three centuries. Imagine the dedication and skill it took to create something so magnificent.'

Zoe reached out to touch the cool stone. 'Thank you for bringing me here, Adib.' He squeezed her hand gently. 'I'm glad you're enjoying it. There's so much more to Lebanon than just Beirut.'

Zoe smiled, 'It's beautiful. And having you as my guide makes it all the more meaningful.'

They continued to explore the site, their conversation weaving through history and personal anecdotes. As they stood in the shadow of the ancient temple, Zoe felt a profound sense of connection—not just to the past, but to the man beside her.

'Adib, this has been an eye-opening experience,' she said softly.

Adib looked at her, 'That's all I wanted, Zoe. To share a part of my world with you.'

They sat silently for a moment, before returning to Beirut.

The troupe had been in Beirut for over a month and were enjoying most of the venues. Zoe sat in the dressing room with the rest of the girls as they got ready. Tonight they were excited as there were some important clients coming to see the show. Ben had said if they were impressed, they had a special black-tie event where they would hire them for the night and pay extremely well. This would be a good opportunity to earn extra cash.

It was almost time to go on stage when Zoe asked, 'Anyone know where Hazel is?'

They all looked at each nodding a big fat no.

'Crap,' said Zoe, 'We will have to adjust without her. Holly you are the best switch dancer. Can you handle it.?'

'Sure. Bloody Hazel. Where the hell is she?'

All of the routines went perfectly well, even without Hazel. Ben came over to them. 'Where the hell is Hazel?'

'She probably eloped with that rich Arab boyfriend,' snarled Suzi.

'You know after her last episode, she has never been late or missed a show since arriving here,' said Holly.

By 10 p.m. there was still no sign of Hazel. 'Isn't that boyfriend of yours his friend?' said Michelle.

'Not really,' said Zoe, 'He is a friend of a friend.'

'Well, don't you have his number, Zoe? Maybe you could ask this friend of a friend if he could find out where she might be,' suggested Suzi, sarcastically.

Zoe went to the lobby and asked if there were any messages. Then asked if she could use the lobby phone. The operator put her through to Adib. He told her he would investigate. She put down the phone. Maybe she was overreacting, but a wave of panic washed over her, sending shivers down her spine. She had a bad feeling. She returned to her room but could not sleep, so paced the room.

The hotel phone rang and woke up Zoe from her fitful sleep. It was Adib. 'I'll be over there in twenty minutes.' That's all he said before hanging up.

Zoe dressed quickly, went down to the lobby, grabbed a coffee and waited. When Adib entered through the revolving doors of the hotel, Zoe ran towards him. 'Any news?'

Adib took her arm and they walked over to a quiet spot and sat down as not to draw any attention. 'I finally got hold of my friend who knows Khalid very well.' He hesitated and bit his lower lip.

'What?' whispered Zoe, unable to hide her fear.

'Well, Khalid got a call. He was told to drop off 115 million Lebanese Lira.'

'What!' exclaimed Zoe.

'That's only a £1000. It sounds a lot more in our currency.'

'When and where?' asked Zoe.

'Don't worry. I have a contact in the police department. They've been keeping tabs on a group that's lingered since the aftermath of the 1970 war. They're a faction of die-hard fundamentalists clinging to outdated ideologies, desperate for funds to procure weapons, and are behind a lot of recent kidnappings.' He Paused. 'The tensions between Christian and Muslim populations will probably lead to another war. Personally, I may be moving to the US, and your company should be thinking about returning to the UK.'

They sat silently for a few minutes. Adib rose from the chair, kissed Zoe on the cheek and said, 'Just tell the others that I have people looking into Hazel's disappearance.'

Despite the picturesque day unfolding outside, Zoe couldn't appreciate its beauty, her thoughts clouded by worry and fear. The other girls joined her for coffee. With a trembling voice, she delivered the devastating news: Shock rippled through the group, silencing their lively conversation as the gravity of Zoe's words sank in.

'What do we do now?' asked Suzi.

'Nothing, Adib is handling it. I'm going to see Ben to alert him of the situation.'

Zoe walked over to where Ben and Dana were trying to enjoy their breakfast. 'Any news?' Ben asked.

'No,' replied Zoe, 'But Khalid and Adib are handling it.'

'We need to call the police,' said Ben.

'No,' Zoe said firmly, her voice tinged with frustration. 'Adib has his contacts. He mentioned that the police either lack the motivation to investigate properly or are deliberately turning a blind eye, perhaps due to corruption.'

'Well, we can't just sit here and do nothing'

'We have to, until we hear back from Adib.'

An hour later, the receptionist glanced up and beckoned Zoe over. 'Miss Zoe, you have a phone call.'

Zoe's stomach clenched, a sharp twist of nauseous as she lunged for the phone, knocking over a half-empty glass in her haste. It tumbled, spinning, before smashing against the marble floor. She barely noticed it. Snatching up the receiver with clammy hands, she pressed it to her ear.

'Hello?'

'Hi, it's Adib.' His voice was low, urgent. 'We are still waiting to hear back, but I will call as soon as I know anything.'

'Why is it taking so long?'

'I think they are doing it on purpose to make sure we follow their instructions. I'll call when I hear something.'

Zoe went over to Ben and the others. 'We've haven't received word from the kidnappers yet.'

Ben's face dropped. 'What?' He exhaled sharply, rubbing his temples. 'This waiting is unbearable.'

Zoe glanced at the others—shadows under their eyes, restless hands drumming against the table, flicking through pages they weren't reading. No one spoke, but the fear was tangible, thickening the air.

'Adib thinks they're doing it on purpose,' she murmured, voice tight.

A heavy silence followed.

Ben looked up; his jaw clenched. 'You mean—deliberate psychological pressure?'

Zoe nodded. 'They want us afraid. They want us compliant.'

Across the room, Suzi shuddered. 'Well, it's working.'

Two hours later, which felt more like four, Zoe received another call from Adib.

'They've named their meeting place. We're moving forward with the ransom.' He paused. 'We've chosen not to involve the police.'

She gripped the receiver, knuckles whitening. 'What? Why?'

'Khalid agreed to pay—he doesn't care about the money.'

Zoe exhaled sharply, running a trembling hand through her hair. 'That's... remarkably generous. But we can't just let them get away with this. It's unacceptable.'

Adib hesitated. When he spoke again, his tone was different—colder, edged with something darker. 'They won't escape.'

A chill swept through Zoe. She straightened, gripping the phone tighter. 'What do you mean?'

'I can't say more. The less you know, the better. Just tell everyone to stay in the hotel. Wait for my call.'

The line went dead.

Zoe stood frozen, her heartbeat drummed in her ears, the weight of Adib's words settling over her like a suffocating blanket. *They won't escape.* She swallowed.

Forcing herself to move, she turned back to the table where the troupe sat, their faces etched with tension. Ben had already cancelled that night's show, using food poisoning as an excuse for two of the dancers. No one had argued. Now, the group drifted in anxious limbo—pacing, flipping through books without absorbing a single word, playing cards with forced laughter that never quite reached their eyes. Eventually, they all returned to their rooms.

The hours crawled by. At exactly 7 p.m., a sharp knock rattled Zoe's door. She crept to the peephole and peered through. Adib stood on the other side. But he wasn't alone.

Hazel. Zoe yanked open the door, gasping at the sight of her friend. Hazel looked exhausted, her skin pale, dark circles shadowing her eyes. Zoe didn't hesitate—she lunged forward, wrapping Hazel in a fierce embrace. A shaky breath escaped her lips as relief crashed over her. Hazel was safe. She was back. But something was off. Adib's face was unreadable. And Hazel, though physically here, felt... distant.

Something had happened. Something Zoe wasn't sure she wanted to hear.

Zoe empathized with Hazel's need for rest and solitude after the ordeal she had endured. Hazel just wanted to take a shower and sleep but promised to catch up later. Zoe invited Adib in. 'Sorry, but I do have some business to attend to. I will call you tomorrow.'

Zoe kissed him gently and thanked him, 'Okay, see you tomorrow.'

She let Ben and the other girls know Hazel was safe and now resting.

12

A Special Event

The group gathered in Ben's room, eager to hear Hazel's harrowing account of her ordeal. As she recounted the terrifying events, her voice trembled. 'I was making my way through the Souk, heading to meet Khalid, when suddenly this man approached me, speaking in Arabic,' Hazel began, her eyes tearing, 'I tried to explain that I didn't understand, but before I knew it, I was being dragged into a dingy room, and they bound my hands and feet.' The room fell silent as Hazel's words hung heavy in the air; each member of the group absorbed in the gravity of her story. With a shudder, Hazel continued, 'I don't know how long I was there,' her voice unsteady. A little later, they yanked the ties from my wrists, shoving a plate of unrecognizable food in front of me. My hands trembled as I picked at it. Then, without warning, one of the men moved closer, his eyes dark with intent. A sickening grin spread across his face.

My heart pounded, but instinct took over. Before I could think, I drove the knife into his arm. Snap. The flimsy plastic blade barely broke the skin. His was shocked, then furious.

He yelled at me as he lunged toward me, but the other man caught him just in time, wrestling him back. Spit flew as he struggled, then he wrenched free just enough to take a wild, furious swing at me. I've never felt such pain.

She touched the big bruise on her cheek, her gaze distant.

'Later that evening, they shoved me into a car and dumped me in front of a café. That's when Adib found me.'

'Oh, my God, you poor thing,' Holly murmured sympathetically, her usual bravado momentarily softened by the severity of the situation. 'You were incredibly brave, Hazel,' she added, her words were genuine as she admired her friend's courage.

'We only have two more shows and that special event to finish our contract,' said Ben. 'Hazel, you can opt out if you like.'

'Thanks, I think I will,' said Hazel.

Ben organised a rehearsal to rearrange a couple of numbers without using Hazel.

'Zoe, get the girls ready. We need to decide which two numbers we are going to do for that special party. And from now on, no one goes out alone.'

The grand ballroom of the opulent hotel in Beirut shimmered with a thousand lights, reflecting like a sea of diamonds and gold. The elegantly dressed guests mingled, their laughter and animated conversation weaving through the air as they sipped endlessly flowing champagne.

As the dancers entered, their eyes widened in awe. The room was a living tapestry of luxury, even more so than the club that they were dancing in: rich velvet drapes and gleaming marble floors, with a wonderfully decorated stage.

The special act from an Arabic dance troupe started the show.

The costumes were all stunningly crafted with sequins and silk.

'Wow,' said Holly, 'I feel like Cinderella.'

Zoe and Holly were mesmerised by a vibrant display of cultural heritage, traditional folklore dancers with intricate costumes and traditional Lebanese music.

'Yeah, there costumes choreography are amazing. I wish I could shake my hips like that,' said Zoe.

The following act was an elegant and timeless, classical ballet performances showcasing intricate choreography of excerpts from *Swan Lake* .

The girls performed one number and quickly returned to the dressing room to change while a lady sang a newly released song called "Zahrat al-Madaen". Later the stage manager explained to them that it translated to "Flower of the Cities." 'It is a popular song for its evocative lyrics and beautiful melody. It reflects themes of national pride and cultural heritage,' he said proudly.

As the troupe performed a very contemporary number, the guests watched with rapt attention. As the final notes of the music faded and the dancers struck their final pose, the room erupted in applause. The girls beamed, their faces flushed with joy and relief. Suzi and Michelle looked over at Holly and Zoe, and smiled.

The troupe then changed to civilian clothes and joined the festivities. They looked around with a mix of excitement and trepidation. Their eyes were drawn to the dazzling array of jewellery worn by the guests—women with cascading diamonds like frozen waterfalls, men sporting cuff links that seemed to capture every stray beam of light.

In a corner of the room, a group of well-known celebrities

were engaged in animated conversation. A famous actress, her neck encircled by a necklace of such grandeur, laughed heartily at a joke. Nearby, a financier with an understated yet clearly expensive watch observed the scene with a keen, almost calculating gaze.

'Do you see that? The necklace she's wearing—it's worth more than my family's house!' said Holly.

That's a lot, thought Zoe as she seeing a photo Holly's family home.

The host, a distinguished gentleman with an impeccable suit and an air of effortless charm, welcomed everyone. It was his daughter's birthday. As he introduced her, his eyes sparkled with genuine admiration as he gestured her towards the stage.

'Ladies and gentlemen, we are thrilled to have these extraordinary talents performing for us tonight. Please, let's give them a grand welcome!'

The troupe told Ben that this night would be remembered as one of the most extraordinary of their lives.

13

London

In March of 1975, the six month contract was over for the troupe. Just in time as Adib's predictions about the Civil war were correct. The Lebanese Civil War was a multifaceted armed conflict that started April of 1975. No one knew how long it would last or how many people would be killed.

On the last day in Beirut, Adib and Zoe had a wonderful meal at his friend's restaurant where her favourite foods, hummus, falafel, tabbouleh and baba ghanoush were in abundance. Zoe asked him what happened with the money and the kidnappers,

'Don't worry, that matter has been settled,' he said, his voice calm and reassuring.

Zoe raised an eyebrow, a playful smirk forming on her lips. 'Damn, you sound like a spy.'

He chuckled softly, a glint of mystery in his eyes. 'What makes you think I'm not?'

She stared at him, searching his face for any sign of a joke. 'What does that make me? Moneypenny?'

He leaned in closer, taking her hand gently. 'No. More like a

Bond girl.'

Zoe felt her heart skip a beat, her cheeks flushing slightly. 'Is that so? Well, Mr. Bond, you better make sure to keep me safe.'

'Always,' he replied with a wink, the air between them charged with unspoken promise.

They burst out laughing, a little too loudly, gathering stares from other patrons.

While their relationship had strengthened over time, Zoe still thought there remained a veil of mystery surrounding him, never revealing certain aspects of his life. They chatted a while and as Zoe was enjoying her favourite dessert of Baklava, Adib asked if she would meet him in London where he had decided to stay for a while. Zoe explained she was under contract for another six months, but they would have a week off before their next gig. She was happy as she knew it would be great staying in his luxurious condo in Knightsbridge, instead of Holly's cramped flat.

The girls landed at Heathrow and said their goodbyes. As Zoe stepped through the threshold of Adib's flat, she was greeted by the grandeur of its expansive interior. High ceilings and large windows flooded the space with natural light. Expensive and traditional furnishings, not quite Zoe's taste, but it suited the place. But perhaps the most remarkable feature of the flat was its prime location in Knightsbridge. Nestled amidst London's upscale boutiques and elegant cafes, it offered Zoe a front-row seat to the vibrant energy of the bustling streets.

He treated her like a queen, but she quickly noticed a shift in the dynamic compared to their time in Beirut. The ambience lacked the romantic allure she had felt there. Additionally, she couldn't ignore Adib's increasingly possessive behaviour, which left her feeling somewhat stifled in her new surroundings. As the week was almost over, Zoe and Adib dined in an upscale restaurant. Suddenly, in a moment that caught Zoe off guard, Adib produced a ring and asked, 'Zoe, will you marry me?'

The shock on Zoe's face was palpable as she looked at the huge diamond on the ring.

'I, uh,' she stammered, her mind racing with uncertainty. 'I didn't see this coming.'

Adib's hopeful gaze faltered, replaced by a look of disbelief. 'You didn't see this coming?' he echoed softly.

'I'm sorry, Adib,' she said, her voice tinged with regret. 'I just don't think I'm ready for this.'

Adib's expression shifted from disbelief to disappointment. 'I thought we were on the same page, Zoe,' his voice barely above a whisper. 'I love you, and I thought you felt the same.'

'I do care about you, Adib. But marriage... it's such a big step. I'm not sure if I'm there yet,' Zoe explained, her eyes pleading for understanding.

The air between them grew heavy with unspoken tension as they lapsed into an uncomfortable silence. The remainder of the meal passed in strained quietude, each bite and sip a reminder of the words left unsaid. Adib's disappointment was evident in the way he picked at his food; his usual enthusiasm dampened.

Finally, Adib quietly requested the bill, signalling an end to the evening's festivities. The walk back to the car was filled with a heavy silence. Zoe felt a pang of guilt and sadness, wondering if she had made the right decision.

Zoe felt awkward, so told Adib that she would stay with Holly.

When they arrived at Holly's flat, Zoe said, 'Let me finish the next contract and I'll come back to see you.'

He opened the car door, kissed her gently, then drove off without a word.

Zoe stood for a moment gathering her thoughts, then knocked on Holly's door.

Holly's eyes widened, 'I thought you were staying with Adib.'

'I'm sorry I didn't give you a heads-up. I didn't have my phone book, so couldn't call you.'

They sat down with a glass of wine, and Zoe explained everything that had happened with Adib.

'Are you sure you made the right decision?' asked Holly.

'No! Oh, I don't know. I am so confused. Will I ever settle down?'

'Let's see,' said Holly, 'Franco, Alfredo and now Adib. You really have a knack for attracting these family men.'

The following morning, Zoe's suitcase was delivered from Adib, by taxi.

Somehow Zoe knew in her heart he would probably never see her again. *She was still too young and restless to settle down. There was so much more to do and see in her life and she knew Adib would want a proper family with children. Was she making a mistake again?*

Unfortunately, Ben's wife fell ill so the contract he had made for the girls was cancelled. Zoe had received a letter from Hazel, so she and Holly arranged to meet her as she said she had some news. She didn't say whether it was good or bad. They met in a pub close by and Holly brought over three glasses of white wine to the table.

'So, how are you?' Zoe asked, 'Are you still seeing Khalid?'

Hazel raised the glass to her lips, taking a sip of wine before letting out a nervous laugh. 'I don't think any man is worth getting kidnapped for,' she quipped, her words laced with a hint of sarcasm.

Zoe and Holly nodded in agreement, clinking their glasses against Hazel's. 'I'm right there with you,' said Holly.

Hazel looked at her friends. 'I have bad news. You know those headaches I was having,' Hazel continued, her voice tinged with concern. 'Well, I had a scan, and it turns out it's a small brain tumour. It's not too serious, but I do need an operation. So, no more dancing for a while.'

Zoe's eyes widened in shock and Holly gasped, as Hazel's words sank in. Zoe leaned in and gave her a tight hug. 'I am so sorry,' she whispered, her voice filled with genuine sympathy and support.

Holly fought back her tears.

'Actually, I've been having a few aches and pains myself,' said Zoe, 'I guess I should pay a visit to the doctor. But maybe it's just old age.' They laughed as they were all only twenty-five years old.

Zoe was disappointed that Ben's contract had been cancelled, but Holly welcomed the break and surprisingly she had decided to visit her parents. She invited Zoe and they caught the train to Brockenhurst. One of the wealthiest towns in Hampshire. Zoe wasn't surprised when they climbed out of the taxi outside of Holly's home. This exquisite four-bedroom, three-bathroom cottage was nestled in the heart of Brockenhurst. It had a perfect view of the New Forest, blending modern living with countryside charm. Inside she observed the large modern kitchen, and a living room with a wood-burning stove. All modestly decorated but with exquisite taste. Zoe found Holly's mother delightful but found it strange hearing Holly being addressed as Victoria. Holly just sat back drinking a large vodka tonic. Apparently, her father was out of town on business.

'I am so glad Victoria has found a lovely friend,' said the mother, her voice warm with genuine relief. 'Her last crowd were, how shall I say?'

'Unsuitable,' added Holly, her tone carrying a hint of disdain. She turned to Zoe with a smile. 'Come on, Zoe, let's go to my room.'

Zoe glanced at Victoria's mother, giving her a polite smile. 'Thank you for having me over, Mrs. Hollywood.'

Mrs. Hollywood waved her hand dismissively, her eyes twinkling. 'Oh, please, call me Camilla. I'm just happy Victoria has someone like you in her life.'

Zoe felt a blush creeping up her cheeks. 'I'm glad to be here.'

Holly tugged at Zoe's hand playfully. 'Come on, we have so much to talk about.'

As they headed upstairs, Zoe could hear Camilla murmuring to herself, 'Unsuitable indeed. Thank goodness for Zoe.'

Once inside Holly's room, Zoe flopped onto the bed, laughing. 'Your mom is sweet, but what's going on between you and her?'

'Nothing. I just hung around with a bad crowd at one time. Plus, mother doesn't like the idea of me dancing. She wants me to go back to uni.'

Zoe looked at her friend, 'She would prefer you to be a doctor or lawyer?'

Holly laughed, 'Yeah, something like that. 'She means well.

But we came to an understanding. She knows I won't stop dancing, so figured when I am old and decrepit, I can run a dance school, so she suggested I study business and finance.'

'Well, that doesn't sound too bad. I mean now the contract has been cancelled, what are we going to do? More stressful auditions?'

Holly looked at her friend and said, 'I could do with a break. Meanwhile, I want to take some modern dance classes.'

Two days later, they were back in London.

Zoe was growing bored of doing temp work when she received a letter from Lynn, an old friend whom she knew from her early days in London. Lynn was living in Italy, working as a DJ in an upscale club, and invited her to come and visit. Zoe jumped at the chance to return to Italy for a holiday.

14

Alfredo

A few days later Zoe hopped on a train from London to Dover. Taking the train might be more time-consuming, but it was a much more enjoyable way to travel; Train travel was comfortable and spacious, you can enjoy the scenery along the way, and you ended up in the centre of cities rather than at some distant airport. You also got to meet interesting people, and on this trip, Zoe met a group of Italians who wanted to practice their English with her.

She left the train and boarded the ferry to cross the channel. A big storm ensued so she stayed above board to avoid sea sickness. Opposite her, a couple, obviously newly married were kissing passionately when the boat rocked and they were drenched with water from the lifeboat situated above them. Zoe felt sorry for them but also stifled her laughter as they made their way below.

Zoe arrived safely in Calais and caught the train to Naples. She hooked up with some other adventurous travellers and the eight-hour journey passed quickly. She met Lisa, a backpacker from Australia. 'I'm going on to Rome after Naples. How about you? Is this your first time here?'

'No,' Zoe replied, returning the smile. 'I've spent time in a few Italian cities a while back. How about you?'

'Oh, it's my third time,' Lisa said with a laugh. 'I just can't get enough of Italy. The food, the history, the people... it's all amazing.'

A young couple from Canada, Mark and Jenna, joined their conversation. 'We're on our honeymoon,' Jenna said, her eyes sparkling with excitement. 'We are also going to Rome and then continue on to other countries for our European tour.'

'Wow, that's fantastic!' Zoe exclaimed. 'Congratulations! How long are you travelling for?'

'Two months,' Mark answered. 'We're planning to visit France, Spain, and Greece.'

Throughout the journey, they shared stories and travel tips. Lisa recounted her adventures in the Australian outback, while Mark and Jenna talked about their wedding and future plans.

At one point, Mark pulled out a map of Rome. 'I've been reading about the best places to visit, but there's so much to see. Any recommendations?'

Lisa leaned over to look at the map. 'Definitely check out the Trevi Fountain. It's beautiful, especially at night.'

'And don't miss the Roman Forum,' Zoe added. 'It's like stepping back in time.'

At a stop in France, Zoe was looking out the window when she saw a man on the parallel train exposing himself. She gasped while Mark cursed and the other girls gave out a nervous giggle. Zoe beckoned the guard and tried to explain what just happened but couldn't think how to say penis in French. After her feeble attempt they all started laughing until they cried!

As the train sped through the picturesque landscapes, they laughed, exchanged addresses, and promised to keep in touch. 'Wow, my address book is filling up. I will need to buy another bigger one, but then have the tedious task of copying all the information into the new book.' said Zoe.

'I use a mini file, where I can just add extra pages,' said Lisa. 'I meet so many lovely people on my travels, I hope I can meet them all again one day.'

The hours flew by, and before they knew it, the train was pulling into Napoli Centrale station. 'Well, here we are. It was great meeting you all,' said Zoe.

'Same here,' Lisa replied, giving her a hug. 'Enjoy Naples, or should I say Napoli! Maybe we'll run into each other again.'

'Take care,' Jenna said, waving as they parted ways. 'And have an amazing time!'

Zoe stepped off the train, glad to be back in her favourite country.

Lynn was working as a DJ in a Naples nightclub. Zoe always felt quite plain next to her as she was an extremely beautiful and petite blonde. She wasn't the most intelligent of Zoe's friends, but she was a lot of fun to be around and attracted men like bees to honey. Most were rebuked for assuming that being English, she was *that* sort of girl. Zoe had to console a lot of disappointed suitors.

Zoe was sitting in the club while watching Lynn compile her record collection for the evening's show when a man´s voice called out, '*Ciao Bella.*'

He greeted Lynn with a kiss before she introduced him to Zoe. He was handsome with dark eyes and tanned skin. '*Ciao*, are you English,' he asked Zoe in perfect English.

'Yes, I am,' she replied.

'My name is Alfredo. If you are alone, would you care to have a drink with me?'

Zoe glanced at him and as she was feeling a little bored, she said, 'Sure, why not.' She followed him to the bar.

He was maybe a couple of inches taller than Zoe and dressed elegantly and stylish. Italian suits were expensive, but they were as essential to young Italian men as leather jackets were to bikers. They settled into a cozy corner of the bar, and Zoe couldn't help but admire his charming demeanour. 'So, do you live here?' she asked, taking a sip of her drink.

Alfredo smiled, his eyes sparkling with enthusiasm. 'No, I'm in town looking for ideas and staff for a new club in a ski resort I'm about to open.'

'A ski resort? That sounds fascinating. Where is it?'

'In a town called Rivisondoli, a few miles from here. It's a beautiful area, and I want to create a place that combines luxury with adventure,' Alfredo explained, his passion evident.

Zoe nodded. 'I've always wanted to learn to ski.'

Alfredo said with a grin. 'It's one of my favourite pastimes. You should come visit once it's open. I'll give you a personal tour.'

She laughed. 'I might just take you up on that offer. I've always been more of a dancer than a skier, though.'

Alfredo leaned in slightly, intrigued. 'A dancer? That's wonderful. What kind of dance?'

'Mostly jazz and contemporary,' Zoe replied. 'I'm part of a touring dance company.'

They went for a walk and talked for hours, sharing stories about their lives and ambitions. Alfredo's charisma and humour made the time fly by. Zoe felt a genuine connection between them, something she hadn't expected when she first walked into the bar. They said goodbye and Alfredo told her he had to go on a business trip but would be back soon.

Lynn spotted Zoe sitting at a table, a dreamy look on her face. She slid into the seat across from her, a curious grin spreading across her lips. 'Alright, spill. You look like you're floating on a cloud. What do you think of Alfredo?'

'He's really sweet and funny,' Zoe said, her eyes lighting up. 'We ended up going for a walk and talking for hours. He's well-travelled, loves animals, and he's a writer too.'

'I didn't know you were a writer.'

'Not a writer per se. I have written a few short stories, but lately I started writing a novel,' said Zoe.

'Good for you. What is it about?'

'An adventure in Italy. It's still in a very rough draft.'

In the days that followed, Zoe and Lynn spent a lot of time together, enjoying each other's company. However, as Lynn's gigs started piling up, her schedule became increasingly hectic, leaving less time for them to be together.

Zoe was glad when Alfredo returned., especially when he asked, 'Would you like to visit my hometown?'

Zoe was a free spirit and went wherever the wind would take her, so said, 'Sure. Why not?'

They travelled to Alfredo's hometown of Mondragone. It was a small village near the sea, a few miles from Naples and famous for its mozzarella. For respectability, Zoe stayed in his business partner's hotel. Giovanni, the owner, was a charming older man, still attractive with his grey hair and piercing blue eyes. His six sons practically ran the hotel for him, while his mother and wife did all the cooking. So far Alfredo had been the perfect gentleman and their overnight arrangements, meant this continued.

Zoe met Alfredo's parents but was a little surprised when he introduced her as his personal assistant. *What the hell was that about?* she asked herself. Later Alfredo explained they had very old-fashioned ideas about courting. By this time Zoe's Italian was quite good but his parents spoke in a heavy Neapolitan dialect. When she spoke, they would turn to Alfredo and ask '*Que diche*' (What is she saying.) Apparently pure Italian wasn't used in that part of Italy. She also noticed a difference in Alfredo's demeanour when they were in his village. If she hooked her arm in his, he'd say '*Non mi toccare,*' (Don't touch me.)

The only entertainment in the village was the cinema -so a night out involved watching a movie that she could hardly understand, munching on caramel popcorn or a stale Mars Bar. She was usually the only female there. She asked Alfredo why most women from the village wore black.

'They are constantly in mourning for a friend or relative, so it becomes a perpetual state,' he said.

Some nights Alfredo would take her into Naples with Giovanni and a beautiful young lady, who was not his wife. Zoe felt guilty as she liked Giovanni's wife a lot, but it was accepted as the norm. The villagers were friendly to Zoe, mostly curious, she thought. They couldn't understand how she could be so far away from her family. Every day she would meet the same people and they would ask, '*Ciao bella, come stai? Come tua madre*' Every day the same questions, 'How are you? how's your mother?' They couldn't understand how a single woman could travel alone.

A couple of weeks passed during which Alfredo had been a real gentleman. Of course, being in his hometown helped.

They were lying on a secluded beach, the sun setting in a blaze of colours. 'Alfredo,' Zoe began, turning to face him. 'You've been so wonderful. But there's something I've been wanting to do for a while now.'

He raised an eyebrow, a playful smile tugging at his lips. 'Oh, and what might that be?'

Without another word, Zoe leaned in and kissed him, her lips soft and insistent against his. He responded eagerly, and soon they were lost in each other, the sound of the waves the only witness to their passion.

When they finally pulled apart, they spent the rest of the evening wrapped in each other's arms, until the chill of the night air and the gritty sand became too much to bear.

'Let's head back?' Alfredo suggested, helping her to her feet.

Zoe nodded, brushing sand off her clothes. 'Yes, please. I need something to wake me up.'

They staggered back to a nearby café, and settled at a small table, Alfredo waved to the waiter. 'Two double espressos, *per favore.*'

'Oh, no,' cried Zoe, 'I still can't handle espressos, never mind a double. Just order me cafe con latte please.'

As they waited, Zoe reached across the table, taking his hand in hers. 'These past few weeks have been incredible, Alfredo.'

He squeezed her hand gently. 'They have been for me too, Zoe. You're special. I knew it from the moment I saw you.'

The waiter arrived with their order, and they clinked their cups together.

'To us,' Zoe said, smiling warmly enjoying the perfectly made coffee.

'To us,' said Alfredo. 'However, if we ever do that again, I'm going to keep my socks on.'

Zoe laughed and suddenly realised that not only were his socks missing but also her beautiful scarf that Adib had bought for her. Perhaps it was a sign that she should let go of the past.

15

Amsterdam & Caracas

The trips away from Alfredo's village were a welcome relief. One time he whisked Zoe off to Amsterdam to meet some of his friends. The Dutch are so laid back and most of them spoke English. On their first day there, the rain kept them home until after lunch, but when the sun finally peeked out, they took a tram towards the museum district. They had packed a picnic lunch so sat in the sunshine near the Rijk Museum, people watching as they ate. Alfredo remarked that the museum was founded in The Hague on 19th November 1798 and moved to Amsterdam in 1808. Alfredo and Zoe were kept busy by accommodating all the tourists asking them to take their photo in front of the museum.

'I feel like Annie Leibovitz.'

'Who's that?' asked Alfredo.

A famous photographer. She was the chief photographer for the *Rolling Stone* magazine. I wish these people could just take their own photos.' Zoe said, handing a camera back to a smiling couple.

'I know,' Alfredo replied, snapping another photo for a

group of friends. 'But it's kind of fun. Everyone's so excited to be here.'

Their next stop was the Bloemenmarkt – the flower market. Zoe couldn't believe how many bulbs were for sale and some of them were enormous.

'Look at the size of these tulip bulbs!' Alfredo said, holding one up.

'Wow, those are huge,' Zoe said, inspecting the bulb. 'I wish I had a garden. In fact, I think I'll buy some for Holly's parents. They have a lovely garden.'

Right beside the flower market, there were several cheese shops offering free samples.

'Let's try some,' Zoe suggested, heading to the nearest shop.

They tried several samples, and each one was more delicious than the last. 'This Gouda is amazing,' Zoe said, savouring a bite.

They bought a little pack of several different cheeses for snacking later. 'This will be perfect for our picnic tomorrow,' Zoe said, tucking the cheese into her bag.

'A picnic,' said Alfredo. 'I do have to do some work. We will be meeting with some of my business associates tomorrow.'

Their meeting was held in a coffee bar. The aroma of freshly ground beans floated through the air as they waited. It was the best coffee that Zoe had ever tasted. Alfredo was amazing. He would speak to her in English, his friends in Italian and the bartender in Dutch without any hesitation.

Their next escapade was to Caracas, Venezuela where Alfredo had more business meetings with his silent partners. Zoe thought they looked like the Venezuelan Mafia, laundering their money. When she hinted as much to Alfredo he laughed. 'You've been reading too many of those mystery novels!'

Alfredo teased.

'Well, I guess my imagination is running wild,' she said, not entirely convinced, but smiling anyway.

Despite her suspicions, Alfredo's friends were wonderful. They were keen to practice their English on her, so she didn't get much opportunity to speak Spanish. 'Your English is fantastic!' she would often say, impressed by their fluency.

'Thank you, Zoe,' one of Alfredo's friends, Carlos, replied. 'But we still need lots of practice.'

She chuckled. 'I'm sure you'll be fluent in no time.'

Zoe often got Spanish mixed up with Italian. One evening, at a Mexican restaurant, she inadvertently caused a stir. 'Could I have some *burro*, please?' she asked the waiter.

Everyone at the table burst into laughter.

'What's so funny?' Zoe asked, her cheeks turning red.

Carlos, still chuckling, explained, 'In Italian, burro means butter. But in Spanish, it translates to donkey!'

Zoe joined in the laughter. 'Oh, my goodness! No wonder everyone was looking at me funny.'

Alfredo patted her hand reassuringly. 'Don't worry, Zoe. They are impressed that you try to speak their language.'

She grinned, feeling a bit better. 'I guess I'll stick to English for now.'

'You're doing great,' Carlos said, smiling. 'And we appreciate the chance to practice English with you.'

Despite her earlier reservations, she was enjoying the company and the experiences Venezuela had to offer.

Caracas, often described as a concrete jungle, was rarely the top choice for tourists to visit. It was congested, noisy, polluted, and in parts, dirty and dangerous. Wandering through unknown streets was risky even in daylight – however she always felt safe in Alfredo's company. One day they travelled up the mountains and ate wonderfully fresh water melon with the locals. The locals were very generous even though they were extremely poor. Such a contrast to the people in their fancy hotel where she and Alfredo were staying.

Their last evening was spent in a huge mansion belonging to Carlos. Zoe and Alfredo were enjoying a lively dinner with their Venezuelan friends and their business associates. The atmosphere was filled with laughter, the clinking of glasses, and the rich aroma of *arepas* and other dishes that Zoe did not recognize. Their friends, Maria and Carlos, were recounting stories of growing up and how they met, their voices filled with nostalgia and warmth. Zoe, followed along with the help of Maria's translations, savouring every moment of this cultural exchange.

Suddenly, the convivial atmosphere was shattered by the piercing sound of sirens. Before anyone could fully comprehend what was happening, a group of police officers burst through the door, their expressions stern and authoritative. The company fell silent and froze in their seats as the officers barked orders. Zoe and Alfredo exchanged bewildered glances with Maria and Carlos, fear and confusion evident in their eyes. The police began checking IDs and questioning everyone in rapid Spanish. Despite their protests and attempts to explain, Zoe, Alfredo, Maria, and Carlos and the other two men, were handcuffed and led out into the courtyard and shoved into police cars.

'I told you they were shady people,' whispered Zoe.

'Maybe you're right,' said Alfredo.

At the jail, the air was thick with the smell of sweat and despair. The officers, stern and unsympathetic, processed their arrival with robotic efficiency. They pushed them into a holding cell. Zoe shivered as she heard the distant sound of murmured conversations among the other detainees. The cell was a small, grimy room with concrete walls stained by years of neglect. A single, flickering bulb provided the only source of light, casting eerie shadows. The floor was cold and damp, and a stench of urine and mould permeated the air. The barred window offered a glimpse of the outside world, but the view was obstructed by a huge stone wall.

As the first light of dawn began to filter through the small, barred windows of the jail cell, Officer Ramirez walked over to the cell where Zoe and Alfredo were being held. The cell door opened, and the officer's demeanour had softened from the previous night's raid. He motioned them to follow him. Zoe and Alfredo exchanged a tired but relieved glance and quickly did as they were told.

In the small, dimly lit hallway leading to the exit, Officer Ramirez turned to face them.

'I'm sorry for the inconvenience you've experienced,' he began, his voice low and sincere. 'There was a mix-up in our operation. We had a tip that proved to be false, and unfortunately, you and your friends got caught up in it.'

Alfredo, rubbing his wrists where the handcuffs had left red marks, asked, 'Will our friends be released soon as well?'

Officer Ramirez nodded. 'Yes, we are processing their release now. This was all a terrible mistake. You're free to go, and there won't be any charges against any of you.'

Zoe, still shaken from the ordeal, managed a small smile. 'Thank you. It's been a rough night, but we appreciate you clarifying things.'

Officer Ramirez handed them a piece of paper with information on how to file a formal complaint. 'If you need to, you can use this. Again, I'm sorry for what happened.'

With that, he opened the door, where the sun was now shining brightly. Zoe and Alfredo stepped out, feeling a rush of relief and exhaustion. As they walked away from the police station, they tried to see the funny side of all what had happened.

'Just chalk it up to another adventure,' said Zoe, 'Maybe it will be fodder for my novel.'

After a quick shower at their hotel, they caught the first flight back to Italy. Their friends had left a message with the hotel clerk saying everything was okay and their future investments were still happening.

16

Rivisondoli Ski Resort

Back in Italy, it was time to move to the ski resort in the mountains of Rivisondoli. Zoe was packing when Lynn asked to meet later as she had some good news.

Zoe sat at a cozy corner table in her favourite coffee shop, a warm cappuccino cradled in her hands. The door chimed, and Lynn walked in, as usual, turning men's heads. She was stunning in her white trouser suit with her blonde hair cascading over her shoulders.

'Hey, sorry I'm late!' she called out, sliding into the seat opposite her friend.

'You look like you're about to burst. What's up?'

Lynn's grin widened, her excitement palpable. 'You won't believe it, Zoe. I got accepted as a Playboy Bunny in London!'

'No way! That's incredible, Lynn! Tell me everything!'

Lynn took a deep breath, her words tumbling out in a rush. 'I went through the interviews and auditions, and it was so nerve-wracking. But they loved my look and personality. I'll be starting next month at the Playboy Club in Mayfair. It's such a huge opportunity – the glamour, the networking, everything!'

Zoe beamed with pride. "I'm so happy for you! a friend of mine told me that becoming a Bunny is no easy feat. Hundreds of women attend auditions. The training program is tough.'

'So I was told,' said Lynn, 'We have to learn the names of 143 liquor brands and memorize twenty different cocktail garnishes. I'm feeling a bit nervous, but mostly excited. It's a big change. I've always wanted to experience London. And this job could open so many doors for me., especially in the modelling world.'

'As long as you stay out of centre page of the Playboy magazine,' said Zoe.

'Hell yeah,' said Lynn laughing, 'What about you?'

'Well, I've decided to join Alfredo at the club.'

Lynn clinked her coffee cup with Zoe's and said, 'Here's to new beginnings. We should be drinking champagne.'

They chatted a little longer before saying a teary goodbye. 'Don't forget to write. I'm tired of losing touch with my friends,' said Zoe. The words triggered a reminder—she still owed Holly a letter. In Holly's last one, she mentioned finishing her university courses and preparing for dance auditions. Zoe felt a pang of jealousy, or was it regret?

She liked Alfredo—a lot. He was charming, spontaneous, and full of life. But was she in love with him, or just swept up in the intoxicating whirlwind of his exciting lifestyle? His wonderful mysterious acquaintances, the late-night drives along the coast, the effortless way he moved through the world with an air of confidence—it was all exhilarating.

And yet, there were moments when doubt crept in. Some days, she felt restless, even bored. Especially when they were surrounded by his friends, all speaking in rapid-fire Italian, their laughter ringing around her while she sat in quiet detachment, smiling politely but feeling like an outsider. She tried to follow their conversations, catching fragments of words, but the effort was exhausting.

Did Alfredo even notice? Or did he assume she was as enchanted by his world as he was?

The drive up the mountain to Rivisondoli was spectacular. Zoe was bundled up with her coat, scarf, gloves and a very warm hat. The resort was only two hours from the airport, so ski weekends, snowboard breaks and short ski holidays to Rivisondoli were perfectly feasible for Italians from Naples and Rome. The wealthier clientele had their own chalets, while others stayed in the hotel. Nearby, there was a grocery shop, a kindergarten, and a library. The library made Zoe particularly happy because she loved to read and explore facts from their extensive collection of English encyclopaedias, which had been donated by one of the regular Italian clients. These clients wanted their children to learn English, and Zoe supposed their education also benefitted from the vast amount of information in these books. Zoe 's curious mind was always researching. She found it amusing that snowboards were actually invented in 1965 but were then called *Snurfers.*

The guests were much more cosmopolitan than she had encountered in Naples and Alfredo was back to his old caring and fun-loving self. Zoe assumed the change in his demeanour was because they were far from his family, and also because the money from the club was rolling in.

At the hotel Zoe worked three evening shifts in reception while Alfredo ran the night club. During the days she had the chance to ski and became quite proficient at the sport. She often went into the village where she met many interesting visitors who were envious of her living in such a beautiful place. One evening, while enjoying a glass of wine and chatting with a group of tourists at a local trattoria, the conversation turned to their impressions of Italy. Sandy, an American traveller said, 'Rome and Naples are amazing, but this place? It's like a dream.'

Zoe smiled, taking a sip of her wine. 'Rivisondoli is idyllic, I agree. The mountains, the quiet, it's perfect. Big cities just don't do it for me.'

A man named Paul, from London, leaned in, curious. 'What do you mean? You don't like the hustle and bustle?'

'It's not that,' Zoe replied, her eyes thoughtful. 'Rome and Naples have their charm, their history and vibrancy. But there's something about the tranquillity of a place like Rivisondoli that just feels right to me. However, I do enjoy London.'

Sandy nodded, her expression dreamy. 'I get that. It's like stepping back in time here, in the best possible way.'

'Exactly,' Zoe said, smiling. 'I love waking up to the sound of birds, not traffic. And the people here, they're like family.'

Paul raised his glass. 'To Rivisondoli, and to finding our own little slices of paradise.'

'Cheers to that,' Zoe agreed, clinking her glass with theirs.

Zoe thought about London and Holly. She truly missed her friend, so she returned to her room to reply to Holly's latest letter. As she read it, a smile spread across her face. Holly had finally admitted that her mother might be right, including a quote from her: *"Darling, you can't dance forever. You need to prepare for another career."* Reluctantly, Holly had enrolled in the course her mother suggested. Zoe sat with pen in hand ready to write but she hesitated as she tried to imagine Holly in a class full of office people. The thought was amusing, Holly with her vibrant personality and unconventional approach, in a room filled with people in suits and ties. It made Zoe chuckle quietly but also led Zoe to a deeper contemplation about her own life and future.

From her early years filled with curiosity and dreams, she had come a long way. Growing up, Zoe had always been the imaginative one. She remembered the countless hours spent dreaming about the future, creating adventurous scenarios in her mind.

After dancing, would her five 'o' levels be enough to get a good paying job? Was she really the type to do ordinary jobs? Over the years, Zoe had faced her share of challenges and triumphs. Each experience had taught her valuable lessons, contributing to her growth as an individual. Now, she found herself at a crossroads. The routine here was beginning to feel monotonous. Her personal life seemed to be on autopilot. The spark that once ignited her passions was dimming. As Zoe pondered her future, she felt apprehension. She wanted to dance again. At this time, she had a lot of spare time on her hands. She read a mountain of novels and wrote a lot, not just in her diary, but created the first draft of her novel. She needed more adventure in her life. She finished her letter to Holly, striving to sound content, but she knew her friend would read between the lines. Afterwards, she took a walk to post the letter, pausing to appreciate the beautiful surroundings.

Zoe and Alfredo were eating lunch when she suggested to Alfredo that she start dance classes in Naples, 'Alfredo, I want to start dance classes in Naples as I need the exercise.'

Alfredo frowned, his fork pausing mid-air. 'I told you, Zoe, it's not a good idea. Naples isn't the place for that kind of venture.'

'But why not? I speak the language; I have the skills. And I could meet some like-minded friends,' she insisted.

Alfredo sighed, putting down his fork. 'It's not just about the language. You don't understand the nuances, the way people think. Especially the men. They can be... forward.'

Zoe crossed her arms, her eyes narrowing. 'Forward? What do you mean by that?'

He leaned closer, his expression serious. 'They'll flirt with you, try to take advantage. You don't know what they're really saying when they complement you. It's a different mentality here.'

The tension in the room was palpable. Zoe shook her head. 'So, what? I should just stay away from any male patron who talks to me?'

'Yes,' Alfredo said firmly. 'I don't want you talking to them. It's for your own good.'

Zoe's frustration boiled over. 'You're being ridiculous, Alfredo! I can handle myself. I'm not some naive girl.'

Alfredo's face hardened. 'This is non-negotiable, Zoe. I won't have you embarrassing me in front of my colleagues and staff.'

She stood up, her chair scraping loudly against the floor. 'Embarrassment. Seriously! You're not listening to me. This isn't about safety or your reputation, it's about control.'

Zoe stormed out of the room, grabbing a small bottle of whiskey from the bar. She wasn't a big drinker, so after a few mouthfuls, the alcohol hit her hard. She stumbled down the lobby, screaming, 'Hey Alfredo, am I embarrassing you now?'

That charade did not go down well with Alfredo or the staff.

Alfredo ordered one of the maids to escort her to her room.

The following morning, Zoe, nursing a terrible hangover, approached Alfredo and apologized. 'We'll talk later,' he said.

The incident was forgotten—or at least buried deep in some neglected corner of Zoe's mind. But the tension between them lingered, thick and unspoken, wrapping around their conversations and turning even the simplest exchanges into a quiet battlefield. The space between them felt colder, the silences stretching longer. Zoe knew their relationship was hanging by a thread, frayed and fragile. Something had to change.

But it didn't.

For two more months, she endured the slow unravelling. His jealousy sharpened, his possessiveness tightening like an invisible leash. What once felt thrilling now felt suffocating. Every question sounded like an accusation; every glance held suspicion. She found herself shrinking, choosing her words carefully, anticipating his moods before they turned into storms. It was all she could take.

One evening, standing in the dim light of their apartment, she realized she could see the end. And she didn't fear it—she welcomed it.

Alfredo was working, immersed in his own world, oblivious to the decision Zoe had already made. She moved quickly, heart pounding but hands steady as she packed her bag, shoving clothes inside without much thought. There was no room for hesitation. She scribbled a short note—no explanations, no long goodbyes—just enough to say what needed to be said. Then, slipping the paper onto the bedside table, she turned and left.

Outside, the midday sun burned bright, but Zoe felt only

the cool certainty of her choice. She found one of the staff members, a kind-faced man who had always been polite to her, and asked if he could take her into town. He didn't ask questions. Maybe he had seen this before. Maybe he knew better than to interfere.

She spent the night in a small, nondescript hotel, the room quiet except for the hum of the old fridge. Sleep didn't come easily, but she didn't mind. By morning, she was on the first train to the airport, her fingers gripping the worn leather of her bag as the countryside blurred past the window. With every mile, she felt lighter.

Boarding the plane back to England, staring out at the clouds, the questions crept in, whispering their doubts.

Did I need to learn to be more patient? Less critical of men? Did I just made another mistake?

17

Newbury

Once again, back in London, Zoe crashed at Holly's flat. She had been feeling guilty about her mother, so decided it was time to visit her. She went to the public phone box. 'Damn it's broken again. Bloody kids,' she said to no-one in particular. She walked over to the next street and found a working phone. She made the call to one of the only neighbours who had a phone and asked if her mother was okay. 'Yes,' said the neighbour, 'and still as cantankerous as ever.'

'Thanks. Could you let her know I will be up there tomorrow.'

'Everything okay?' asked Holly.

'Yes,' said Zoe. 'I'm not looking forward to the visit, but I have to go.'

When she returned to Holly's flat, she explained where she was going.

Holly looked at her and said, 'By the way, I have a phone in the house. It is a party line.'

'Okay, lucky you.' said Zoe.

Holly laughed, 'Slight problem, the other tenant Mrs Coleman talks a lot, so you have to ask her politely, to finish her conversation so you can make a call.'

'Well, if you get bored you can always listen in,' said Zoe.

'Before you go up north, let's go shopping. That should cheer you up.' suggested Holly.

They both had saved their earnings and were ready for a shopping spree. They went to their favourite store called Biba, the iconic fashion store, which became famous in the swinging sixties and seventies. It was founded by the Polish-born fashion designer Barbara Hulanicki a couple of years ago, and it was surprisingly affordable. Holly bought the pink gingham dress with a distinctive cutout at the back of the neck, accompanied by a matching triangular kerchief. This dress had gained celebrity appeal, as it had been worn by the iconic Brigitte Bardot. Zoe had simpler tastes so bought a pair of high purple, suede boots and a white mini skirt.

Zoe's trip up north was bearable. She had learned just to let her mum talk and be criticised. Luckily, Zoe managed to get two tickets for the local theatre and her mother thoroughly enjoyed a decent rendition of 'Jesus Christ Superstar'.

'That was surprisingly good,' her mum said as they exited the theatre, her eyes shining with excitement.

'I thought you'd like it,' Zoe replied, smiling.

Her mother always loved going to the theatre and listening to opera, but her limited finances rarely allowed her the opportunity. Also, her hearing was failing slightly.

They walked to a nearby family pub for a quiet drink. Her mother wasn't a drinker but enjoyed a port now and then. 'Two ports, please,' Zoe ordered at the bar.

As they sipped their drinks, her mother started in on her usual topics. 'You know, Zoe, you really should think about settling down. All this traveling around can't be good for you.'

Zoe nodded, trying to keep the peace. 'I know, Mum. I'm working on it.'

Her mother sighed, taking another sip of her port. 'I just worry about you, that's all.'

'I know you do,' Zoe said softly, 'but I'm happy with my life right now. There will be plenty of time to settle down.'

Her mum looked at her, eyes softening. 'As long as you're happy, that's all that matters.'

Zoe was surprised as usually her mother was more critical of her. Maybe getting out of the house put her in a good mood. Now, Zoe felt even more guilty for not being around, now that her brother was also travelling abroad. She was sorry that she had missed Jonathan as it was a while since they had seen each other. She also wished her mother had a proper carer, but on her budget, they could only afford someone to do a bit of housework and some shopping.

The town hadn't changed much. Separate groups of men and women—or rather, boys and girls, as Zoe felt much older than most of them—still gathered in the usual spots. The evenings were bitterly cold, but the girls were skimpily dressed, believing that alcohol would keep them warm.

Zoe called her old childhood friend Dot, and they met at the Royal Arms pub, an old hangout of theirs. Dot had lived in the same flat and worked the same job ever since leaving school. But she was always fun to be with, recounting some of the difficult days they had spent on caravan holidays.

'The moods of my mother sometimes made things difficult,' Zoe said, taking a sip of her drink. 'Remember the time she accused me of sleeping with that sailor we met at the camp? It wouldn't have been so bad, but I was still a virgin then.'

'Yeah, I remember that,' Dot said, laughing. 'Didn't your mum lock you out?'

'Yes,' Zoe replied, shaking her head. 'I spent the night under a tarpaulin on one of the fairground rides. I was so scared, but at least it was dry.'

Dot chuckled. 'Those were the days, huh? Full of drama, but somehow, we always made it through.'

'Yeah,' Zoe agreed, smiling, enjoying the trip down memory lane.

Two days later, Zoe hugged her mother goodbye. 'Take care, Zoe.'

'I will, Mum. See you soon.'

Zoe boarded the train for London and watched as her mother waved goodbye. She had insisted on accompanying Zoe to the train station.

Back in London, Zoe felt a wave of relief and guilt wash over her. She loved her mother, but she was glad to be back in her own space, ready to dive into her life in the city.

Holly had just returned from one of her dance classes when she excitedly mentioned an upcoming audition to Zoe. The event was to take place at the residence of Beryl Denise, a renowned talent agent. 'Count me in,' Zoe said eagerly. She made it a point to attend as many auditions as possible, using each opportunity to hone her skills and boost her confidence.

On the day of the audition, Zoe and Holly found themselves among a select few participants. While many girls aimed to secure roles closer to home in London, Zoe and Holly had no such reservations. In fact, they welcomed the prospect of dancing abroad, especially considering London's perpetually dreary weather. They felt a surge of excitement at the thought of potentially performing under the sunny skies of Spain.

At the end of the audition, Zoe whispered to Holly, 'That routine was so easy, or am I just getting really good?'

'It was a little complicated, but we knocked it out the park.'

The agent offered a job to them both. They were to be replacement dancers for a Spanish Company, touring Spain, for the fiestas. The main attraction was *Andrés Pajares Martín*, a top Spanish actor, director, writer and comedian, in theatre, film and television. *Andres* started as a comedian in 1968, but he preferred theatre performances and was looking for dancers to work in his company that would be travelling around Spain.

They had a week to learn the routines along with two other girls, Hilda and Tobi.

Once again Zoe couldn't help pulling out that encyclopaedia and discovered the name Tobi came from Hebrew/Greek origin and meant "God is Good" and Hilda from old Norse meaning "Battle Woman."

'We'll see if they live up to their names,' said Holly

I wish there was another way to do research. These encyclopaedias are so heavy - impossible to carry around, thought Zoe.

18

Spain

The week passed quickly and the dancers all met up in Heathrow airport - destination Madrid. It was a three-and-a-half-hour flight and Zoe slept all the way. A bus was waiting to take them to the hotel. It was the end of May and the weather was perfect. The hotel was not as nice as the one in Beirut but much better than the ones in Italy.

The other eight dancers were Spanish, including four boys. The principal dancer, Marisol, was very tall and beautiful and her partner Mikael, was not only her dance partner but also her husband.

After rehearsals ended, the company all boarded a not so, pristine coach without toilets, and their journey started. It was an interesting one to say the least. Many times when they arrived at a venue, all they did was eat, do the show, (often two a night) and arrive back at the hotel, exhausted and ready for a hefty gin and tonic. The gruelling schedule left little room for anything else.

There were times when they had to get back on the bus to travel through the night to the next venue. Sleep was hard to come by, especially with the Spanish dancers practicing their Flamenco handclapping. The incessant clapping drove the girls mad, especially Holly.

One night, Holly had enough. 'For the love of God, can you please stop that clapping?' she snapped, glaring at the Spanish dancers.

One of them looked up, confused. '*No entender,*' she said, shrugging.

Zoe tried to mediate. 'Holly, calm down. Let me try.' She turned to the dancers and, using exaggerated gestures, mimicked sleeping and then pointed to the clapping hands. 'Por favor,' she said, hoping her plea would be understood.

The Spanish dancers giggled, but the clapping did cease for a while. However, it wasn't long before the rhythm picked up again, even more spirited than before.

'This is impossible!' Holly groaned, throwing her hands up in frustration. 'Why can't they just understand?'

'I think they do understand but pretend not to.' Zoe sighed. 'Winning this argument is like trying to catch smoke with your hands. Everyone ends up frustrated.'

And so, the nights continued with a mix of exhaustion, tension, and the relentless rhythm of Flamenco claps echoing through the cramped bus.

For some reason, the rest of the company took a dislike to the English girls and throughout the ten-month tour, some were really quite nasty to them. One person who was helpful was the stage manager Santiago, who fancied Holly. When they were in Cadiz, as a treat, he took them to the beach for a relaxing afternoon. As they lounged in the sun, Zoe turned to Holly, a grin spreading across her face. 'This is paradise. We needed this break.'

Holly nodded, sipping on her drink. 'Absolutely. But it's a shame we have a show tonight.'

The group eventually packed up and headed back, but they soon found themselves stuck in a massive traffic jam. Zoe glanced at the clock on the dashboard, her smile fading. 'Oh no, we're going to be late.'

Santiago tried to navigate through the congestion, but it was no use. By the time they reached the venue, the show was about to start. They rushed inside and quickly changed, for the opening number, no time for makeup.

Later, their company manager Mario, who was perfectly bilingual, entered the dressing room, his face a mask of irritation.

'Not only did you make the show start late, but you looked like a bunch of pale faced hobos.'

'We got stuck in traffic,' Zoe explained. 'We're so sorry.'

Mario shook his head. 'Sorry isn't good enough. You know the rules, so you're all fined.'

Zoe groaned and turned to Holly. 'Great. Just great. A perfect end to what was supposed to be a perfect day. You know the name Mario means warlike.'

Santiago looked apologetic. 'I didn't think the traffic would be that bad. I'm sorry, everyone.'

Zoe forced a smile. 'It's not your fault, Santiago. We just have to deal with it.'

The choreographer, Jerry Jerome was English, and he also took a liking to the girls. He was happy when they got the new routines down faster than the others. He was very creative. One number was very bluesy, where they all sat on a stool before sashaying downstage smoking a cigarette. The Greek wedding number started with them all lighting matches to illuminate the setting and was brilliant although many times it was a struggle to get them lit and stop them from going out.

Sometimes the stages were too small for twelve dancers. One stage, in particular, was especially challenging due to its cramped size and a winding staircase that had to be navigated to get to the stage. During the opening number, with everyone wearing big headdresses and lots of feathers, Zoe had an unfortunate encounter. After the opening number, one of the male dancers aggressively yanked on her headdress, causing her to fall to the floor. She might have been seriously injured if Santiago hadn't intervened, stepping between them just in time.

'Bitch! Don't you ever block me again,' yelled the dancer, as Santiago dragged him away.

'What a drama queen! There was no room on that bloody stage, so complain to the manager,' said Zoe in a calm voice.

They reported the incident to Equity and also took the opportunity to seek their advice about another matter. They had been asked to sing in the opening number. *Bye bye London, Bye bye London, Hello Madrid, Hello Madrid.* However, their contracts stated they were hired as dancers, not as singers. On Equity's advice they asked for more money and got it and sang the silly song for the rest of the tour.

The company toured all over from place to place, a few days here, a week there, north, south from Madrid to La Coruna, and through many small towns and villages. Some of the bigger towns and main cities were Barcelona, Medina del Campo, Murcia and Sevilla. The country had such a strong history, Hilda would drag them out to visit every cathedral ever built. Tobi spoke a little French, Hilda spoke fluent Portuguese, Holly spoke a little Spanish and Zoe spoke Italian, so between them they always managed to get around and have a lot of fun. However, it wasn't all glamorous. Sometimes when they arrived at a venue, they had to find their own accommodation.

It was a blazing summer afternoon when the girls, arrived in Seville. They had slept well on the bus, so they were in a good mood. There was just one tiny problem—they couldn't find any accommodation. 'How hard can it be to find a place?' said Holly.

Dragging their suitcases through the cobbled streets of Spain, they passed countless "No Vacancy" signs. Their next stop was the bustling tourist information desk, a hotspot of chaos and confusion. Zoe, ever the sensible one, approached the frazzled attendant. 'Excuse me, do you have any recommendations for places to stay?'

The attendant sighed and handed over a dog-eared brochure. 'You can try these,' he said, pointing to a list of hotels. 'But there is a big festival taking place this week. Good luck!' They lugged their suitcases to the nearest café that had a public phone close by.

Zoe took charge and armed with a handful of pesetas made a few calls. She flopped down on the chair. 'Everything's either booked or costs a fortune!'

'This is hopeless,' Tobi groaned, 'Maybe we should just sleep on the beach.'

'Well, we can't stay here,' Hilda said. 'Let's just start walking and see what we can find.'

'Or we could ask the locals. They might know a place,' suggested Zoe.

As luck would have it, an elderly woman was sweeping her doorstep nearby. Holly, with her basic Spanish, approached her. '*Hola, señora, Sabe un hotel para nosotros?*'

The woman looked confused, but a young girl came over and translated. They motioned for them to follow and led them down a winding street to a quaint little guesthouse. The sign read *Pensión María*. Inside, a matronly figure bustled about.

'Do you have a room for four?' Zoe asked, holding her breath.

'*Sí, chicas.* You're in luck. We have one room left.'

They were shown to a small but charming room with two sets of bunk beds. It wasn't the Ritz, but it was perfect.

The night was young, and there was no show that evening, so they freshened up and headed out in a good mood. After all, they had a room, a roof, and each other—what more could they need?

Sometimes they would book a twin room in an expensive hotel and all four of them would sneak up to the room. They also cooked in the room on Hilda's one-ring heater, making sure the maids didn't see it when they cleaned the room. Tinned meatballs featured on their menu often which made Zoe think about becoming a vegetarian. They even slept in the theatre once when they couldn't find a room. They had a few near disasters. One time Hilda and Tobi were in a room when a piece of the ceiling fell directly onto the spot where Hilda's head had been resting moments earlier.

They arrived in Leon and it was freezing cold. They went to bed wearing their jazz bells and anything else from their limited wardrobe. They did not have many clothes packed, so when they got tired of wearing their own, they would swap clothes with each other. It was funny to see the petite Hilda in a shirt belonging to big, bosomed Tobi.

19

The Bus Crash

The early morning sun had barely begun to rise as Zoe, Holly, Tobi, and Hilda dozed in their seats on the tour bus bound for Madrid. The rhythmic hum of the engine and the gentle sway of the bus had lulled them into a deep, peaceful sleep. The journey had been long, and the weariness of the road had taken its toll. Zoe was the first to stir, her head resting against the cool window. Holly, next to her, was curled up with her hoodie pulled over her eyes, snoring gently. Across the aisle, Tobi and Hilda had finally fallen asleep after discussing their plans for Madrid.

Suddenly, a loud, jarring noise shattered the air as the bus lurched violently, its tires screeching against the pavement while it swerved out of control. The passengers awoke with a start, panic instantly surging through their veins. Everything seemed to happen in a flash: a terrifying lurch to the side, and the bus tipped over. When the bus finally came to a stop, the world was turned upside down. There was a moment of eerie silence, broken only by the hissing of steam escaping from the engine and the faint groans of other passengers. Zoe's eyes fluttered open, and she found herself hanging sideways in her seat, the seat belt straining against her chest. She felt disoriented, her mind struggling to process what had just happened.

'Holly! Tobi! Hilda!' Zoe called out, her voice shaky. She fumbled with her seat belt, her fingers trembling as she released it. She dropped to the side, her body hitting the wall that was now the floor. 'Is everyone okay?'

'Yeah...I think so,' Holly's voice came from where she had landed, not wearing a seat belt. She crawled over to Zoe, her hands and knees pressing against the glass of the windows, which were now beneath them.

Tobi groaned as she extricated herself from the tangle of seats and belongings. 'What the hell just happened?' she muttered, wincing as she touched her shoulder. She looked around, seeing the overturned bus in disarray, with bags and scattered belongings everywhere.

Hilda carefully maneuvered through the debris, her glasses askew. 'We need to get out of here,' she said, her voice steady despite the situation. 'The door is probably blocked, but the windows are big enough for us to crawl through.'

Zoe nodded, still trying to shake off the shock. 'Okay, let's go,' trying to sound braver than she felt.

One by one, they crawled through a broken window that had shattered upon impact Zoe threw her jacket over the edge to avoid the sharp fragments of glass. The cool morning air hit their faces as they emerged, and for a moment, they just stood there, taking in the scene. The bus lay on its side, skewed across the road, with smoke curling up from under the hood. The other dancers were slowly gathering around, some slightly injured, most just as dazed as they were.

Zoe looked at her friends, checking them over. Holly had a small cut on her cheek, Tobi was rubbing her shoulder, and Hilda had a scrape on her knee, but otherwise, they were unharmed. 'Is everyone okay?' Zoe asked again, her voice firmer now.

'Just a few cuts and bruises,' Holly replied, her hand brushing the cut on her cheek. 'But yeah, we're okay.'

Tobi glanced around, squinting against the brightening sky. 'Let's just make sure everyone else is okay.'

Together, they moved to assist the other passengers, their initial shock giving way to a quiet determination. The four of them, knew they would never make it to Madrid on time, but they were alive, and that was all that mattered.

Santiago listened to Mario and translated for the girls. The manager was calm but urgent as he spoke to someone on the other end of the line, his words carried on the morning breeze.

'Yes, we've had an accident. We're on the highway just outside of El Casar. No, no major injuries, thank God, but we need another bus out here as soon as possible,' the manager said, pausing to listen before continuing. 'How long? Okay, just get here quickly, please.'

He hung up and slipped the phone into his pocket, rubbing his temples as he took a deep breath. He then turned his attention to the bus driver, who was sitting on the grass nearby, looking pale and shaken. The driver, a man in his late fifties, was holding his head in his hands, clearly distressed by what had happened.

Mario approached him carefully, kneeling beside him. 'You okay, Javier?' he asked gently, his eyes narrowing with concern.

Javier lifted his head slowly, his face etched with guilt and exhaustion. 'I... I don't know what happened,' he stammered, his voice heavy with remorse. 'One minute everything was fine, and the next... I must have dozed off. I swear, I wasn't drinking. I'm just so tired. The last couple of shifts have been brutal.'

After a tense moment, Mario nodded. 'I believe you, Javier. You're a good driver, but you've been working too hard. This could have been a lot worse.'

Javier swallowed hard, his hands trembling slightly. 'I'm so sorry,' he whispered, barely able to meet the manager's eyes. 'I let everyone down.'

The manager placed a reassuring hand on Javier's shoulder. 'We're all just glad no one was seriously hurt. That's what matters now. The company will take care of this, and you're going to get some rest. We've already got another bus on the way. It should be here in about an hour or so.'

Holly, overheard the conversation and understood the gist of it. She shared a glance with Zoe, who was now nursing a small cut on her arm. 'Sounds like the driver just got too tired,' she murmured. 'It's a miracle we're all okay'

'Yeah,' Zoe agreed, glancing back at the overturned bus. 'Could've been so much worse.'

Tobi and Hilda walked over to join them, both looking a little more composed now that the initial shock had worn off. 'We should just sit tight until the new bus arrives.'

The four of them found a spot on the grass a little way from the wreckage, sitting together in a small circle as they waited. Luckily there was a farm nearby and the farmer and his wife came over offering refreshments: water, coffee and baked goods.

As they finally reached Madrid, Zoe felt a mix of relief and sadness. Back to where their journey had begun. As she prepared backstage, Santiago approached her.

'Zoe, you have a visitor waiting at the stage door,' he said, his eyes twinkling with curiosity.

'A visitor? Who could it be?' she wondered aloud.

When she reached the stage door, her eyes widened in surprise. Standing there with a bouquet of flowers was Alfredo, a warm smile on his face. 'Alfredo! What are you doing here?'

'I couldn't let you finish your tour without seeing you again,' he said, handing her the flowers.

Zoe's heart fluttered with mixed emotions. 'Thank you, Alfredo. I really appreciate this, but I have to get ready for my entrance.'

She promised to meet Alfredo later. They arranged to meet at a cozy Italian restaurant nearby. That evening, they had a wonderful meal together, reminiscing about the past and catching up on their lives. Alfredo's presence was comforting, but Zoe knew she had to be honest.

'Alfredo,' she began gently, 'I'm grateful that you came all this way to see me. But you need to understand that our relationship is over. I've moved on, and I hope you can too.'

Alfredo looked at her, sadness in his eyes. 'I understand, Zoe. I just wanted to see you one last time. To say goodbye properly.'

They finished their meal with a bittersweet farewell. As they parted ways, Zoe realized she had forgotten to ask him how he had tracked her down. But perhaps some questions were better left unanswered.

20

An actor's life

It was the winter in the UK when Zoe and Holly returned from their tour of Spain.

'Bad timing,' said Zoe. 'I hate this weather.'

'Me too,' said Holly.

For something different, they joined a talent agency and began working in commercials and movies, primarily as extras. The competition was fierce, but neither of them were fully invested in that kind of career. One day, their agent asked them to prepare a couple of numbers to perform in a gay bar.

'Are we really doing this?' Zoe asked, her eyes wide with a mix of apprehension as they rehearsed their routine.

Holly grinned, adjusting her costume. 'Absolutely! It'll be fun, and who knows, it might open up new opportunities.'

One of the numbers was from *Cabaret*, a piece Zoe found particularly challenging as she had to sing and dance. Despite her doubts, she delivered a stunning performance and was met with roaring applause.

'You were amazing out there!' Holly exclaimed, hugging Zoe tightly after they left the stage.

'Thanks,' Zoe replied, 'I didn't think I had it in me.'

Encouraged by this success, Zoe joined a local theatre company and was given a small part, in the upcoming play. She hadn't acted since her school years, so on opening night, she was extremely nervous. She adjusted her costume and peeked out from behind the curtain.

'I don't know if I can do this,' she confessed to Holly, who was backstage for moral support.

'Remember *Cabaret*?' Holly said, placing a reassuring hand on Zoe's shoulder. 'You've got this. Just breathe and be yourself.'

She stood behind the curtains, her heart beating fast against her rib cage, like that of a weakened gazelle running bewildered and exhausted from a fierce lion. She broke into a sweat and her hands shook like an alcoholic deprived of their daily dosage. Her mouth was dry and her throat tightened. She wanted to run, like that terrified gazelle. - *such is stage fright.*

She could hear the excitement of the crowd through the heavy velvet curtains. Friends calling over to other friends, laughter and the coughs. The small polite cough, the throaty cough and the downright disgusting phlegmy cough.

'One minute to curtain,' yelled the production assistant, rushing past Zoe, clipboard in hand. He looked back and gave her a querulous look, making sure she was ready.

Backstage the cast were bustling around in their period costumes, primping and laughing, ready for the big moment. Zoe wondered if she was the only nervous actor here. The heat was intense and the old dress she was wearing smelled of mold and was extremely itchy. Her shoes gripped her feet like Japanese foot binding, and she felt the make-up melting and smudging her already stained ruffle.

Zoe stepped onto the stage. The lights were blinding, but she felt a surge of adrenaline. She found her mark on the stage floor. Other actors took their places, crew stood ready in the wings. The curtain rose. Zoe stood there staring into blackness, her eyes adjusting to the glaring stage lights. The audience had become part of the play. They are now an eager crowd of the Elizabethan era, waiting for the horrific moment to occur. As she delivered her lines, the nerves slowly melted away, and she found herself immersed in the performance, reconnecting with a passion she thought she had lost.

Zoe turned to her executioner – stage fright gave way to stage presence. Lady Jane's blood coursed through her veins: I AM Lady Jane Grey. The words flowed easily.

'If I must die for England, so let it be. But first, hear my story'

Her monologue ended and she exited stage right. She joined Holly and they continued to watch the play backstage.

As the applause died down, the director came and congratulated her. 'You have a knack for this.'

Zoe thought maybe, but the stress was just too much.

Christmas was approaching, and their agent found them a position at Selfridges as demonstrators of Fisher Price toys. It was a fun job that got them into the spirit of Christmas, despite neither of them typically enjoying the holiday. Zoe's family was up north, and Holly couldn't stand the idea of spending Christmas with her snobby crowd of relatives.

One evening, as they were setting up a display of colourful toys, Holly glanced at Zoe. 'You know, this isn't so bad. I think I'm actually starting to like Christmas a little.'

Zoe laughed, arranging a row of plastic animals. 'Yeah, who knew working retail could be so festive? Plus, the kids' excitement is contagious.'

Holly nodded, watching a little boy's face light up as he played with a toy train. 'It beats the usual family drama, that's for sure.'

'Agreed,' Zoe said, her smile fading slightly. 'I don't really miss my family, so spending it with you makes it a lot more fun.'

Holly grinned, nudging Zoe with her elbow. 'Right back at you. We'll make our own Christmas; one we actually enjoy.'

Selfridges store in London was a special place. It hadn't changed since the first time Zoe had worked briefly in the boutique in 1968. That was the first time she had worn blue jeans. Standing on the stairs looking down to the ground floor, all Zoe could see was a sea of black veils as most of the clientele were Arab women. They had an abundance of money and of course nowhere to shop until they flew to London.

As the days passed, Zoe and Holly found themselves laughing more, sharing stories, and creating their own holiday traditions. On Christmas Eve, after the store closed, they sat at home drinking champagne.

'I got you something,' Holly said, handing Zoe a neatly wrapped package.

Zoe's eyes sparkled with surprise. 'You didn't have to!'

'I wanted to,' Holly replied with a shrug. 'Open it.'

Inside, Zoe found a vintage ornament, a tiny ballerina that looked remarkably like her. 'It's beautiful, Holly. Thank you.'

Holly smiled. 'I saw it and thought of you.'

Zoe handed over a gift to Holly, a small box containing a pair of delicate earrings. 'To match your style and spirit.'

Holly's eyes widened as she put them on. 'They're perfect. Thank you, Zoe.'

In that moment, surrounded by festive decorations, they realized they had created a holiday experience that was uniquely theirs—filled with joy, friendship, and a newfound appreciation for Christmas.

After Christmas, Zoe carried on doing extra work and managed to find a small flat she could afford. She spent some of her savings on head shots so she could do some acting and modelling. These odd jobs didn't make her rich but kept the bills paid.

For entertainment, she joined a Baptist church where actress Della Reese served as the minister. Every time Zoe walked in, she was warmly greeted and hugged by the well-endowed black women of the congregation. It felt comforting and motherly, a stark contrast to her own thin mother, who rarely hugged her. Zoe joined the choir, where she and another woman named Elizabeth stood out as the only two skinny white sopranos.

Dancing became an impossibility after Zoe's recent visit to the doctor which had revealed a diagnosis of arthritis. The persistent pains she experienced on a regular basis suddenly made sense in light of this new medical information. So, dancing was not in the picture anymore. Holly said a bittersweet goodbye to Zoe when she went off to dance with a troupe in Los Angeles. Zoe was happy for her friend, but that was a place she had always wanted to visit - maybe one day.

21

Katherine

Zoe had a few casual friends, but Holly was very precious to her. She felt a void when Holly took off to America.

One Sunday Zoe received a phone call from her friend Andre, whom she had met in Beirut, but when he had moved to London, they had lost touch. He had left the war-torn Beirut for a more peaceful life in the UK. He dealt with antiques and specialised in Russian Icons. Zoe hadn't seen him since Beirut and one day she happened to be stumbling around an ice rink with her old friend Eileen. when all of a sudden someone grabbed her and twirled her across the ice. It was Andre. He was an excellent skater. From then on, they had kept in touch.

'Hello, Zoe, I want to invite you to lunch. I want you to meet someone.'

'Who?' she asked.

'Just get your arse over here and you'll see.'

She wondered why he was being so mysterious. Maybe he had finally found a girlfriend. Andre lived in an expensive apartment in Knightsbridge, lavishly decorated with antiques and Persian rugs. Zoe jumped off the tube at Knightsbridge station and walked along Kensington Street, window shopping in all the expensive stores, wishing she could spend some of her savings. But her lifestyle was so unstructured she had to hang onto her money until she found another job, whatever that may be.

Ten minutes later she rang Andre's doorbell. He opened the door and gave her a huge hug. In the living room was a beautiful red head sitting gracefully on the wing back chair drinking tea from a china cup.

'Zoe this is Katherine. Katherine this is Zoe.'

'Pleased to meet you,' she said with an accent Zoe couldn't quite detect. 'Just call me Kat.'

As they continued talking, Zoe discovered an unexpected connection.

'You know,' Kat began, taking another sip of her tea, 'I used to dance in Beirut before we met. I was dating a guy named Nick at the time. He was a friend of Andre's.'

Zoe's eyes widened in surprise. 'No way! When I was in Beirut, I dated Adib. He was also a friend of Nick's. What a small world!'

Kat laughed, shaking her head. 'Seriously, what are the odds? So, you knew Nick too?'

'Yeah, I did,' Zoe replied, smiling at the coincidence. 'When Andre called me, I thought he was going to introduce me to a girlfriend.'

Kat grinned, leaning back in her chair. 'Nope, definitely not. We are just friends.'

Zoe nodded, still amazed by the connection. ' Who would have thought we had Beirut in common?'

'I guess it was meant to be.'

'Agreed,' Zoe said, raising her mug in a toast. 'To small

worlds and unexpected connections.'

'To small worlds,' Kat echoed, clinking her mug against Zoe's.

'This calls for a real drink,' said Andre as he stood holding a bottle of champagne.

'So, where are you staying Kat?' asked Zoe.

'Actually, I'm not sure. Andre said I could stay with him until I find a place. It has to be dirt cheap as I don't have a work visa yet.'

'You can stay with me if you like. I only have a sofa bed, but I would appreciate a little extra money.'

'That's so kind of you.'

After a meal of Arabic food, Andre drove them to Zoe's flat.

'I rarely drive, but I didn't want Kat traipsing through London with that heavy case.' He carried it to the door and hugged them goodbye.

Kat was very intelligent, humorous and well-travelled. She and Zoe became instant friends and roommates. Kat helped Zoe by paying a little towards the bills. They made inquiries about obtaining a visa. Unfortunately the UK introduced more restrictive immigration laws, which made it progressively harder for Australians and other Commonwealth citizens to work in the UK without a formal visa.

Determined not to let this deter her, Kat turned to Zoe's agency, a small but resourceful operation known for helping out young travellers.

Zoe told Kat, leaning in conspiratorially over a cup of tea in her tiny flat. 'Official jobs are tough to come by these days, but there are still plenty of people in this city who need a reliable pair of hands and don't ask too many questions.'

Kat nodded, understanding the unspoken implications.

'What kind of work are we talking about?'

Zoe smiled. 'The agency said nothing too shady. Mostly odd jobs—housekeeping, baby-sitting, maybe helping out in a few pubs or small shops. They pay cash, so it's all under the table. It's not glamorous, but it'll keep you afloat.'

Over the next few weeks, Kat found herself taking on a variety of these odd jobs. In the mornings, she would help Mrs. Green, an elderly widow in Chelsea, with her shopping and light housework. In the afternoons, she'd make her way to a local pub, The King's Head, where she'd assist the owner with cleaning and occasionally serve drinks to regulars. On weekends, she'd look after the children of a busy working couple in Notting Hill, ensuring they were entertained and fed while their parents were at work.

It was hard work, and the pay wasn't much, but it was enough to cover her rent and keep her in London, which was all Kat really wanted. Despite the under-the-table nature of the jobs, she felt a sense of independence and adventure, living in a city that was both thrilling and challenging.

As time went on, Kat's network grew. She met other Australians and travellers who were in similar situations, and they would often swap tips about where to find work.

Zoe and Kat sat drinking cheap plonk in their local pub. 'I know your experience in London isn't what you initially imagined, but it is full of the unexpected twists that made for great stories. You and I could write a book about it all one day.'

Yet even under those circumstances Zoe felt they had a decent life. Zoe would make a meal, out of whatever was leftover in the fridge, being named by Kat as "Queen of the leftovers." After doing the dishes and popping a few bob into the meter of the heater, they would snuggle under a blanket and turn on the old black and white TV that a friend of theirs had donated. There they were, whisked away to another time when Fred Astaire and Ginger Rogers floated across the screen.

'I heard there was a documentary about Australia,' said Kat. 'Which channel?'

'BBC, I think.

'Okay, we have nothing else planned, let's watch it,' said Zoe. They looked at each other. 'Go one then, your turn to change the channel.'

'But I'm so comfy,' said Kat.

'So am I. It's your choice to watch it.' Kat unravelled the blanket and got up to change the channel. 'It's not working.'

'Move the rabbit ears,' said Zoe slightly irritated.

After a bit of fiddling with the settings, the picture finally cleared up on the screen. Kat, settling into her chair with a sigh, remarked, 'I wish they'd invent something where you could just sit in your chair and speak your demands directly.'

Zoe looked at her, eyebrows raised. 'Don't be daft,' she replied with a chuckle.

'No, seriously,' Kat insisted, 'like what we see on Star Trek. Imagine being able to just talk to the TV and have it do whatever you want.'

Zoe stifled a laugh, shaking her head. 'Right, that'll be the day,' she said, her tone tinged with amusement.

With the budget being tight, television became their primary source of entertainment for the months that followed. It was a humble yet satisfying escape, a reminder that sometimes the simplest pleasures can provide the greatest comfort.

22

The Escort Service

Zoe was perusing the newspaper ads when she saw one for escorts and thought, Why not? Kat joined her and they arrived at a fairly respectable looking establishment, filled out some forms and listened to the orientation. Some girls left but as Kat and Zoe were the adventurous type, they stayed. They sat with eight other girls. Zoe and Kat laughed quietly as Zoe said, 'I feel like a wallflower at a high school dance.'

Men came in and chose whomever took their fancy. Kat, looking her glamorous self was chosen early on by a bespectacled, scrawny man.

By 10 p.m. Zoe and two other girls were sitting watching TV, when the owner invited them to go out and eat. Consolation prize, thought Zoe.

The following day, Kat recounted her uneventful night. 'We ate dinner and chatted,' she said, twirling a strand of hair around her finger. 'He was quite a lonely man but a real gentleman.'

Zoe raised an eyebrow. 'Really? I thought he seemed a bit... off.'

Kat shrugged, smiling. 'Appearances can be deceiving. He just needed someone to talk to. It wasn't the exciting night I expected, but it was nice in its own way.'

'Well, at least you got dinner,' Zoe replied with a smirk. 'The rest of us ended up at an all-night diner with the manager.'

Kat laughed. 'Hey, free food is free food.'

'True,' Zoe admitted, sipping her coffee. 'But next time, I hope I get picked by a rich geezer and get whisked away on his private jet to Paris.'

'Dream on,' said Kat, but you never know. Sometimes the least interesting people can surprise you the most.'

Zoe smiled. 'Maybe you're right. Here's to better luck next time.'

A week later, they received a letter from the police. The escort agency had been raided and they were called to be witnesses. 'How exciting, my first time in a police station,' said Zoe.

After a short interview, the DCI realized they were not the usual sort to be involved with such seedy operations. He leaned back in his chair and sighed.

'Ladies, you don't strike me as the type to get mixed up in this kind of thing.'

'We really aren't,' Zoe said earnestly. 'We had no idea what we were getting into.'

The DCI nodded. 'I believe you. But you need to be more careful. This isn't a game.' He stood up and motioned for them to follow him. 'Come on, I'll give you a ride home.'

They followed him out to his sleek Jaguar. As the car sped through the streets, the DCI glanced at them through the rear view mirror. 'Consider this a lesson learned. Stay away from anything like that. Human trafficking is a big business.'

'We will,' Zoe promised.

Kat added, 'You don't need to tell us twice.'

The DCI pulled up to their building and they climbed out of the car. Before they could thank him, he gave them a stern look. 'Next time, use your heads. It's a dangerous world out there.'

'Got it,' said kat.

'Thank you,' Zoe added.

The DCI gave them a final nod before driving off. They watched the car disappear, feeling a mixture of relief and gratitude.

'Well, that was intense. No more adventures for a while.' said Kat.

Zoe laughed softly. 'Agreed.'

A few days earlier, Zoe had received a letter from Holly, she had finished her contract in Los Angeles and was in Spain with her latest beau. So, it was a surprise when Holly showed up at her door.

All three of sat in the local wine bar and caught up with their lives.

'Why did you leave Spain?' said Zoe.

'Well, the boyfriend turned out to be a bit of a loser, plus I had to put up with his snoring every night and over amorous attempts of his admiration for me. Seriously I've only known him for three months and he wants to move to London and live with me. So I dumped him.'

'Good,' said Zoe. 'I missed you.'

All three were unemployed so they often got together with a cheap bottle of plonk to commiserate. During one of these get-togethers, Zoe picked up a local magazine and glanced through the ads. One in particular caught her eye.

'Hey, look at this,' Zoe said, holding up the magazine. 'There's an ad here for air hostesses. They say no experience necessary.'

Kat and Holly leaned in to read over her shoulder.

'Really?' said Kat, 'That sounds like fun.'

Holly nodded, 'And it's not like we have anything else going on. Why not give it a shot?'

'Yeah! It could be a great opportunity. Plus, we could all be together.' said Zoe.

'Cheers to new beginnings,' Holly added, raising her glass.

'To new beginnings,' Zoe and Kat echoed, clinking their glasses together.

Zoe stood up, 'So do you have any change? There's a phone box just outside and today it actually works.' She made an appointment for all three of them for the following day.

Dressed to impress Holly grabbed a taxi and picked up Zoe and Kat on the way.

'I slept in,' said Zoe.

'Hence that stupid wig,' said Holly.

'I love this wig,' said Zoe.

They walked up the steps to a meeting room in the Savoy Hotel. As they entered, they were immediately ushered to a penthouse suite where two Arab-looking gentlemen and and a white gentleman sat at a desk reading some files. The setting was elegant, but the atmosphere was tense.

'Good morning, ladies. Thank you for coming in today. Please, have a seat,' said the white guy with an American accent, gesturing towards the chairs. They sat down, exchanging curious glances. 'Let's start with some introductions.

Could you please tell me your name and a little about your background?'

After the introductions and a few other questions, the Arab man turned to Zoe, 'Final question for you—what do you think is the most important quality for an air hostess to have?'

Without hesitation, Zoe replied, 'I believe adaptability is crucial. Each flight is different, and being able to handle any situation that arises is key.'

'Thank you, ladies. Before you go, we need to see you walk across the room.'

Zoe, Kat, and Holly stood up. Zoe and Kat, who had done some modelling, strutted confidently across the room. Holly, a natural poser, followed with her own flair.

'Very good,' the other Arab gentleman said, nodding appreciatively.

As they returned to their seats. The American man leaned forward. 'One more thing,' he said, eyeing Zoe. 'Are you wearing a wig?'

Zoe hesitated for a moment before nodding. 'Yes, I am. Sometimes when I don't have time to wash my hair, I wear a wig.'

'Could you remove it, please?' he asked, his expression unreadable.

Zoe took off the wig, letting her long, unwashed hair fall to her shoulders. The men were obviously relieved.

'Thank you,' the American said with a smile. 'We just needed to be sure.'

A brief conversation in Arabic ensued and then the American said, 'We would like to offer all of you a position, if you are interested.'

All three shook their heads in agreement.

'We will send you the contract to sign, so be ready to leave in two weeks time.'

As they left the room, Zoe turned to the others with a smirk. 'Well, that was interesting.'

Kat chuckled. 'I can't believe they thought you might be bald.'

Walking down the steps of the Savoy, they couldn't help but feel a sense of triumph.

'We nailed it,' Kat said.

Zoe nodded. 'Absolutely. Now let's get out of here and celebrate.'

'Drinks on me,' Holly said, grinning.

23

Saudi Arabia

Two weeks later they landed in Beirut. They had to have a physical and get their visas before flying to Saudi Arabia. They had been hired as crew members for Saudi Arabian Airlines.

As they stepped off the plane at King Abdulaziz International Airport in Saudi Arabia, a peculiar scent greeted them, aged spices unfamiliar to their senses. The pathway outside of the airport was lined with vendors peddling beautifully coloured Persian carpets, adding to the sensory overload of their arrival.

'Good grief,' muttered Holly under her breath, wrinkling her nose at the unfamiliar scent.

Kat, on the other hand, regarded their surroundings with fascination. 'Oh, I find it rather intriguing,' she said, 'It's like stepping into a whole new world.'

Holly shot her a skeptical glance. 'Whatever you say. It's nothing like Beirut.'

Holly and Zoe shared a room in the Jeddah Hotel while Kat shared with a new friend called Shauna.

After a day of rest, their training began. The intensity was gruelling, particularly when they found themselves in the middle of the Red Sea on a scorching hot day. One of the toughest drills involved jumping into the water fully clothed, swimming to a dinghy, and climbing aboard. The choice to wear jeans proved to be a poor one, as the heavy fabric weighed them down, but fortunately, they were all strong swimmers. Kat and Zoe consistently reached the dinghy first, with Holly close behind, and they would help the other girls aboard.

By the end of the day, they were all sunburned, and muscles they hadn't even known existed screamed in protest. The exhaustion was palpable. One girl, however, didn't make it through. She admitted she couldn't swim, which led to her immediate dismissal. Had she lied on her application?

Kat and Shauna, joined Zoe and Holly in their room.

'For me,' said Zoe, 'the best part of training was going down that slide.'

'Yeah,' Holly replied, 'but I can't imagine passengers actually leaving their wallets and glasses behind in that situation. Those are essential, especially if the plane exploded.'

'Don't say that!' exclaimed Kat. 'You'll jinx it.'

'Just stating the facts ma'am,' said Holly sarcastically.

After training they all had separate schedules. Zoe's first flight was from Jeddah to Ryad. Before take-off the Captain came to welcome her and handed her a bottle of water. She said cheers, took a sip and almost choked. All the crew laughed. They had spiked the drink with *Sadikki*, the home-made alcoholic brew. This was moonshine, made by some American engineers. The brown coloured liquid represented scotch and the clear one was supposed to be gin. Both tasted like diesel fuel to Zoe.

Holly didn't care too much for Kat. She often found her too gregarious and somewhat of a know-it-all, so Zoe knew she would be happy when she and Zoe had the same schedule. After a few local flights Zoe and Holly got their first long haul to London. It was raining so they went out and splashed around like Gene Kelly, as they hadn't seen rain for several months. People thought they were a little nuts. After non-stop rain, the novelty wore off and they couldn't wait to get back to the sunshine. Most of their time off in London was spent shopping as there was nothing much to buy in Saudi Arabia. However food was extremely cheap, so they saved a lot of money.

It was early afternoon on a Thursday when Zoe and Holly were prepping for a flight to Ryad. They were told a certain passenger was boarding first. Zoe and an Arabic speaking crew member stood by the door and welcomed him aboard.

The perfunctory greeting of the flight attendant was said in English and Arabic.

'Good evening, Welcome aboard. Ahlan wa Sahlan.' (Welcome with open hands)

'Good eve . . . SIR! WAIT!'

A six foot five, black man stood before them, dressed in a robe, carrying a long, curved wicked-looking sword, known as a scimitar.

'Sir, I'm sorry. You cannot take that in the cabin,' said Zoe.

He looked down at her and smiled, baring his gold teeth, not understanding a word, so the other attendant repeated in Arabic, politely explaining that the sword could not be taken in the cabin. They called the Captain who came out and secured the weapon in the cockpit.

Of course - it was Friday tomorrow, the day for beheadings in the town Square. The pilot also informed Zoe that this man was the head executioner. Zoe wished she spoke Arabic so she could have had a conversation with him, as she was sure he would have some good stories to tell. She just couldn't imagine people gathering in the town square for such an event. Was this country still in the Middle Ages?

Zoe found out that a couple of years prior, King Faisal had been assassinated by his nephew, who was found guilty of regicide and executed three months later in the town square, by this man who was now on her plane.

At this time, Saudi Arabia was relatively unknown to many Westerners. Only those who came for work, mostly Americans, ventured into the kingdom, as tourists were generally not allowed unless they were visiting family. These expatriates were eager to hear how western women navigated life in such a different culture and often expressed a desire to meet up once they were settled.

All three women had experienced a bit of Middle Eastern culture while dancing in Beirut. Although they were not required to wear the hijab in Saudi Arabia, they showed respect for local customs by covering their bare shoulders and wearing loose clothing, especially when visiting the bustling Arab market known as the Souk.

They also had to establish a reputation, as non-Arabic women were not treated with much respect. So on a flight if a Saudi man hissed or clicked his fingers for their attention, they would point out politely that there was a call button if he needed help.

After some time, Zoe came to realise that royals were abundant in the Kingdom. She was introduced to Amir—whose name, ironically, translated to "Princess." Despite her royal title, Amir was a rebellious spirit. She defied conventions, by smoking weed and spending her time mingling with foreigners, a lifestyle far removed from the typical image of a princess.

'Zoe, how would you and your friend like to go on a yacht for a day?'

How could Zoe refuse. On their first day off Holly and Zoe boarded a mega yacht that stretched over 150 meters in length, with a gleaming hull made of polished aluminum and steel. The name was in Arabic, so Zoe never got a translation. There were spacious outdoor lounges, dining areas, and panoramic observation points. A dedicated helipad sat on the uppermost deck, allowing the prince and his guests to arrive in style, and the rear deck housed a stunning infinity pool with a waterfall edge. Amir gave Zoe and Holly a quick tour of the 12 guest suites, each of them uniquely designed, featuring themes inspired by cities like Riyadh, Jeddah, and Mecca.

Apparently today there were only 15 staff but when there was a party there could be up to 40. The yacht often cruised along the pristine coastlines of the Red Sea, docking at private islands or exploring coral reefs. It was also used for high-profile events, from royal gatherings to philanthropic galas, reflecting the prince's influence and lifestyle.

It was complete luxury, every detail exuding opulence and excess. Yet, as Zoe took it all in, she couldn't help but wonder how much good could be done if the wealth were directed toward more meaningful causes.

24

Ramadan, Hajj & Bedouins

In March Zoe and Holly were informed they would have to do some extra flights for Ramadan, which is the ninth month of the Islamic calendar, and the month in which the Quran was believed to be revealed to the Islamic prophet Muhammad.

Fasting during the month of Ramadan is one of the Five Pillars of Islam. The month is spent by Muslims fasting during the daylight hours from dawn to sunset. This was especially challenging for the day workers, many of whom were from Yemen. Working under the scorching sun all day, they weren't even allowed to drink water. Zoe and Holly often witnessed men collapsing from heat exhaustion. It was equally challenging for the flight attendants. During the day flights, there was little to do since passengers refrained from eating or drinking. But as soon as the sun set, there was an immediate rush of requests for water, with passengers suddenly eager to rehydrate all at once. The calm of the day would instantly transform into a hectic flurry of activity as Zoe and Holly and other flight attendants scrambled to try to meet everyone's needs simultaneously.

At other times, Zoe and Holly would catch men changing from suits to robes in the galley. Holly would glance at Zoe and sigh, 'My God, we have to put up with this for the entire month. It's bad enough we have to hear the 'Call to Prayer' five times a day.'

Zoe and Holly were fortunate to have their room at the back of the hotel, away from the nearby mosque, but even then, they were still aroused by the 5:00 AM call to prayer. 'Seriously, it sounds like cats wailing,' Holly would complain as she plugged her ears. Zoe, being a much sounder sleeper, eventually adjusted to the early wake-up calls and managed to get used to it.

Five weeks later, a new challenge arrived: the time for the Hajj. The Hajj is a significant spiritual pilgrimage to the holy city of Mecca in Saudi Arabia, which every adult Muslim is required to undertake at least once in their lifetime. It marks a period of intense devotion and communal unity. During this time, the atmosphere around the hotel became even more charged with activity and reverence.

For women participating in the Hajj, it was a rare moment of respite from the strict dress code; they were allowed to remove their hijabs (head scarves) while performing certain rituals, which was a unique and significant change from their usual attire. This exception provided them with a brief sense of liberation amidst the deeply spiritual and structured rituals of the pilgrimage.

As the city and the hotel prepared for the influx of pilgrims, Zoe and Holly had to adapt which, added another layer of complexity to their already demanding schedule.

Since planes were not permitted to fly directly into Mecca,

Zoe and Holly boarded a flight from Cairo to Jeddah. The aircraft was filled with many passengers—Muslims from various countries—who were experiencing air travel for the first time. During take-off the cabin was filled with hushed murmurs of prayer, fingers thumbing through prayer beads, and eyes closed in silent devotion to cover up their fear of flying. Some passengers were simply drivers responsible for transporting pilgrims to Mecca.

On the evening flights, Holly and Zoe assisted the pilgrims with their needs, offering them water and assurances during the two-hour flight. Many of them were embarking on Hajj for the first time. Despite the demands of the job, from managing the crowded cabin to accommodating special needs and dietary requests, they felt a unique sense of purpose. Holly and Zoe found themselves deeply touched by the collective spirit of faith and the unity that transcended language and cultural differences.

Once they landed in Jeddah, buses waited to take the pilgrims on the final leg of their sacred journey to Mecca. For most Muslims, Hajj was more than just a religious duty; it was a journey of inner growth, unity, and a deeper connection with their faith, leaving them profoundly transformed by the experience of their journey to Mecca.

Zoe and Holly had a rare day off together and decided to meet up with their friend Abdul, an Egyptian who had a broader perspective than many of the Saudi men they knew. He suggested they take a trip to the vast Arabian Desert, a place he loved. Stretching north to the Syrian Desert and west to the Red Sea, the immense expanse of the Arabian Desert is largely within the borders of Saudi Arabia. Excited by the idea of adventure, Zoe and Holly eagerly accepted his invitation.

They had been invited to a "sheep grab" as the westerners called it. Zoe had a quizzical look on her face. 'Are we visiting someone's house. I mean how else would they cook lamb in the desert?'

Abdul smiled, 'My dear ladies, in the Saudi desert, lamb is often cooked using traditional methods that have been passed down through generations. One of their methods is slow cooking the lamb in a pit beneath the sand, which helps to retain moisture and infuse the meat with a unique, smoky flavour. You will love it.'

'Interesting,' said Holly, 'This should be fun.'

They arrived at a remote spot where a group of men sat in a circle, their faces lit by the glow of a small fire. Abdul parked the jeep and stepped out, warmly greeting his friends. He introduced Zoe and Holly, who had draped scarves over their heads out of respect for the local customs, aware they were the only women present. The men nodded politely, acknowledging their presence, while Zoe and Holly felt intrigued by the unfolding experience.

Tea was served in small glass cups without milk. In Saudi Arabia, tea is a central part of the culture, and drinking it is a social ritual deeply tied to hospitality. Zoe took a sip while Holly sniffed it and whispered to Abdul, 'What is that strange smell?'

'It's infused with cardamom or cloves and lots of sugar' he replied.

'I like it,' said Zoe.

'Good,' said Abdul, 'Because in gatherings like this, offering tea is a sign of respect and friendship, and you will be offered several rounds.'

Holly drank the first one, screwing up her face. Zoe elbowed her. Without anyone noticing, Holly managed to dump the next two cups into the sand.

The main dish of lamb was tender and flavourful, and Zoe and Holly eagerly devoured several pieces with their hands, savouring each bite. 'Do we have any napkins?' Holly asked, wiping her fingers on the edge of her scarf.

'Come with me ladies,' Abdul said, gesturing for her to follow. They walked behind him as he crouched down, rubbing his hands in the desert sand. The fine grains absorbed the grease, and then he poured water from a tank stored in his jeep to wash them clean. Zoe smiled, impressed by the simple, practical method. 'When in the desert, I suppose,' she thought with a grin.

They thanked the group of men and said their goodbyes, before taking a quiet stroll under the vast desert sky. The desert at night had an eerie feel—dry bushes rustled in the gentle wind, and now and then, small creatures, perhaps scorpions or beetles, scurried across the sand in the moonlight. As they walked, they spotted a tent in the distance, dimly lit by a small fire. A group of Bedouin men sat around it, their traditional robes flowing in the flickering light. Abdul approached one of the men, speaking to them in a different dialect.

'Okay, ladies, you've been invited in,' Abdul said, holding the flap of the tent open. Zoe and Holly ducked as they entered, the warm, tent's interior. As Abdul followed them inside, the women quickly covered their heads and faces with colourful scarves.

'I'll explain who you are, and then I'll leave so the ladies can relax,' Abdul assured them, speaking softly. He then addressed the Bedouin women in their dialect and left the tent.

The women, now at ease, dropped their veils and smiled, motioning for Zoe and Holly to sit. One young boy sitting near the fire spoke up in hesitant English, 'You are welcome here. Please, sit with us. My name is Nayef, because I am tall for my age.' His shy smile helped break the tension, and Zoe and Holly, grateful for the hospitality, settled in to enjoy this rare and intimate desert experience. When a man entered, some women covered their heads while others didn't. So, Zoe asked Nayef, 'Why do some women cover their heads and others do not?'

Because some of the women were related to him, they were allowed to uncover their faces in his presence. As various men came and went from the tent, likely out of curiosity about their visitors, the women adjusted their coverings accordingly. Some covered their heads and faces as the men entered, while others, more relaxed, kept their veils off.

One older woman, who didn't have a scarf, simply lifted one of the layers of her dress to cover her head. Her practical solution made it hard for Holly to stifle a giggle.

Once again, they had to endure numerous cups of tea before they said goodbye.

On the way home, Zoe turned to Abdul and asked, 'How did you know their dialect so well?'

Abdul smiled and replied, 'My mother was actually part of a Bedouin tribe before she met my father. I grew up listening to her speak, so I picked up the accent and some of the dialect over the years.' His response revealed a personal connection to the culture, adding depth to their experience in the desert.

25

Party time

Another day off together, Holly wanted Zoe to go to a party, but she was reluctant as she didn't feel very energetic after being poorly the last few days.

'Come on Zoe. It will do you good to get out,' insisted Holly.
'I still don't feel a hundred percent.'
'No problem, you can come, sit on a sofa and people watch.'
Zoe could see she wasn't going to give up so agreed to go.

For all the foreigners, the entertainment was a visit to various company compounds for a movie or a party, as there were no social gatherings in the city. This particular party was hosted by their American friends from the Peace Corps. Everyone enjoyed their get-togethers, because they were the only people lucky enough to have real alcohol.

Like Holly suggested, Zoe sat on the sofa and people-watched while drinking water with a lemon in a tall glass, pretending it was gin. The smoke from the cigarettes bothered her and she wanted to leave but their driver had left and wouldn't be back for a couple of hours. *Damn, I wish women were allowed to drive. It would make life a lot easier,* thought Zoe.

Because of this law, women were assigned a driver for a small fee. Later that evening Zoe spotted their designated driver in another room chatting with the Arab-speaking females, so they decided to let him enjoy himself for a while. This was a great opportunity for him, as Saudi men and single women weren't allowed to socialize with each other. However, Zoe noticed a drink in his hand and hoped it was soda, as alcohol was forbidden in the Muslim religion.

Everyone was having a good time, especially Holly. She was beautiful and sensuous, and men flocked around her, which made the other girls a little envious. She looked at Zoe every so often to make sure she was doing okay.

Zoe let out a great yawn.

'My goodness, is it past your bedtime?'

She looked up and blinked. In front of her stood *Adonis*, a tall, muscular blue-eyed blond man.

'I ... er ... not really,' she stuttered.

'Hi, my name is Ed.'

'Hi, I'm Zoe.'

'Can I get you a drink?'

'Thanks.'

'Let me guess, gin tonic?'

'Actually, it's just water.'

'You're not a tea-totaller, are you?'

She laughed. 'Definitely not, I've been sick and my stomach is not ready to handle booze.'

'Bad food?'

'No. Crazy as it sounds. In these stinking hot temperatures, I came down with a cold.'

'Are you a stewardess?'

'Yup, what else in this place?'

'You probably got sick from one of the passengers.'

'Probably.'

They chatted the rest of the evening and suddenly Zoe didn't feel ill anymore, probably due to the attention from this gorgeous man. He had a captivating smile and perfect teeth. Not only was he handsome, but extremely interesting and witty. Although French Canadian, his accent was more Canadian than French. He was a Civil Engineer and had been in Saudi Arabia for eighteen months. Although it wasn't his favourite place to work, the money made it more bearable.

'Sorry to break up this love tryst, but we have to leave,' said Holly.

'Okay.' said Zoe, making a face at her then turning back to Ed. 'Well, it was a pleasure meeting you.'

'Pleasure is all mine. How can I get in touch with you?'

Zoe's heart raced. She thought he'd never ask. 'We're at the Jeddah Palace Hotel. Make sure you have a few *Riyals* to pay the house boys and that should guarantee delivery of your messages.'

The females from the airline were based on the second and third floor of the Jeddah Palace Hotel. The only males allowed on those floors were the house boys, who brought them messages and cleaned their rooms. (Zoe always sprayed after their visit to get rid of the smell of sweat) The only house phone available was for airline use so they relied heavily on the house boys to bring them notes from friends, for a few *Riyals*.

Before they left the party, Zoe paid a visit to the bathroom and as she made her way back, she bumped into Ed. She felt awkward, not knowing what to say. No need, he planted a passionate kiss on her lips. Her heartbeat doubled and all she could do was smile. That sensation lasted until she got to the car.

Their driver was crashed out in the back seat.

'Oh darn it,' said Holly. 'What are we going to do?'

'Well, you've been drinking so I guess it's up to me.' She dragged the *Gutra* (head gear) from their drunken driver and threw it around her head and face. It was much heavier than she expected and it smelled of sweat and Sandalwood. She held back a gag.

'You are not going to drive,' shrieked Holly. 'If we get stopped we both could go to jail.'

'How else are we getting home? Don't worry, it's late no one will see.'

It was strange driving along in the dark, on muddy roads with no street lights. The temperature had dropped to sixty degrees, but Zoe was still sweating. They saw a group of men sitting by a cafe. Zoe's pulse raced and her palms were wet. Her heart beat enough to rattle her ribs. Holly just ducked down and Zoe thought she was praying. Another five minutes of driving, they arrived safely back at the hotel. Zoe parked a little way down the street so no one would see her get out of the driver's seat. She threw the headgear over the driver and they left him there to sober up. Holly and Zoe ran up the stairs laughing until they couldn't breathe. Catching her breath Zoe said, 'Wow, I don't want to do that ever again. It's not good for my heart.'

26

Edmond

Over the next two months Ed waited for Zoe at the airport after each of her flights and then discreetly drove back to his place. They had fun, making love, talking about their hometowns and drinking wine that Ed had acquired from their Peace Corps friends. After only two weeks, he had declared his love for Zoe and told her if she went back to Canada with him, they would have a great life. They would take ski trips, mini vacations to New York and visit Europe. This sounded very exciting to Zoe.

On her days off Ed taught Zoe to scuba dive. Her first dive, Ed explained they would only go down about sixty feet, accompanied by an experienced diver called Hagen Schmidt. He wanted to take some photos with his new camera.

Zoe adjusted her mask one more time, her heart pounding with a mix of excitement and nerves. The sun was hot on her shoulders, and she could feel the gentle sway of the boat beneath her feet as she stood on the edge, peering down into the clear, turquoise water. Zoe's hands trembled slightly as she clutched the sides of her mask, taking a deep breath, while Ed watched carefully. Hagen gave her a thumbs-up. She nodded back, her mouth dry despite the humid sea breeze. Then, with one final gulp of air, she took a giant stride forward and plunged into the cool embrace of the Red Sea.

The first sensation was of the water wrapping around her like a blanket, cooling her sun-warmed skin. As she adjusted to the underwater world, Zoe's nervousness began to ebb away, replaced by awe. She slowly released the breath she had been holding, bubbles rising up around her like tiny silver beads, catching the light from above. She started to descend, her fins gently propelling her downward. The noise from the surface quickly faded, replaced by a muffled silence that was almost meditative.

As she sank deeper, the underwater world unfolded in front of her like a living canvas. Bright corals, in hues of purple, orange, and yellow, stretched out like an endless garden beneath her. Schools of vibrant fish darted through the corals, moving in perfect harmony, creating a spectacle of colour that Zoe had only seen in documentaries. She was mesmerized by a parrot fish nibbling on the coral, its scales shimmering in the sunlight filtering down from the surface.

Zoe's breathing steadied, each inhale and exhale through the regulator making an eerie sound. She felt a sudden rush of joy, floating in a world few people ever truly see. A sense of weightlessness enveloped her, and she gave a small kick to explore further. To her right, a clown fish peeked out from a swaying anemone, its tiny eyes blinking curiously at this new visitor. Suddenly, a shadow passed overhead. She glanced up to see a majestic sea turtle gliding gracefully through the water, its flippers moving with a slow, powerful rhythm. It moved past her with an almost otherworldly calm, completely unfazed by her presence.

She glanced at Ed, who had been watching her closely. He nodded approvingly.

For the next few moments, Zoe let herself be immersed in this dreamlike world.

When it was time to surface, she felt a twinge of reluctance, but also a surge of accomplishment. As she broke through the surface and pulled off her mask, and released her regulator, gasping in the salty air, she couldn't help but laugh. She had done it — her first dive. She called out to Ed, 'That was amazing.'

They inspected the equipment, and Ed and Hagen were surprised to see that she still had air left. 'You must have been incredibly relaxed down there to have air left,' Hagen remarked.

Hagen had taken a bunch of photos and a month later, he showed Zoe the book: C*olourful Saudi Arabian Red Sea.* There was Zoe on page fifteen, in front of white coral, her long hair swirling around her face.

The following week, Zoe was able to go on her second dive with Ed and Hagen. Zoe felt the cool rush of seawater envelope her as she descended into the blue depths for the second dive of her life. She loved this part of diving—the feeling of being weightless, like flying through a strange, underwater world.

Ed swam a few feet ahead, his fins gently fluttering as he explored the coral reef. Schools of vibrantly coloured fish darted around them, and Zoe was entranced by the vibrant coral formations that stretched as far as she could see.

About twenty minutes into the dive, something caught Zoe's eye—a shadow gliding along the sandy bottom. She squinted through her mask, heart quickening as she recognized the broad, flat shape of a nurse shark. It moved slowly, almost lazily, its body swaying with the currents. Zoe had seen pictures of them before, and she knew they were generally harmless to humans. Still, seeing one up close was a different experience. A mix of awe and a small thrill of fear washed over her.

She signalled to Hagen, her hands closed as if in prayer, the underwater signal for sharks. He turned and gave her a thumbs-up, his eyes wide with excitement. Zoe knew she could trust his judgment; he had experience with sharks and a massive scar on his leg to prove it. They carefully swam closer, keeping a respectful distance. Zoe's breathing quickened, and she took a moment to calm herself, steadying her breaths through the regulator. The shark seemed unbothered by their presence, gliding gracefully over the seabed as if it were alone in the ocean.

Zoe was mesmerized. She forgot about time, about everything except the shark's slow, rhythmic movements and the way it seemed to float effortlessly. It felt like she could watch it forever. Then, suddenly, the shark swam away. Zoe exhaled slowly, realising she had been holding her breath. She glanced down at her pressure gauge and felt a jolt of panic shoot through her chest—her air was dangerously low. She was nearly out.

Zoe tapped the reserve, but the needle hovered near empty. Her heart thudded. How had she missed it? The combination of excitement and her faster breathing had drained her tank much quicker than expected.

She turned to get Hagen's attention, her movements urgent, and made the "out of air" signal—a hand slashing across her throat. Hagen's eyes widened behind his mask, and he quickly swam toward her, pulling out his regulator in order to buddy breathe.

Zoe grabbed the regulator and pressed it to her lips, inhaling deeply three times as her lungs filled with precious air. Relief flooded through her, but fear kept her from taking it out of her mouth. She couldn't hand it back. Ed, seeing her panic, had to share his regulator with Hagen, and the three of them began their ascent, tethered together like divers on umbilical cords.

Zoe clutched Ed's arm, trying to keep her breaths steady, her eyes darting between him and the shimmering surface above. Each second felt like a minute. She could feel her heartbeat pulsing in her ears. The water gradually grew lighter, and she could see the surface growing closer. Her mind raced with every foot they climbed, hoping they'd make it without any more complications. Finally, they broke through the surface, greeted by the warm sun and the sound of waves gently lapping against their dive boat.

Zoe pulled the regulator from her mouth, gasping in the salty air, her heart still pounding. She turned to Ed and mouthed, 'Sorry'.

'That was close,' he said, breathless but grinning.

Zoe managed a shaky smile, adrenaline still coursing through her veins. 'Next time,' she panted, 'I'm definitely keeping a better eye on my reserve air.'

Hagen was not too happy with her, but Ed was so sweet, quickly forgiving her, remembering that she was not a certified diver.

'I think it's best I train you a little more before venturing back down.'

Later that evening in bed, he said, 'I have something to tell you.'

'That sounds so ominous,' she replied, grabbing her glass of wine.

'I'm married.'

'What?' Zoe's hands trembled and she spilled some of the wine over the bed cover. She thought her heart stopped for a few beats. This was supposed to be the love of her life. 'You ba ... '

'Wait, before you get upset, let me explain.'

God, why me? Why do I have so many problems with relationships?

'My wife was over here with me and hated it. I told her it was only for a couple of years, but she wanted to return home immediately. Then she added that she'd had enough of me and wanted a divorce.'

Tears brimmed Zoe's eyes. 'Why did you wait so long to tell me?'

The look on his face softened, 'She left seventeen months ago and filed for divorce, so I thought it would be done by now. However, I need to go back to Canada and sign the papers.'

Zoe swallowed some wine so her voice would work. 'Well, yes! Of course you have to sign the papers in person.' She shook her head. 'When do you leave?'

'My contract is up next month.'

A tear rolled down her cheek. 'Then what happens?'

'We can meet up in London and talk about arrangements for you to join me in Canada.'

Zoe had thought a lot about her future. It would be exciting spending her life with Ed. But all this reality was starting to sink in. Their romance in this Arabian desert was very "cloak and dagger" which added to the excitement. *What if, when we were in normal circumstances, the dynamics changed, like it did with Adib? What is wrong with me? Why can't I just let go and learn to love someone unconditionally?*

'Mmm, Canada. Snow.' said Zoe.

'But the summers are great.'

'I'll miss diving in the Red Sea, jaunts in the Prince's yacht and visiting exotic places like Bombay, Dubai, Paris and of course London.'

'Don't worry we'll do a lot of travelling, but I can't guarantee knowing any Princes.'

Zoe laughed, 'Don't worry, you are my prince. Yacht or no yacht.'

Did that sound too corny?

27

Arabian Nights

Zoe found it hard to concentrate on her job. She couldn't hand in her resignation until she heard from Ed. Meanwhile, she carried on as normal. Holly and Kat were the only ones who knew about her plans. Kat kept asking Zoe if she was sure about her decision and tried to persuade her to stay.

The job had lost its sparkle and excitement, and Zoe often called in sick. She started to party hard and drink like she knew how to drink. One night she got smashed and threw up in the lobby of the Jeddah Hotel. That was a very embarrassing moment, and it triggered a deep visceral rejection of Grand Marnier. Her other friends sensed something was up as they knew Zoe wasn't usually a heavy drinker. They tried to get her to open up but even though she was tempted to tell them her plans, something kept her from taking them into her confidence. It might have been a suspicion that each one of them would suggest a completely different course of action that Zoe knew would result in greater confusion. Then a telegram arrived:

Urgent relay to Zoe. **stop**, *Love you.* **stop**, *all finished here.*

stop, *am yours, will meet you London or Paris this month.* **stop,** *advise me of hotel and date after October 5 Ottawa.* **stop.**

Edmond.

It arrived almost eight weeks after Zoe last saw Ed. She jumped for joy as she held it in her hand. She had a London turn already scheduled. It was only a three-day trip but Ed quickly arranged to meet her at the St George hotel near Oxford street.

The hotel was in a great location for Holly and Zoe to shop for clothes, right in the middle of London. Not surprisingly there wasn't much choice for Western women in Saudi Arabia. They always took advantage of their international flights, especially London or Paris and made a beeline for Selfridges.

They arrived back at the hotel at the sacred hour of four o'clock – teatime in England. Zoe jumped in the shower while Holly made tea. The warm cloak of the water lulled her into a trance, and she quickly found herself in a state of relaxation.

But once again, her mind raced, speeding through moments in her life when she had taken decisive and life changing steps... steps that were stepping stones of destiny. She saw a common thread. Her outer shell, reflected a tall good looking, confident girl with a bubbly personality, but internally troubled and full of doubts. The warm water cocooned her and even when Holly yelled that tea was ready, she couldn't break out of her thought pool. She was about to leap an ocean to another continent and marry a man she was crazy about, but would it last? Would it be a gluttonous feast that would end far too soon and leave her reeling with emotional indigestion in a land far away from home. But where was her home? Her hometown of Newbury, London., Europe? She didn't feel attachment to any place.

Luckily, they were staying in a three star hotel – the water stayed warm through all her mental voyaging.

'Are you ever going to emerge? Tea's gone cold. I'll make another pot,' said Holly, with a hint of annoyance. 'You don't want to look like a wet rag when Ed arrives.'

Zoe thought that Holly would think she was indulging herself, but she wasn't. She was desperately searching for who she was.

'Don't worry, he loves me any way I look.'

The shower curtain pulled back and there stood Ed holding an engagement ring in his hand. 'You're right. Now will you marry me?'

Totally naked and dripping wet she hugged him tightly. All her doubts swirled down the drain. Soon his clothes were soaked. They laughed. 'If I wasn't sharing this room with Holly, I would make you take off those wet clothes and join me,' said Zoe, kissing him.

'No need,' he said, as he climbed into the shower, fully clothed. As the water dripped down his face, his beautiful blue eyes looked at her lovingly and his smile made all her doubts disappear. *Perhaps Ed might just be her soulmate.*

Zoe threw some soap at him, and they giggled like a couple of teenagers. Grabbing a huge soft bath towel, Zoe climbed out of the tub while Ed undressed and took a proper shower.

Holly had arrangements to meet some friends, so Ed and Zoe ate lunch in the hotel restaurant. The ring was on her finger and she kept looking at the beautiful Opal, every chance she got.

'Do you like it?'

'Like it? I love it.' she said grabbing his hand, almost knocking over the wine glass.

All of this was a little overwhelming. Zoe was not very good at expressing her emotions verbally, so she squeezed his hand tightly.

'I'm glad. I heard from Holly you preferred opals to diamonds, which is a little unusual.'

'Well, you should know by now, I am a little unusual.'

'True,' he agreed.

'By the way, I think that was one of the weirdest and funniest proposals ever,' she said.

'I had bigger plans but that seemed so much more spontaneous,' he said with a beautiful overtone of true love in his voice.

'To you and me forever,' he said, raising his glass.

The waiter brought their soup, piping hot and steaming. Her mind raced. *Forever, wow that's a long time. Why can't I just relax and go with the flow and enjoy this now moment.*

The next morning, Zoe called the airline and told them she had food poisoning. It wasn't too far from the truth as she did have a bad stomach, but she knew it was from nerves. Human Resources accepted her excuse which gave her another four days to spend with the man she was very much in love with, which could be considered a sort of sickness.

Even though Zoe had lived in London for a couple of years, she had never done the tourist thing. Ed wanted to see the sights, so they decided to start with the pinnacle of London Culture, a pub crawl. London had a lot of great pubs, so they travelled around by the traditional London Black Cab.

First stop – *The Red Lion* on Parliament Street, just down the road from Big Ben.

'Two Watney's Red Barrel and two Cornish pasties,' Ed called across the crowded bar to the career barmaid, who looked like an extra from Oliver Twist.

'Right luv! here's the beer. Grab a seat and I'll bring the pasties to ya,' she roared back.

'It's a weekday, why is it so crowded?' asked a confused Ed.

'Typical lunch crowd,' said Zoe, 'True English fayre.'

English food had a bad rap, but the cook at *The Red Lion* could make three sausages and onions, look like a gourmet meal.

'I just read that there's been a pub on this site since 1434,' said Zoe, looking up from a tattered brochure. 'The cooks obviously learnt from their predecessors how to fry a sausage.'

'You know a lot about pub history?'

'No, a good friend's father told me when he knew we were going on a pub crawl and gave me lots of info on the most popular ones. One more fact about this pub. Every prime minister is reputed to have had a working lunch here, and I can see why it is believed that a young Charles Dickens used to be a regular visitor. By the way, did you know he was born in 1812?'

'A walking encyclopaedia, you are,' said Ed.

Three pubs later they arrived at the *Prospect of Whitby*, which was London's oldest and most famous riverside pub, dating back to 1520. The tavern was formerly known as *The Pelican* and later as the *Devil's Tavern*, on account of its dubious reputation. It was a meeting place for sailors, smugglers and cut-throats.

Finishing off a couple of pints they then travelled to Baker Street, to visit the Sherlock Holmes Museum and the pub named after him. After dinner they took a walk in Hyde Park and listened to all the soap box politicians. Ed was 6'1" and as they walked, he towered above everyone. Zoe felt proud to be by his side as he held her hand tightly.

They rested the following day, indulging in a cream tea at the Dorchester Hotel, then sipping wine in a trendy bar.

'This city never ceases to amaze me,' Zoe said, leaning back in her chair, sipping a very expensive wine. 'There's always something new to discover.'

Ed smiled, raising his glass. 'And I'm glad I get to experience it with you.'

Their last day proved exhausting, visiting sites like Tower Bridge and Buckingham Palace.

'I can't believe how much we've crammed into one trip,' Ed said, wiping his brow as they walked along the Thames.

Zoe laughed. 'That's London for you. Always an adventure.'

Their final meal in London was at Mayfair's La Gavroche, Michel Roux Jr.'s famous fine-dining restaurant, offering luxurious French food and impeccable service at absolutely crazy prices.

'This place is incredible,' Ed remarked, looking around at the elegant decor.

'It's my first time here,' Zoe replied. 'I was told the food here is just out of this world.'

Ed wasn't rich, but since there was nowhere to spend money in Saudi Arabia, he had saved a considerable sum. He didn't mind splurging once in a while.

'To us,' he said, lifting his glass to Zoe. 'And to many more adventures.'

'To us,' Zoe echoed, clinking her glass against his.

However, Zoe had a bit of a guilty conscience. The money spent on the meal was a week's salary to a lot of people. It made her think of how frugal her stepmother had been to benefit her and her brother. Her family were the only ones on the street to go out on regular outings, whereas a lot of the neighbour's children would play outside the pub while their parents enjoyed a few pints. The only thing that took away some of the guilt was that Zoe sent a few pounds home every month. If Zoe had taken her mother to an expensive restaurant, she would certainly have known which fork to use. She had learned a lot when she was a downstairs maid for a rich family. She had taught Zoe a lot and the knowledge she gained from Franco, her Italian fling, also added to her experience.

The mini vacation ended too soon. Neither she nor Ed wanted to leave London, but Ed had to get back to Canada for work and Zoe had to hand in her resignation with the airline.

28

The Cairo Affair

After her extended trip to London, Zoe had to finish her schedule. This particular trip made her think she would never see Ed again!

The rumble of the landing gear grew louder, and the plane shook viciously. Flight 7289 arrived in Cairo at 11 a.m., exactly one hour late. Lana and Zoe left their jump seats and prepared for deplaning. As usual chaos erupted as passengers grabbed their bags from the overhead compartments and fought to get off the plane. The Boeing 737 was only half full so fortunately, deplaning only took a few minutes.

Zoe stood at the plane door with her eyes closed taking in the sounds and the smells of Egypt. The warm dusty air was filled with a fertile, rich mix of spices, incense and animals. Over time she had come to enjoy the various aromas which were intoxicating and exhilarating. She was glad Holly had not been scheduled on this flight as she would have been moaning all the way. She loved Holly, but she could be difficult to handle at times.

Zoe felt a tug at her sleeve. 'Come on Zoe, stop daydreaming. We have to get this plane ready for boarding.'

Lana headed toward the cockpit and Zoe followed. It was her first time working with Lana and she wasn't looking forward to it at all. Lana had a reputation for being difficult; she had been with the airline since it started and her dealings with other crew members were reportedly quite unpleasant. Still, it was just a quick turnaround, so Zoe knew she would be able to handle it. She had had plenty of practice with Kat.

'Sorry sweeties, change of plans,' said the flight engineer turning to them. He had less personality than a slice of white bread.

'One of these days I'm going to hit him,' whispered Lana. 'I hate being called sweetie or darling'

'What kind of change?' Zoe asked, stifling a giggle.

'The "Big Guy" just commandeered the plane,' he replied with a stupid grin on his sunburnt face.

The "Big Guy" he was referring to was actually the King of Saudi Arabia, a man who was very popular with the people and had earned a lot of respect for all the changes he had brought to the Kingdom. Apparently, he and his Queen needed to return home urgently, so he commandeered their plane with his personal crew.

That meant an unexpected layover in an exciting city like Cairo. Zoe was ecstatic. However, Lana had a different opinion and snarled, 'Damn, this always happens. I'm so sick of it. Now we have to face an angry mob of disgruntled passengers. I just don't get enough money for this kind of shit!'

After a hectic two hours in the airport, dealing with the displaced passengers, Lana and Zoe were finally able to relax in a comfortable hotel room. They chatted over a pot of chamomile tea, getting to know each other a little. Due to a big convention in Cairo, hotel rooms were scarce, so they were forced to share a room. With no change of clothes and the prospect of a night out, they paid a visit to the *Souk*. Their uniform consisted of trousers, so they had fun haggling prices on a couple of colourful, comfortable tops. A short walk and a tasty snack calmed Lana down. She was actually being pleasant.

'This is your first time here, so let's do something exciting,' she said.

An hour later they were on horseback riding around the ancient pyramids, following a group of Swiss tourists. They decided horses would be a lot more comfortable than the lazy looking camels. Even Lana who had seen the pyramids many times, was awestruck by the sheer size and splendour of them. The sky glowed red and orange and the fluffy clouds floated by slowly. They were far enough from the bustling city to enjoy the quietude. Neither of them wanted to listen to the German-speaking tour guide, so they sneaked off, confident they could rejoin the group when it was time to go back to their hotel.

Lana sighed, 'You know I never get tired of seeing these wonders of the world. They are so ... magical. It's amazing to feel the mysterious power that emanates from them.'

Zoe nodded her head in agreement. Lana was showing a gentler side of her personality that most people hadn't experienced. It was late so they reluctantly turned back. Suddenly Lana's horse stumbled, and she went flying. Zoe dismounted and ran over to her, not thinking about securing the animals, who immediately trotted off into the desert.

'Come back you silly asses,' Zoe yelled.

'They're horses,' said Lana dryly.'

'Oh, you do have a sense of humour. Well, if you aren't hurt too badly, let's start walking before it gets dark.'

Lana moaned but showed less irritability than usual as Zoe helped her up. They walked for fifteen minutes in what they fervently hoped was in the right direction.

'What's that?' asked Zoe, when she heard a loud noise. Standing still they were unable to see anything except sand and the distant city lights, so continued walking, a little more cautiously now. Zoe noted that in the short time together they had built up a certain amount of trust in each other. Strolling through the desert at night is eerie, dark and silent, but peaceful. The only signs of life were small lizards that scuttled across their pathway leaving their cockroach dinner behind in their haste. Then they heard the noise again and something flapped and swooped right above their heads.

'My God! Vultures! Can't they wait until we're dead?' screamed Zoe.

'Very funny,' replied Lana, sarcastically.

If they hadn't had been so nervous they would have admired the strange bird with its wingspan of six feet and fierce black eyes. It circled a few times then flew off and disappeared into the night sky. Lana and Zoe were really tired and dragged their feet in the warm sand.

'How much further?' moaned Zoe.

'How the hell should I know?' snapped Lana.

'You've been here many times before.'

'Right, but I usually travel by jeep. Look I can't go any further, my ankle really hurts.'

'I'm sure it's not much further, I can see lights.'

'Bloody hell woman, didn't you hear me. I hurt.'

'Okay, we'll rest here for a bit.'

Lana shook her head. 'Don't you ever get mad?'

'Yes, like right now.' said Zoe, feeling the blood rush to her head. 'You're getting on my nerves. If you hadn't fallen off your stupid horse, we'd be home by now.'

'My horse wasn't stupid, I was.'

Zoe looked at Lana but didn't say anything. After a couple of minutes, they both laughed and flopped down on the sand. It felt warm and coarse and stuck to their sweaty bodies. The slight breeze grew stronger, blowing sand around them. They needed to find shelter. Zoe had heard about sandstorms, but never experienced one until now.

'I am so hungry,' said Zoe, wiping the sand from her face, which only made it worse.

Lana laughed, 'That's the problem being so thin, no spare fat for emergencies.'

As they rested, they gazed upwards. The bright stars sparkled like diamonds in the sky and the moon round as a penny, rose smiling down on the *Great Pyramid of Cheops,* where a cloud resembling *Tutankamuns'* ghost floated by. The wind was picking up and they prayed a sandstorm was not developing.

Zoe was surprised at how calm Lana was. *What if they had to spend the night here?* That was not a comforting thought to Zoe.

Lana sighed, 'You know the *Pharaohs* treasures stored within the tombs have only added to the mysterious and supernatural aura surrounding them. Considering all the research and studies carried out, the techniques and construction still remained a secret. Look at that view. Makes you forget about schedules, cars and airplanes, a rushed lifestyle with no time to enjoy nature.'

Zoe looked over at the *Sphinx*. 'Look at that statue. I can't imagine how the Egyptians built that. How ominous he is with that lion's body and human head. His face is generally believed to represent the face of *Pharaoh Khafra*.'

'You're well read,' said Lana, suitably impressed.

At that moment a rumbling sound came towards them. The pounding of horses' hooves and dark figures appeared on the horizon. 'You are aware there are bandits roaming around the outskirts of the city,' said Lana quietly.

Zoe gave her a nervous look and glanced over at the oncoming doom. 'They look like three horsemen, or is it just a mirage? What do you think? Run, wave to them, or hide?'

'I couldn't outrun a snail at this point,' replied Lana. 'My stomach aches, and it hurts to swallow. I need water desperately.'

'The only way to hide is to lie down and pretend we are part of the sand dunes,' joked Zoe.

Both were pessimistic about the success of that ruse and thirst marred their judgment.

'Considering our options, let's risk it,' said Lana, forgetting about her pain as she jumped up and waved her arms.

'Over here, over here,' they yelled. Thankfully it was the rescue team from the horse ranch.

'When the horses returned riderless, it was obvious you two were in trouble,' said one of the riders.

That night the girls slept soundly and by morning felt refreshed as they made their way to the airport. The crowd was hostile, waving tickets in the air and yelling in languages neither of them understood.

'I think I would rather be lost in the desert than face this lot,' said Zoe, lifting a case that weighed more than 70lbs.

Lana agreed wholeheartedly. She was in an exceptionally good mood. 'Zoe, I want to thank you for last night. You're a very patient human being and I appreciate your tolerance of a tired old stewardess. You've helped me look at some things in a different light. I think it's time to retire.'

'Think nothing of it. I enjoyed myself. After all, you could have stayed at the hotel and missed all the action.'

'I'm glad I didn't,' said Lana firmly, touching Zoe's shoulder before turning away.

Lana grabbed the microphone. 'Ladies and Gentlemen, may I have your attention? ... '

Zoe watched her with intensity. *She was in control. That's what she was known for, a take charge, get things done attitude. She felt privileged to have worked with her.*

The sun was already high, the heat was intense, and the air was humid and thick with the fetid stench of hot angry bodies, sweating profusely. The airport had no air conditioning, the plane was late and the catering hadn't arrived. Lana looked over at her new friend, rolled her eyes and said,

'Living the Dream ... '

29

Montreal

Two months later, which felt like four, Zoe was air-bound for a new life. The lights were low. The sound of snoring and the purr of the plane engine echoed throughout the cabin. Zoe couldn't sleep and thought it might have been all that coffee she had drank accompanied by a real tasty croissant, in Charles de Gaulle airport. *Or was it because she was too excited and nervous at the same time.*

The Boeing 747 jet rose effortlessly into the sky. Zoe was not a nervous flyer but on take-off and landings, she was mentally prepared to act in a bad situation. The training from the time in the airline stayed with a person, even years later.

She gazed out of the window at the fluffy white clouds. *No turning back now. This is it.* She was feeling much more confident on her decision. Living in the middle of a desert was sort of exciting but it would have soon got old. She missed culture, going to movies or the theatre., so that was another reason to look forward to the new life ahead of her.

Once the plane reached cruising altitude, Zoe tipped the seat back and looked forward to the benefits of flying in first class.

The man next to her looked as tense as a parolee at his parole hearing.

'Are you alright?' she asked.

'I hate flying,' he whispered, as though he didn't want to make it public. His accent was smooth, not American, probably Canadian.

After a surprisingly tasty meal and a couple of glasses of red wine, the cabin lights dimmed and the male passenger relaxed as he snuggled up to a complimentary pillow and blanket, and was soon sound asleep. Thank goodness he wasn't a snorer.

Zoe closed her eyes but still couldn't sleep, once again hoping she had made the right decision. When Holly accompanied her to the airport, she had asked again if she was making the right decision, 'Are you sure you know what you're doing?'

Zoe laughed nervously, 'Of course not, I love Ed, but don't get a roommate.'

Zoe wondered if Holly felt abandoned, as she did find it a little difficult to make new friends.

The sound of the landing gear coming down brought Zoe back to the present. She returned her seat to the upright position, fastened her seat belt and prepared herself for the landing, and the rest of her life.

Montreal airport was buzzing. The customs agent opened her passport and asked with a very strong accent, 'Are you here for a holiday?' Zoe had to say yes as she wasn't sure about the immigration laws. 'Enjoy your stay in Canada,' he said in a perfunctory manner.

The luggage had already arrived by the time Zoe passed through immigration and customs. The flight had been full and people were pushing to get to the crowded carousel before their cases disappeared for the second time.

Ed had asked her to meet in Montreal so they could do some sightseeing before travelling to Ottawa. *Sight-seeing*, she pondered. *First thing I will need to do, is to buy some warm clothes.*

It was November and freezing. A thick layer of snow and ice blanketed the airport buildings. Dressed in only a cotton sweater, a short skirt and leather jacket, Zoe ventured out, the icy wind hurt her nose and ears and she almost slipped; Her arms flailing around as her suitcases slid away. A porter helped her and she retreated immediately back in to the warm airport. *Yikes, will I ever get used to this?*

Luckily Ed arrived within moments. He threw her suitcases in the trunk, then gave her a tight hug, which was welcome both for the emotional value and the body warmth. In the car he handed her a bouquet of flowers. She wanted to kiss him, but her lips were too cold. Instead she laid her cold hand on his. He squeezed it gently before changing gear and speeding off to the hotel.

Next day Ed had a business meeting, so Zoe went shopping. A warm coat, hat, scarf and gloves later, she wandered around this curious town built for some unexplainable reason in the frozen tundra of an arctic like wilderness – or so it seemed like that to her, after relocating from the sun drenched dunes of the Middle East. She had a little problem communicating as most of the people she encountered had an accent very different to her school French. They also mixed English words with their French, which Zoe found amusing.

Edy had arranged to meet at a cafe near the hotel so Zoe wouldn't get lost. She sat by the glowing fire and enjoyed the best French Onion Soup she had ever tasted. The walls were hung with wonderful paintings, all done by local artists, according to the friendly waitress.

Ed joined her eventually and ordered a coffee.

'Aren't you going to eat,' Zoe asked.

'No, let's go out, there is so much I want to show you. This is such a great city.'

Ed, it turned out had grown up here. 'Why did you move to Ottawa if you like it so much?'

'Work. But I do come here often on weekends.'

Montréal is the largest city in Canada's Québec province. This particular year it was getting ready for next year's summer Olympics, which Ed promised to bring Zoe back to visit. The city buzzed with activity, showcasing its unique blend of French and English influences in architecture, cuisine, and arts. The city's lively festivals, charming neighbourhoods, and welcoming atmosphere made it a popular destination in Canada.

30

Ottawa

Zoe and Ed arrived in Ottawa the following day. Ed owned a condo in a lovely part of town, overlooking the Rideau canal - which at this time of year was frozen over. The canal was built in the eighteen thirties and the workers were made up of mostly British Garrison soldiers. When the work was completed, the military were the lock masters. At that time, the Rideau Canal was world famous as a skating pathway where well-wrapped Canadians and international tourists skated cheerfully along, occasionally pulling off for a mug of hot chocolate. The canal was almost five miles long and it was a magical experience, and Zoe enjoyed watching people slip, slide or glide their way up and down this ribbon of ice.

'I guess I'll have to learn to skate now that I'm in Canada,' said Zoe, as they warmed themselves in a cosy coffee shop.

'It's fun. Don't worry. I'll teach you.' he said.

True to his word, Ed taught Zoe how to skate like a local. In no time it became her favourite pastime. She did land on her butt more than a hundred times but the moments between were graceful and joyous, and to her – a dancer – she was in heaven ...albeit, an icy heaven. However, after sweltering in the high nineties in Saudi Arabia, it was hard to adjust to freezing temperatures with a windchill factor of frostbitten noses. *Will I be able to enjoy living in these conditions? I can't wait for summer to arrive.*

'I wonder what kind of job I can do here.' said Zoe.

'We don't have to worry about that just yet. Relax, get to know the area before looking for a job.'

Ed had a business trip to New York so they planned to drive down together. Unfortunately the agents wouldn't let Zoe cross the border as she had a British passport and still no American visa.

'Never mind, I'll be back tomorrow and we'll take the long way home,' Ed said cheerfully.

The only accommodation close by was a seedy Motel 6, a popular, cheap place for travelling salesmen. Her room didn't even have a fridge so she kept a six pack of beer outside in the snow, one of the few blessings of frigid weather. That evening she bravely ventured out to find somewhere to eat. She precariously crossed a dual carriageway to find herself at the Ponderosa, not the beautiful ranch from the TV show, but a chain restaurant, specialising in beef. She ordered a small, medium rare steak. Their idea of small was certainly not hers, as she slid away the plate with a third of the dead beast still on it. She moved to the bar and chatted to the bartender as she was the only customer. Back in her room, the phone rang. It was Ed. He was excited as he had closed the deal and would be back from the Big Apple early the following morning.

He arrived with a bottle of her favourite wine and some chocolates. They were tempted to stay a while to make out, but the room was too gloomy. Instead they visited Niagara Falls, which is linked with the US by the Rainbow Bridge. The sight was beautiful as the water cascaded down into the Niagara River. However, they were freezing, so decided to take the elevators to a lower, wetter vantage point behind the falls, on another day, preferably during the summer.

After the Christmas Holidays, Zoe applied for a job at the Bank of Montreal as a teller. It turned out that she couldn't work with only a visitor visa, so she and Ed found it necessary to get married. It was a small affair at City Hall with their close friends, Julie and Antoine as witnesses. They were planning on having a full, white wedding in the summer so they kept this quiet from both their families.

That winter and Spring, they had a wonderful time. Every spare minute was spent with each other, making new friends, snuggling together watching TV or visiting Ed's family for scrumptious home cooked meals. Unfortunately these family visits proved a little difficult for Zoe as they insisted on speaking French, which was tiring as their accent was so difficult to follow. They took a couple of road trips, back down to Montreal, over to New York and Ogunquit in Maine.

On one of those trips to Montreal, they met up with Julie. Her father was working at the Montreal Olympics and he invited Ed and Zoe to come and visit. It was an exciting time as it was the first Canadian city ever to hold the Olympics. However the city spent millions over their original budget, including the village which housed the athletes. This event almost bankrupted the city.

Zoe and Ed were given the grand tour and were introduced to a few of the players from the Yugoslavian basketball team, who were celebrating winning a silver medal. Ed was tall but these athletes towered above him. Then on to the Gold medal winner in weightlifting, Soviet Vasily Alekseyev. He was 6'1" and weighed 345lbs. Zoe said to Ed, 'I would have liked to have seen his food bill.' Then they were introduced to the Canadian swimming team. Most of the swimming gold medals went to the Russians, but Julie's dad took them to have lunch with Canadian Becky Smith who managed to win a couple of Bronze medals.

Unfortunately, they didn't feel completely comfortable walking around due to the presence of armed guards and police. This heightened security was a response to the Munich massacre, a tragic event during the 1972 Summer Olympics in Munich, West Germany, where the Palestinian terrorist group Black September took eleven Israeli Olympic team members hostage and killed them, along with a West German police officer.

They decided to wait for their real wedding and two years flew by. Their lives had become a routine. However, once again Zoe was feeling restless and having doubts. Unfortunately, life was becoming a bit boring. She wondered what had happened to the plans for ski trips, jaunts to New York, and mini vacations to Europe. To make matters worse, she was working in a bank—the first nine-to-five job since leaving school. Ed was sweet and kind, treating her like a queen, but she felt trapped. Weekends had also become monotonous. Saturdays were spent going to a movie with friends, followed by dinner. Sundays were reserved for visiting his parents and after dinner the conversation changed to French, which Zoe had a problem following. Doing the same thing every week was not Zoe's idea of fun. Even going out for a drink had become a chore.

'Why go out and spend money on drinks when we have a cupboard full of alcohol?' said Ed.

Holding back her frustration, she replied, 'Money isn't the point. I could drink orange juice. It's the idea of being with other people or just people-watching.'

Zoe always made it a point to kiss and make up after an argument before going to bed.

That night, as Ed drifted into sleep, Zoe quietly turned over and switched on the soft glow of the night light. Careful not to disturb him, she reached for the bedside table and gently slid open the drawer. She pulled out the envelope. Leaning back against the pillows, she unfolded the letter from Holly, her eyes scanning the words she had read earlier that day.

My dearest friend Zoe, how are you? I miss you terribly. It's just not the same in the desert without you. Kat has met someone, a pilot, and they are serious. They are talking about getting married and moving back to the states. I don't care for him very much, but if he makes Kat happy, so be it. I am now thinking about returning to London and going on a few auditions. I need my dance fix.

Take care, write soon.

Love you lots Holly.

Zoe returned the letter to the drawer, exhaling a deep, weary sigh. A wave of longing washed over her as she realized just how much she missed Holly—not just their late-night talks and inside jokes, but the way Holly had always been there to listen to Zoe's doubts and fears.

At that moment, another truth settled in, one she had been avoiding: the honeymoon phase with Ed was well and truly over. The glow of newlywed bliss had faded, replaced by the sharp edges of routine and boredom. She was beginning to see marriage not as an endless adventure, but as a series of compromises—some of which felt like losing pieces of herself.

Restlessness crept in. She grew irritable, snapping at Ed over trivial things, and found herself making excuses to be out of the house more often. Nights spent together turned into nights apart, as she threw herself into socializing without him. Her friends noticed the shift. When Ed wasn't around, she seemed lighter, more animated, like a Zoe they had never seen before. It was as if marriage had placed an invisible tether on her, one that she hadn't even realized was there until now.

She let out another sigh, deeper this time. Maybe, without even meaning to, she had checked in her Free Spirit the day she said, "I do."

She should have listened to Holly and Kat on whether she was making a mistake as they knew her track record with relationships. But she had had faith that this one would work out. After all, her philosophy was not to regret anything in life for not trying. However, a pattern was forming. In the past she had moved towns, even countries to work or follow a man.

31

The Break up

As time went by, Zoe and Ed's relationship became increasingly strained. The laughter and warmth that had once defined them were now overshadowed by tension, distance, and frequent arguments. Zoe could feel Ed watching her, searching for answers in her silences, and she knew he had realized something was seriously wrong.

Zoe had left the job at the bank and was deciding on what kind of job to pursue. Was this the reason for her irritability?

One evening, after yet another day of walking on eggshells around each other, Ed finally spoke. His voice was steady, but there was an unmistakable weariness in his tone.

'We need to figure this out. We can't keep going like this.'

Zoe hesitated before answering, her gaze fixed on the floor. 'I know,' she murmured. 'It's been hard for both of us.'

They had retreated to a quiet café, a place they used to visit in happier times. Now, the dim lighting and the low hum of distant conversations only added to the weight between them. For weeks, they had barely spoken beyond the necessities, the distance growing like an unspoken wall between them.

But tonight, they both knew it was time—time to finally talk to either salvage what was left or accept that it was slipping beyond their grasp.

Zoe traced the rim of her coffee cup with trembling fingers, then finally broke the silence. 'I feel like we've been drifting apart.' Her voice was soft but edged with an unmistakable sadness.

Ed sighed, running a hand through his hair before leaning forward. 'I know I haven't been there for you like I should have,' he admitted. 'I want to do better. I want to understand you more.'

For the first time in a long while, Zoe felt something flicker in her chest—was it hope?

'Maybe we can start over,' she suggested.

Ed studied her for a moment, then nodded slowly. 'Yeah, maybe we can.' He reached across the table, his fingers brushing against hers. They stayed at the café for hours. Somewhere between the second and third bottle of red wine, they promised to try. She let him hold her hand, let herself believe, just for a moment, that things could be fixed, or was it the alcohol dulling her brain?

'I miss how we used to be,' Ed said, his voice thick with emotion. 'I want us to be happy again.'

Zoe squeezed his hand. 'So do I. I'll do whatever it takes.'

But even as she said the words, even as she leaned into Ed's embrace, she felt something tightening in her chest—a familiar suffocation, like when she had gone diving and found herself running out of air. She wanted to believe her own promise, but deep down, she knew the truth. Some things, once broken, could never be fully repaired.

Promises were only words, and in the end, words weren't

enough. They never did have that big wedding. Three months later, after one final, explosive argument, Zoe left.

It had started over something small—just another night of her staying out late with friends, another unspoken disappointment hanging between them.

'You seem to prefer being with them rather than staying home with me,' Ed said, his voice clipped.

Zoe hesitated. 'No, it's just...'

'Then go move in with them!' he snapped, grabbing his car keys.

Zoe had never seen him like this before. But something inside her snapped, too. Every frustration, every resentment, every moment of pretending came rushing to the surface, and suddenly, she was shouting back.

'If you want to be an arsehole, go ahead! Run back to your mummy!'

Ed spun on his heel; his face dark with fury. 'Go to hell!' he shouted, slamming the door behind him.

The apartment was silent. Zoe stood there, her heart pounding, the weight of finality settling over her.

Well, I guess this is it. Another botched relationship.

Her mind raced. *Why couldn't I make it work? Do I always blame others when things go wrong, or is it just me? Am I too impatient? Do I get bored too easily?*

A new, more pressing thought took hold. *Now what? Where will I live? Will Ed and I stay friends? Will we ever get back together?*

She already knew the answer. Ed didn't come home that night.

By morning, Zoe had packed her things. She stuffed her life into two suitcases—the same ones she had arrived in Canada with—and left without taking a single penny from Ed.

She went to stay with her friend Julie. And just like that, it was over.

Julie, Zoe's new friend, had broken up with Antoine, so she offered Zoe a place to stay until she sorted her life out. Julie was a pretty blonde, a little shorter than Zoe, and a lot of fun. They went out drinking and dancing, often venting about their exes, though Zoe never felt too bad about Ed. She believed the breakup was her fault.

Every morning Zoe boarded the number three bus to go to work. She befriended the driver Tom, so if she arrived late at the bus stop, Tom would wait for her, much to the chagrin of the other passengers.

It was one of those hot, sunny mornings. She was late and sprinted to catch the bus. Unfortunately, it was a different driver. She jumped on just as the doors were closing and collapsed into the only vacant seat. She was breathing heavily, wiping her brow, when a handsome man next to her, offered her a bottle of water.

'Here, you look like you need this,' he said with a warm smile.

She took a big swig and handed back the bottle. 'Thank you. That was just what I needed.'

He shook his head and gently pushed her hand back. 'It's okay. You keep it.'

Grateful, she took another sip. 'I'm Zoe Hunter, by the way.'

'Jason Hadley,' he replied, extending a hand. 'I don't usually take the bus, but my truck broke down this morning.'

Zoe noticed his rugged look: brown wavy hair that needed styling, brown eyes, and tanned skin. He was casually dressed in blue jeans and a T-shirt, which showed off his glaring, obvious biceps. There was something reassuring about his presence.

'Bad luck about the truck,' she said, and thought, good luck for me.

Three stops later, Jason stood up and squeezed past her. 'This is my stop.' He reached into his pocket, pulled out a card, and handed it to her. 'Give me a call sometime.'

Zoe took the card, feeling a spark of excitement. 'I will. Thanks again for the water, Jason.'

He flashed another smile before stepping off the bus. Zoe watched him walk away, feeling like the day had suddenly taken a very interesting turn. Very nice, she thought. How long do I wait before calling him?

She decided to be brave and called him the next day. They had a couple of dates before she invited him back to the flat for dinner one Saturday night. Julie was supposed to be out with friends but they had cancelled, so she joined them for dessert and a couple of glasses of wine. They all laughed talking about experiences of past disastrous relationships, until midnight. Jason was a chauffeur part time so he had to leave as he had an early morning run.

'Wow!, he's really cute,' said Julie. 'And a nice person.'

That night turned out be the last date with Jason. He and Zoe were supposed to go to the movies the following Tuesday but he cancelled. Apparently he had to work.

'Hey Julie, do want to go the movies with me?' Zoe shouted through her closed bedroom door. She banged on it. No answer. It turned out she did go to the movies...with Jason.

What a cow, thought Zoe. They could have at least told Zoe what they were up to.

32

Marilyn

Zoe took a sick day from work and scoured the local paper to find her own place. Nothing! Nice place, right area, wrong price.

It was all so depressing, so she decided to pay Ed a friendly visit. She didn't call him as she wanted to surprise him. It wasn't far so she walked, as it was a beautiful sunny day. She went to the apartment building, got in the elevator and pressed number eight. It was all so familiar ... and reassuring. As the elevator clicked from floor to floor, she began to wonder if she had made a huge mistake leaving Ed.

She stepped out the elevator determined to explore a new beginning for their relationship. Ed was a good man. He was loving and kind. So, she would tell him what happiness was to her, listen to what happiness was to him. Maybe they could reach middle ground.

Full of hope and confidence she reached for the door bell. There were voices coming from inside the apartment, so she pressed her ear against the door and listened. Ed was chatting away as he does, and a cheerful, female voice was cooing and tittering, encouraging him and lots of laughter.

It was less than two months since I left. Was it just a friend or someone more intimate. Did I know her? She felt sick and jealous. Not knowing who it was or the situation, made her feel even worse. The blood drained from her extremities. She went weak at the knees and crumbled in a ball on the floor and cried. They didn't hear her. No one came and said, 'Wow! are you okay lady?' She just sat there like a blob on the cold, tiled floor weeping into her own, cold hands.

Come on Zoe, this isn't like you, said that little voice inside. She got to her feet, wiped away the tears, straightened her new mini skirt, spun with the grace and attitude of a Prima Ballerina, and strode off to the elevator.

This is my life, I'm setting the barre a little higher next time.

A few days later, she bought a beaten up Toyota, which wasn't great to look at, but got her from A to B. She fondly named it her "trashmobile". She took a long drive to gather her thoughts. She passed by the canal. Happy memories there. But no more feeling sorry for herself. She parked the car and sat down in the cafe, on the rather uncomfortable bench and drank a couple of glasses of wine. On the way, she had picked up a different newspaper. She needed a place of her own where she could seriously begin her life again. She glanced through the want ads - Bingo! An apartment was available in an older, but trendy area, called the *Glebe*, not far from down town. She found a phone box and dialled the number.

'Hi, I'm phoning about the place to rent.'

'Who's this?' came a somewhat confused voice from the other end.

'My name is Zoe and I want to rent the place that's advertised in the paper. Is it still available?'

'I don't know, hold on a sec...'

Zoe's heart thumped."

'Look honey, the owner is out and won't be back for an hour.'

Zoe grilled the lady on the other end for details. Apparently she was just a friend, waiting for the owner who was called Janice, to return.

'She's very kindly picking up my groceries so I told her I would answer the phone. Here's the address, come on over.'

Zoe jumped into her "trashmobile" and zoomed off. Twenty minutes later, she knocked on the door. The owner had just arrived back. She was probably only a few years older than Zoe. The apartment was perfect. One bedroom, a cozy living room and a well equipped kitchen, but the real selling point was the cute, little garden, complete with a few Rose plants and a small Rhododendron bush, which reminded her of her mother's garden.

Zoe thought she must have been the sort of person Janice was looking for, because she was the one determined to get her to take it – or else the place was haunted and she'd been through a hundred tenants in the past year!

A week later Zoe was unpacking her belongings. She needed furniture; the sofa she had ordered had arrived which she slept on until she had enough money to but a real bed. While living with Ed, he had paid most of the household bills while Zoe was responsible for the groceries. Anything left over, she saved for a rainy day, or snowy day since she was in the land of long winters.

Not long after moving in, Zoe met her neighbour from across the road. She was in her garden, tending to a bed of vibrant flowers. Zoe decided to introduce herself and walked over. 'Hi,

I'm Zoe. I just moved in.'

The woman looked up, wiping her hands on her jeans. 'Hello! I'm Marilyn. Nice to meet you.'

Marilyn dressed very casually, wearing no makeup, and her blonde hair was cut in a bob. Despite their differences in appearance, they clicked immediately.

'I couldn't help but notice your garden. It's beautiful,' Zoe said, admiring the neatly arranged plants.

'Thanks, it's my little sanctuary,' Marilyn replied with a smile. 'Originally from Yorkshire, England. What about you?'

'Also from the north, A town called Newbury, a few miles north of Newcastle. It's quite different here.'

Marilyn laughed. 'Sure is! So, what brought you to this side of the world?'

'A man.'

Marilyn looked at her with a knowing look. 'Yep, can't live without them, can't live with them.'

They chatted for a while, and Zoe quickly realized Marilyn was extremely intelligent, funny, and great fun to be around. One afternoon, as they sipped tea in Marilyn's garden, Zoe asked, 'So, what do you do, Marilyn?'

Marilyn leaned back in her chair, 'Well, I've been the Chief Planner for the Central Core of the City of Ottawa since 1973. The first woman to ever hold that position.'

Zoe's eyes widened. 'Wow, that's impressive!'

Marilyn shrugged modestly. 'I've got a zillion degrees and run a twelve unit apartment at the same time. But what I really love is to ride around on my old pedal-backward-to-brake bicycle. It's quirky, but it gets me where I need to go.'

'You're like a modern-day Renaissance woman,' Zoe said, genuinely impressed.

Marilyn chuckled. 'Maybe. Or just a bit eccentric. But people seem to like me.'

Zoe nodded. 'I can see why. You're amazing, Marilyn.'

Marilyn smiled warmly. 'And I think you're pretty amazing too, Zoe. I'm glad you live close.'

From that day on, their friendship flourished, with Marilyn making Zoe's transition to her new home even more delightful.

Before joining the Bank of Montreal, Zoe held a temporary position at an event company, which supplied men and women for special events. However, when they were really in a bind, Zoe would step in. She once dressed as a Playboy bunny, and another time, she donned a cowgirl outfit.

Marilyn enjoyed hearing this , so one evening, when she returned from a formal City Hall party, she met Zoe for a nightcap. 'I was talking about you tonight,' she said, 'I mentioned how you made a few dollars by posing provocatively on car hoods or dressing up like a Playboy bunny. You should have seen their faces! The younger Women's Lib members at City Hall were shocked and said, 'You mean your friend does THAT?' But the men were intrigued, and one of them even wants me to set you up with a date.'

Zoe just laughed, amused by the reaction.

They both enjoyed going out for a few pints to the local pub (well close enough for Canadian standards) meeting new friends and just having a good laugh. As it happens Marilyn was from Yorkshire and an awesome beer drinker. Zoe was pretty good coming from Newbury, but Marilyn could drink her under the table nine times out of ten.

Over the next few months, Zoe met a lot of Marilyn's crazy

friends. These were edgy, witty people who Zoe loved spending time with. She now realised that Ed and his low key world had deprived her of the person she really was. The 'me' she wanted to be. Zoe attended a few super cool parties and had a great time. She made people laugh, she let her hair down. She even tried smoking a joint. That didn't work out as it caused her to have a coughing fit. She decided to stick to wine and wit as the best road to hyper-fun. She loved Ottawa and its people although it was still hard for her to get used to all the snow, even if the sun still shone brightly. And predictably, working in the bank soon became tedious.

She found herself in a new chapter of her life, yet despite the changes, there was a lingering sense of unfulfillment. She pondered over what her true purpose was in this new phase, what she was meant to achieve. Reflecting on her aspirations from childhood, she remembered her dreams of becoming a dancer and a flight attendant, both of which she had accomplished. However, beyond those achievements, she found herself adrift, lacking clear objectives. She realized she needed to channel her focus, yet her impatience often led her astray, akin to climbing a towering oak tree and being lured by intriguing branches, only to return to the trunk in search of something more fulfilling. It was a pattern she recognized as being easily sidetracked.

While she harboured ideas and goals, she struggled to formulate concrete plans to achieve them. Looking back, she could discern numerous clues and hints guiding her path. Due to her arthritis, she couldn't return to dancing; maybe an easy class for the exercise. The financial situation loomed over her. Embarking on a new business venture seemed appealing, yet the need for startup funds presented a significant hurdle.

33

The Travel Agent

Zoe poured a cup of tea, took a couple of chocolate digestive biscuits, picked up the newspaper and settled down on the sofa, determined to find a better job. Nothing appealed to her. Most vacancies were for the City of Ottawa and she certainly didn't want to be a civil servant. She would have to be a bored banker until she found something more interesting.

A few days later she was dining at Mamma Grazzi's, a family run, Italian restaurant where she had spent many evenings alone. She was finishing up a plate of Spaghetti Carbonara when the waiter brought her a glass of red wine.

'I'm sorry, I didn't order that.'

'*Si, Signorina,*' the waiter smiled, 'I know, but the gentlemen over there sent it.'

'He did?' she asked redundantly and peeped around to see who he was referring to.

'*Si*, his name is Guiseppe. He's a regular and he remarked on how well you managed the spaghetti and asked if you were Italian.'

She raised her glass and turned to Guiseppe and said, '*No, sono Inglese, grazie.'*

Guiseppe smiled and saluted back. He was an older, weathered gentleman and fortunately he wasn't hitting on her. She turned back to her meal then finished off with a strong coffee. It arrived with the grinning waiter and a plate of Tiramisu, which needless to say she hadn't ordered. She turned again to thank Guiseppe, but he was standing right behind her, grinning. 'How come you speak Italian so well?' he said in a rich soft voice.

'I lived in Italy for a while,' she said, flattered by the compliment.

'Let me guess, Napoli.'

Zoe laughed. 'How do you know, I thought I had a pure accent.'

'Here *mia cara*, this is my business card. I own a travel agency and would love to have someone like you work for me.'

She took the card and read Guiseppe's Travels. She tried to look calm and collected while her heart beat hard enough to rattle her ribs. '*Grazie molte Signor*!' she said, as he sailed out the door. She stared at the card, knowing the job was already hers and said to herself, *I'm a travel Agent.*

Mr Clark, her boss at the bank wasn't happy when she handed in a week's notice.

'Why?' he stammered, 'You are such a good teller and you can really go far in this company.'

'I want to travel and explore the world but I can't do that on a two week holiday each year. In the travel industry I can go somewhere every month.'

By then he knew he wouldn't be able to change her mind. He smiled and Zoe thanked him for being a cool boss. A week later she said good bye to him and her colleagues and left.

After a relaxing weekend, she was ready for Monday. She jumped into her car and arrived exactly at nine at Guiseppe's office. It was closed. Not a good sign.

She parked and went into the coffee bar next door and ordered a grande cafe latte.

'Excuse me, do you know anything about Guiseppe Travel Agency next door,' she asked the Barista, named Lorenzo.

'Whaddya want ta knowa,' he replied in a strong Italian accent.

'I was supposed to start work today, but there's no one there.'

'Donta worry, hesa always late,' laughed Lorenzo. 'Relax, just waita here.'

Zoe sat by the window, where she could keep an eye on the comings and goings next door. Then just as Lorenzo had predicted, at nine fifteen, Guiseppe, strolled into the coffee bar.

He smiled when he saw her. 'Looks like I will have to give you a set of keys.'

The weeks flew by as she trained to be a travel agent and also cleaned up the very disorganised office. Guiseppe was an educated and clever businessman but with old fashioned values. As well as booking flights and hotels mainly for the Italian community, he also charged his fellow mwn wnd women a fee for filling up various forms, like for visa and passport applications, as most of them could not speak or even write in English.

Zoe's dream was coming true. Almost every month she went on a business trip (known in the travel industry as *fam trips*) these were given by companies and hotels who wanted to promote their business, although sometimes it felt like a bribe, the way she was treated; free flight, hotels and meals. She travelled to the Bahamas, Jamaica, The Cayman Islands, New York and Florida. Most were weekends so she found herself always so exhausted on Mondays.

The longest trip Zoe ever took was to Miami, Florida. Zoe extended the stay due to the distance and jet lag. It was there she met Captain Brian Armstrong. He was the captain of a huge yacht, complete with several staterooms and a helicopter for emergencies. The galley was crafted from beautiful oak wood, giving it a warm, luxurious feel.

Captain Brian had kind brown eyes and wavy brown hair, and he kept himself in excellent shape. 'I've worked on boats since I was eighteen,' he told her Zoe one evening as they stood on the deck, watching the sunset. 'Studied hard to get my captain's license. This job is my dream come true.'

'Sounds like you've really found your calling,' Zoe replied, admiring his dedication.

'Yeah, the owners are great, the pay is high, and they rely on me to plan all their trips,' he said, his face lighting up with pride.

Zoe could tell that Brian liked her. He treated her like a queen, always attentive and considerate. Yet, despite his efforts, the chemistry between them just wasn't there. She preferred men who took initiative and didn't constantly ask what she wanted to do.

One evening, after yet another round of polite inquiries about her preferences, she finally said, 'Brian, I appreciate everything you do, but... surprise me! I like a bit of spontaneity.'

Brian looked taken aback for a moment, then smiled. 'You

want surprises? Alright, I can do surprises.'

The following day, Zoe found a note slipped under her hotel door. It read: 'Meet me on the deck at sunset. Dress comfortably.'

Intrigued, she followed the instructions. As the sun dipped below the horizon, Brian appeared, holding two glasses of white wine.

Zoe smiled, genuinely touched. 'This is perfect. Thank you, Brian.'

'Come with me,' he said.

They walked below deck. He had invited her to have supper with the crew, which was quite an honour as they were old school and were suspicious of women being down in the galley. Later that evening, Brian said, 'Tomorrow, I have another surprise for you. Be ready at noon.'

The next day, he took her on a tour of a nearby island, then Zoe and Brian found themselves on a secluded stretch of beach; the golden sand warm beneath their feet. The waves whispered softly, their gentle rhythm harmonizing with the distant rustling of palm trees. Zoe, with a carefree laugh, dipped her toes into the cool water, while Brian watched her with a smile. The world felt miles away, and in that tranquil moment, it was just the two of them, lost in the serenity of their own private paradise.

As they prepared to return home, Zoe realized that Brian's thoughtfulness and genuine effort were qualities she deeply appreciated. However, as he tried to persuade her to stay in Florida and be with him, she just wasn't feeling anything more. She could only treat him as a good friend and possibly a contact for the future.

'I have to admit, Brian, you've surprised me,' she said, as

they walked along the beach, 'but we can only be friends.'

'Well, you know where to find me if you ever change your mind.'

Did she let another good man go?

At the agency, Zoe was becoming very proficient in the travel industry and many times managed the office on her own when Guiseppe was at 'business meetings'. She knew from other sources, he had a mistress. However she was enjoying work and knew that travel was her future. Most flights had to be booked by looking in the OAG (Official Airline Guide)

She had made many friends in the industry but Gino, a Canadian Italian from Alitalia was her favourite. He was a middle aged married man with two children. A few pounds extra, probably due to his wife's cooking which, Zoe had tasted many times when they invited her to their house. His wife Paula, was so typically Italian and always asked why she was not with her family. When Zoe spent time with them, she felt like she was back in Italy.

Over time Gino, could see that Zoe worked very hard and was also impressed with her language skills, so eventually with his recommendation, she was offered a much more lucrative position with American Express Travel Agency.

Sadly she said goodbye to Guiseppe, but he wasn't too disappointed as he told her he was ready to retire and go back to Italy.

34

Budapest

The American Express agency was the corporate side of the industry. It was extremely hard work, booking flights and accommodation via phone calls to the airlines and individual hotels. It was at this time, Zoe was introduced to computers. They basically were way of keeping track of their clients.

Six months had passed and Zoe was feeling bored. *What is wrong with me? Why do I get bored so easily?*

Zoe's good reputation had spread throughout the tight community of the travel world and fortunately she was made an offer she couldn't refuse. She received an unexpected correspondence from a renowned Texan tour company offering her the position of Lead Travel Coordinator. The role promised not only a substantial pay raise but also the opportunity to design and oversee exclusive travel experiences in the Bahamas and Jamaica. Excitement bubbled within her as she read through the offer details—this was exactly the kind of challenge and adventure she had been craving. Without a second thought, Zoe accepted the offer, eager to leave behind the monotony of her previous job and embark on a thrilling new chapter in her career.

Before leaving for this new job, Zoe opened her mail to find an invitation to her brother Jonathan's wedding in Budapest, Hungary. This came as quite a surprise as she didn't even know he was dating anyone. Naturally, she got a great deal as a travel agent and flew out for ten days.

Jonathan had met his future wife, Jazmin when she was travelling through the UK, with Servas.

Servas is an international, non-profit organisation encompassing a network of hosts and travellers. The purpose of the network is to help build world peace, goodwill and understanding by providing opportunities for personal contacts among people of different cultures, backgrounds and nationalities.

Jazmin was a really good match for him. Two brainiacs. Zoe arrived a few days before the wedding, so she and Jonathan could spend some quality time together. As both of them were travelling these days, Zoe felt this was a time when they really bonded. They reminisced about childhood, some of the good memories they shared and filled in the gaps of their own individual lives, as they had always lived so many miles apart.

The marriage took place in a hall with the Justice of the Peace, all in Hungarian, with a translator by Jonathan's side. Zoe sat next to a wonderful elderly lady, who spoke English and was an ex ballerina and enamoured Zoe with her stories.

At the end of the ceremony, Jonathan was asked, 'Will you take this woman to be your wife?' There was a long pause as the translator was explaining to Jonathan. This caused a few chuckles with the guests. Also apparently, there is no "You may kiss the bride" in Hungarian ceremonies.

Their mother couldn't attend as she was suffering a few

more aches and pains than usual and Jonathan thought she might have a slight touch of dementia.

Simon, Jazmin's cousin played tour rep as he showed Zoe around Budapest, a beautiful city, the ninth largest in Europe. St Stephen's Basilica, named after the first King of Hungary was their first stop and then the neo-Gothic architecture of the Hungarian Parliament building, which was partly inspired by London's Palace of Westminster. Simon turned to Zoe and said, 'Did you know there's a law which states nothing can be built higher than the dome of the Parliament building.?'

'I think that's a great idea. Too many cities spoil the skyline with tall buildings.'

There was so much more to see, but Zoe found herself spending a lot of time with Jazmin's extended family. They loved to eat, and knock back the national drink of Hungary called Pálinka, a fruit brandy that, to put it frankly, could well topple a horse.

Jonathan and Zoe hadn't seen each other in ages, and though they had kept in touch through letters, nothing compared to sitting across from each other, sipping coffee, and reminiscing in person. The café was cozy, filled with the rich aroma of roasted beans and the hum of quiet conversations around them.

Zoe wrapped her hands around her cup, smiling. 'It's so good to finally see you, Jonathan. Letters are great, but chatting with you in person is so much more fun.'

Jonathan chuckled, stirring his coffee absentmindedly. 'Exactly. I've got so many stories that I couldn't possibly squeeze into a letter.'

She raised an eyebrow playfully. 'Oh? Sounds like you've

been up to something interesting. Tell me everything.'

Jonathan leaned back, grinning. 'Well, for starters, I finally made that trip to Japan I always talked about. Spent two weeks wandering through Tokyo, Kyoto, and some tiny village in the mountains. It was incredible.'

Zoe's eyes widened. "No way! Japan has been on my list forever.'

He took a sip of his coffee, thinking. 'Kyoto's temples were breathtaking, but honestly, the food? Life-changing. I had this bowl of ramen in a tiny backstreet shop—best thing I've ever eaten.'

Zoe laughed. 'Of course, your highlight would be food. That reminds me—remember when we used to go to the beach with mum. We always craved those fish and chips.'

Jonathan groaned with a nostalgic smile. 'I loved spending the day at the beach, but the aftermath? Not so much. Dragging all those bags, dealing with wet, sand-covered towels, then cramming onto a packed bus for half an hour—only to face that endless trek from the bus stop home? Pure torture.'

Zoe shook her head, laughing. 'Yeah, but remember we were the only kids on our street that got to go to the beach. Most of neighbours only got as far as the local pub.'

Zoe described her travels when she was dancing.

'Do you miss it?'

'Yes,' said Zoe. But my arthritis is getting worse.'

'What are you doing about it?'

'I am trying some natural remedies, so we'll see how that goes. Anyway that's enough about me. Tell me how you met Jazmin.'

They sat back, letting the easy flow of conversation continue, filling in the gaps that letters could never quite capture.

Saying goodbye to her brother was bittersweet. Also, over time, she had grown close to many of Jazmin's relatives, feeling like part of an extended family. But sadly, with Jonathan and Jazmin's move to the UK, she never had the chance to see them again.

35

The Bahamas & Jamaica

Two weeks later, as Zoe stepped off the plane and onto the tarmac of the small airport in the Bahamas; the warm, tropical breeze instantly enveloped her, carrying with it the scent of saltwater and blooming hibiscus, and the lush greenery of the island framed the scene like a postcard. The sun, bright and welcoming, melted away any tension or fears about the job ahead of her.

Due to the restrictions of her work permit as a non-Bahamian, Zoe found herself in a unique, albeit challenging, routine. Every month, she worked diligently for three weeks in the Bahamas, then back to Canada for one week before she could come back to Bahamas. Her other destination was Jamaica, which at that time was focused on addressing its own economic and employment challenges, which made the process of obtaining a work visa more rigorous. The constant travel was exhausting, and the back-and-forth disrupted any sense of normalcy, but Zoe embraced it as part of the adventure, knowing that this was the price she had to pay for living and working in paradise.

When she was on location, she would work shifts from 6 a.m. to 10 p.m. and 4 p.m. to 7 p.m, during which time she helped the guests with local information, and arranged various trips around the island.

On her time off, Zoe found it challenging to completely escape the hotel patrons. Even when she was relaxing on the beach, soaking up the sun and enjoying the sound of the waves, guests would often recognize her and approach with questions. 'Where's the best place to eat?' they'd ask, or 'How do I get to such and such a place?' Despite the interruptions, Zoe didn't mind. She genuinely loved helping people, and each question gave her a chance to share her knowledge of the island. She had read up and was able to talk about the area like a local. She could tell them: The Bahamas consists of about 700 islands and 2,400 cays, but only around 30 of them were inhabited. They are also home to some of the world's deepest blue holes, including Dean's Blue Hole (202 meters deep), making it a paradise for divers. Her favourite fact, was that one of the most famous attractions in the Bahamas was Pig Beach, where friendly wild pigs swam in the crystal-clear waters.

During her time working on the yacht, she had little opportunity to explore the places they visited. But now, she finally could, and she felt truly blessed. This was a wonderful lifestyle—at least for now. That is, until restlessness inevitably set in.

In Jamaica she would travel with the bus driver Malique to pick up the new arrivals from Montego Bay airport. He was the son of the owner of the bus company and was a very popular man. Women would come back each year just to be with him. On more than one occasion Zoe had to come to his aid by keeping some of his adoring women separate. He was a tall muscular Jamaican, charming and charismatic. He was also a great entertainer on the two hour bus ride to their hotel in Ocho Rios.

This particular day, he was on form and the bus was full of excited tourists heading from the airport. The Jamaican sun was shining, and Zoe stood at the front, holding a microphone, while Malique navigated the winding roads with ease, occasionally glancing back at the passengers.

'Alright, folks, welcome to Jamaica! Dis is Malique, your driver for today, and da lovely lady up front is Zoe, our tour rep and my personal sunshine!'

'Oh, stop it, Malique. You're just trying to get out of trouble for being late this morning.'

'Late? Me? Nah, man, I was just running on island time. Besides, you know you can't start the party without me!'

'That's true,' said Zoe. 'We did miss our daily dose of bad jokes. Speaking of which, how many of you are ready for some of Malique's world-famous humour?'

A loud cheer came from the tourists.

'Ah, mi audience! Okay, Why don't skeletons fight each other?' he paused. 'Because they don't have the guts!'

A few cheers and groans erupt in the bus.

'See what I mean? He does have a talent for making people laugh, even if it's with the cheesiest jokes around.'

'Cheesy? Zoe, mi jokes are like da finest reggae—timeless and full of soul!'

'If by soul you mean corny, then sure, Malique.'

'Alright, folks, I promise the scenery will get better than the jokes. Look to your right, you'll see the beautiful Dunn's River Falls.'

'And if you look to your left, you'll see me, da most handsome bus driver in all of Jamaica!'

'Malique, if you keep this up, we'll have to get you your own reality show.' She turned to the passengers, 'Okay, let's focus on the journey, everyone. We're almost at Ocho Rios, where the adventure really begins!'

'That's right! And don't forget, I'll be here to entertain, drive, and maybe even teach you a dance move or two.'

'And I'll be here to make sure Malique stays on the road and out of trouble.'

'Together, we make one unforgettable team. So sit back, relax, and get ready for da best vacation ever!' said Malique.

The tourists applauded and started to ask Zoe questions.

Malique had to concentrate now, as the last part of the journey was a narrow road on a steep mountain.

The bus pulled into the hotel and the tourists disembark, still chuckling from the ride.

Zoe looked at Malique, 'You really do make this job fun, you know that?'

'I try mi best. And who knows, maybe one day I'll wear you down and you will go to dinner with me.'

'Dream on, Malique. But keep the jokes coming. They do make the ride a lot more enjoyable.'

Often Americans who had just arrived in Jamaica for the first time would ask Zoe what language the locals spoke. She would explain that the official language of Jamaica is English, but the unofficial language is a Patois, which included dialects such as Creole, Patwa, and Bongo Talk with many words borrowed from African languages. Sometimes people thought she sounded Jamaican with her slight Northern English intonation.

This kind of life really suited her although she couldn't do dance classes on a regular basis, being home just for a week at a time. But it was all fun and she was lucky to have Marilyn keep an eye on her flat.

In the Bahamas, it was a lot calmer, no Malique and no long bus rides.

It was a place of vibrant change and burgeoning tourism. Nestled in the Caribbean, this archipelago of around 700 islands and cays was increasingly becoming a hot spot for tourists seeking sun, sand, and sea. Zoe loved their many festivals, with Calypso and reggae music. However, despite the tourism boom, there were significant economic disparities. Many Bahamians benefited from the growing economy, but poverty and unemployment were still issues in some areas. Also the rapid development for tourism raised concerns about environmental impacts, particularly on the delicate marine ecosystems.

Zoe got along well with the staff of the hotels and in Jamaica, they would take her to their local haunts and family parties. Often she was the only white person in the crowd. Even as a non local, they all treated her with respect and she always enjoyed their company.

However it didn't take her long to see how some of the tourists were prejudiced and treated the staff like servants. Some of the locals acted as tour guides for a few dollars and Jamal, a friend of Zoe's was excited when he was invited to go to Texas. However, on his return he told Zoe that when he arrived there, he was greeted very coldly and had to return earlier than expected.

The blacks, and even Zoe, as she hung out with them, also experienced prejudice from the white hotel employees. One day she was working at the reception desk, when a tourist asked her if his wallet had been found. Zoe looked in his room pigeon hole only to find his key.

'No, I'm sorry sir, there is nothing here but your room key.'

'I knew it,' he yelled, 'That damn housemaid has stolen it.'

'Zoe couldn't believe what she was hearing. He demanded to speak to the manager, who happened to be an American, to make a complaint. To cut a long story short, the wallet had been found and put in the wrong pigeon hole. Not soon after the manager called Zoe to his office. She had never really liked him. His scrawny physique and balding head couldn't be overlooked as he had a personality to match his ugly form. He accused Zoe of not taking care of the tourist and said, 'You cannot trust these people!'

Zoe shook with anger and said, 'These people are wonderful and kind. They are poor and work hard. The local crime is minimal as their livelihood comes from tourism.'

That didn't go down well. He looked at Zoe with contempt.

'You know I don't think you're suitable for this job, please leave on the next plane out.' he said with an irritating southern drawl.

'With pleasure,' she yelled. 'I don't want to work with a bunch of racists.'

36

The Countess

Zoe was upset about leaving such a perfect job, but she couldn't tolerate racism. Back in Ottawa, she found herself scouring the newspaper ads once again. Eventually, she started working as a waitress at a nearby Holiday Inn. The salary was minimum wage, but the hours were flexible, the tips were good, and they provided free meals.

Needing to fill her creative side, Zoe was excited when she saw an ad for auditions for an international folk dance troupe. Although she hadn't danced in a while, she had maintained her fitness by exercising every day. At 35, she was still in great shape, although her arthritis would flare up occasionally. It had also been a long time since she last auditioned, so she felt very nervous.

The audition went well. Jan, a classically trained dancer from Holland, led the troupe. After injuring his shoulder, he transitioned to folk dancing. He enjoyed it so much, he started his own company.

After eight hours of waitressing, Zoe was exhausted, her feet were sore, but as soon as she stepped into the studio for rehearsals, a wave of energy surged through her. The familiar scent of sweat and rosin, the sound of music echoing through the space, and the sight of other excited dancers reinvigorated her. They began with a thirty-minute ballet warm-up, then transitioned to a lively piece from Hungary, followed by a rhythmic number from Macedonia. The routines were intricate and required focus, though they weren't as physically demanding as the jazz numbers she used to perform. Still, they pushed her in different ways, keeping her engaged and excited for each new challenge.

In the dressing room, the original members introduced themselves. They were much more friendly than other dancers she had met. They were quite a mixed bunch with various levels of dance training.

'Hi everyone, I'm Zoe. It's great to be here.'

'Nice to meet you, Zoe. I'm Maria. Where are you from?'

'Originally from England, but I've been in Ottawa for a while now. How about you?'

'I'm from Portugal. I moved here a couple of years ago. This troupe has been like a second family to me.'

A tall girl with hair cascading down her back said, 'Hey, Zoe! I'm Rebecca. I hear you've got a background in jazz. That's awesome!'

'Yeah, I did jazz for years, but when I got arthritis it proved to be a bit too strenuous. Folk dancing is a bit new to me, but I'm really excited to learn, and hopefully my aching joints won't suffer too much.'

Another girl came over, 'You'll love it. It's different, but it's so much fun. I'm Elena, by the way. I've been with the troupe for three years.'

Jan joined them, 'I see you're getting to know everyone, Zoe.

This is a great group.'

'Yes, they are all so friendly. It will take me a while to remember all their names.' said Zoe.

They performed dances from all over Europe, Greece, Hungary, Czech Republic and Macedonia. Jan was very strict making sure they got all the steps correct in each dance. Zoe often wonder why, as most of the audience couldn't tell the difference between a Czárdás, a traditional Hungarian folk dance, or a dance originated in the Czech Republic. The costumes were heavy and Zoe was sure she had lost a few pounds during those hot summer events, which also involved many quick costume changes.

After one performance, Jan asked the company to stay around because he wanted them to meet someone. Excitement buzzed through the dressing room as they speculated about who it might be—perhaps a celebrity?

Jan returned with a short stocky woman, sporting a plain brown dress. Her hair was short and her tanned face quite wrinkled.

'Hey everyone, this is Countess Helena de Silaghi Sirag.'

'Okay, just drop the countess and call me Bobbie, like all my friends.' she said laughing.

Bobbie, with her roots in Transylvania had a name that inevitably triggered thoughts of Dracula for most people. Zoe couldn't help but smile to herself. She had once delved into the lore of Dracula and discovered that the infamous character was based on a real historical figure, Vlad the Impaler. Vlad was a brutal ruler known for his gruesome method of impaling his enemies on long, sharpened stakes, leaving them to die slowly. While Bobbie's name evoked chilling tales, she herself seemed warm and down-to-earth, a fascinating contrast to the dark history behind her heritage.

Bobbie explained to the company that after the Second World War she had left the communist controlled territory and eventually made her way to Canada with her husband Stephen in 1949 and they landed in Ontario after a brief period in Italy.

She was an oil painter and a believer in the paranormal. Amongst her skills she was a self-described time traveller; had the ability to astral travel. During these out-of-body excursions she reported visiting different star systems and interacting with the spirit forces she encountered. These encounters then became the subject of her paintings.

Bobbie once said in a press interview, 'Yes, I am a weirdo, but I am a creative weirdo.'

None of this made any sense to Zoe, but she was aware that what Bobbie experienced, was possibly a far more important matter than anything Zoe would ever encounter.

Bobbie had watched the troupe dance and wanted to meet them all. Zoe didn't know why but she felt a special bond with her. She enthralled Zoe and most of the dancers with her accounts of her fascinating past.

After a short time of getting to know Zoe, Bobbie made an unexpected but intriguing offer: she wanted Zoe to become her personal assistant. The opportunity meant leaving behind her role in the dance troupe and relocating to a small town called Burlington, not far from Toronto. For Zoe, the decision was a welcome change. Dancing had become increasingly difficult due to her arthritic joints, with aches and pains emerging in places she hadn't known existed. Additionally, Ottawa still held lingering memories of Ed, and she felt ready for a fresh start. Though Zoe was saddened to part ways with Marilyn, they promised to keep writing letters on a regular basis.

The Countess lived in Burlington, in a grand structure with a curtain wall reminiscent of a castle, which took Zoe by surprise. The property featured a massive iron gate that was locked each evening at 10 p.m. Inside, there was a room entirely dedicated to displaying Bobbie's paintings. There was a lot!

Every time there was an art show, Zoe had to lug the paintings into the van, drive to the event and unload. There was usually someone to help her at the event but the work was very demanding.

Whenever Zoe experienced pain, Bobbie would give her a massage, and miraculously, the pain would disappear for a while. Zoe also preferred to avoid medication, opting instead for natural supplements.

The city of Burlington saw an increase in commercial and industrial development as it was located between Toronto and Hamilton. It also hosted various events and festivals and was becoming one of Canada's largest free music festivals. Even with all of this going on it wasn't a city that Zoe enjoyed. Also the job with the Countess became too demanding and actually not as exciting as Zoe imagined it would be. Here we go again, thought Zoe.

After only nine months, Zoe spoke with Bobbie. 'Bobbie, I love you and your art, but unfortunately the job is getting too much for me, so I will have to hand in my notice.'

Bobbie was sorry at her decision but understood Zoe's dilemma.

Zoe made the decision to move to Toronto, a bigger and more cosmopolitan city.

37

Toronto

Zoe picked up a local newspaper from the hotel where she booked a room for a week. Her eyes landed on what looked like the perfect place. She grabbed the phone and three days later was living in a lovely flat in the centre of town. Three days after that she was reporting to her first day of work. Two blocks from her flat, the Crock and Block, quite a strange name for a restaurant, but a popular place. They served good portions at reasonable prices: Prime rib with Yorkshire pudding was one of the most popular meals, especially Sundays. The staff were very friendly and lots of fun.

Zoe immediately hit it off with Suzi, a 5ft barrel of laughs. For someone so small, she was an adventurous outdoors girl and very strong, both physically and mentally, a keen sailor so they swapped stories of their travel adventures.

Suzi had the best laugh ever and even laughed at Zoe's attempt to tell some really bad jokes. She was very kind and thoughtful especially to her family. She and Zoe soon became best friends and spent a lot of time together ... until she got married.

Suzi left the restaurant but they stayed in touch, but Zoe wasn't keen on her husband, who was a controlling person and did not like Zoe at all.

One day Zoe was going through the job listings in the paper. She liked the restaurant but still had the urge to do something in travel. That's when she saw an ad for flight attendants. She quickly made an appointment for an interview. The company was impressed by her experience with Saudi Airlines, knowing how difficult that would have been. Surprisingly, Zoe was hired immediately. It was a small airline called Worldways Canada, whose main business was flying hockey teams around the country.

During training, the girls would encourage Zoe to volunteer to do the demonstrations as they knew of her prior experience, but Jean, the instructor found it annoying and was a little jealous of her popularity. Jean was about forty-five, with bleached blonde hair and no sense of humour. There were only fifteen in the class and Zoe became friends with two of them, later being named the three Musketeers as they always had each other's backs. Billy, a gay man who kept them laughing with his crude remarks and loved helping them with their makeup. He was quite annoyed when he was told to cut off some of his curly locks. In retaliation, he shaved his head completely. Thank God, it suited him as Zoe thought a lot of white men with bald heads looked like skin-heads, or cancer patients. Shirlene was a little reserved and liked to stick to the rules. She had perfectly groomed blonde hair and always dressed smartly and typically reserved and cautious. She only loosened up when Zoe and Billy took her out for a few drinks. She stepped out of her comfort zone for the first time in a while. As the night wore on and the cozy bar's warm lighting and lively atmosphere worked their magic, she began to relax. The laughter and easy conversation flowed effortlessly, and with each sip of her drink, Shirlene's usual reserve started to dissolve. By the end of the night, she was sharing stories and jokes with Zoe and Billy. Zoe, while finding Shirlene's stories a bit dull and her jokes lacking in humour, couldn't help but feel a sense of warmth. Seeing Shirlene so relaxed and engaged, enjoying the evening with genuine delight, made Zoe pleased to witness her friend letting go and having a good time.

Zoe surprised herself when she came first in the final written exam. Only one more practical to go. They sat in the local bar and made fun with some of the things they had to do, especially the makeup. Jean, the instructor, unbeknownst to them, happened to be in the same bar and saw them lampooning the training. The next day Zoe was called in to HR and dismissed for unprofessional conduct. She guessed Jean hadn't had enough to drink to find it as hilarious as they all had.

Zoe took it badly. The whole experience was devastating so hid in her apartment for three days. By the third day, Suzi called to say she was getting concerned as she hadn't heard from her. Through the tears, Zoe explained briefly what had happened. Within thirty minutes, Suzi was knocking on the door with a bottle of *Malbec*, which helped Zoe drown her sorrows. It was kind of ironic as Suzi was going through her own challenges since she had separated from her husband. Zoe always saw him as a miserable man, so assured her it was all for the best.

A week later Suzi called. 'I have a great job for you. I'll be over in fifteen minutes.' Once again, the alcohol was flowing. This time they popped the cork on a reserve bottle of Champagne that was aging, a little beyond the expiry date, which Suzi had kept a little too long, for the right occasion.

Zoe was feeling a little tipsy and laughed, 'They should make champagne glasses bigger.'

'So, listen,' said Suzi, '*The Balmy Arms*, which is an English pub, is looking for a hostess for their restaurant. I work as a waitress and I'm sure there will be a waitress position open soon.'

The Balmy Arms was as close to an English pub that a Canadian company could manage, and it had a very successful restaurant serving English food until about eight and then the real drinking would begin. Suzi put in a good word for Zoe who started the following week.

Commuting all the way from downtown was tiresome so she moved closer to a really nice area on the shore of Lake Ontario, called the "Beach." It was inexpensive and trendy, and she shared with two sisters, Dolores and Rose. Someone suggested she buy a place, but her free spirit resisted; the idea of owning property felt like a chain, tethering her to one spot.

Dolores taught massage in the local beauty school, so often used Zoe as a model in return for free massages, which really helped her arthritis, especially after a busy night at the pub. The Balmy Arms was a great place to work. There were lots of people Zoe's age and a few eligible men who found Zoe attractive and interesting. Zoe hadn't dated anyone seriously since breaking up with Ed and she still wasn't ready for a serious relationship.

After only a short time, Zoe was promoted to waitress and earned loads of money from tips. She was good at what she did. New Year's Eve she made over five hundred dollars, so Suzi and Zoe celebrated the following day.

'Happy New Year, Zoe! How are you feeling?'

'Happy New Year, Suzi! So far, so good. I'm feeling optimistic about the coming year. How about you?'

'I'm excited! I've got some new projects lined up and a few resolutions I'm actually looking forward to keeping. Did you make any resolutions?' asked Zoe.

'I did! I'm focusing on taking better care of myself this year—less work and more relaxation. Maybe start dating again,' said Suzi.

'That sounds like a great plan. You deserve to find the right man.' said Zoe as she lifted her glass. 'Maybe I need a good man. Here's to a fantastic year ahead, filled with new adventures and great memories.'

'Cheers to that, Zoe. May the new year be full of joy and new experiences for both of us.'

By the end of January, Zoe moved up to bartender, which was even more fun and more lucrative. By this time Suzi had moved on as she had finished university and became a teacher. Luckily Zoe had made friends with Karen, the other bartender. She was an attractive girl with her long blonde hair and blue eyes. She could be a little moody at times but was good fun. Unfortunately, Zoe realised her moods were affected by her cocaine habit, so eventually stopped hanging around with her. This made her think about Holly and how she missed her friend.

Usually about five o'clock, the ex-pats would arrive. Most of them worked in the film industry and would sit and drink about four or five bottles of *Newcastle Brown Ale,* then complain about one thing and another.

'In England, it's this, or it's that.'

Zoe would say, 'Why don't you go back to England if you're not happy here.'

But of course, they earned much more money than they would back home. Zoe felt like their psychiatrist. One time the pub was having an anniversary party and Zoe finally got to meet the wives. One of the regulars' wives came up to Zoe and thanked her.

'Why?' she asked.

'Well,' the wife replied. 'The husbands come in here every night and complain to you about work, so by the time they get home, they don't have to vent their problems to us.'

Zoe smiled and thanked her.

Within two years Zoe became assistant manager. During her time there, she made so many friends, and had lots of dates, but nothing serious.

38

Romance and Poetry

One Halloween Zoe went to a friend's party, dressed as Raggedy Ann. It was a fun party as she danced and chatted with friends. Just before dark, she was kidnapped by Roy Rogers and carried off to another party. His name was Marc, another French Canadian, as she thought about Ed, who was also French Canadian. They decided not to reveal their real identities until they met up again as they were getting along so well, without knowing what they actually looked like.

Marc, alias Roy Rogers, turned out to be very attractive with spiked blond hair and intense blue eyes. He was a wiry energetic man, so their first date was a long walk in the park. It was a bit chilly but sunny, then stopped at his favourite restaurant for a huge plate of steaming pasta.

Their following few dates were films and meals. One date he took her to his local bar. He frequented it often as they allowed him to play the piano. He bought Zoe a glass of white wine, then sat at the piano. 'Ladies and gentlemen, mesdames et messieurs, I would like to dedicate this song to my beautiful friend over there.'

Zoe was in shock as she listened.

Annalogy

It doesn't matter where and when
somehow we met
And I will never forget
What I felt there and then.

It was a strange sensation
   some kind of vibration
   outside of space and time
   beyond any rhyme.

I heard this music in my head
   but it wasn't mine, it was yours instead.
   And every word you spoke
   turned into a note.

You are to me
   a source of inspiration
   It's stronger than me
   I cannot resist your attraction

When I play piano
   I'm really trying to say
   Yo te quiero
   I love you.

Everyone applauded as Zoe downed her drink. Oh my God, thought Zoe, that was a bit much. They had only known each other for two weeks and now he was declaring his love.

   Marc joined a red-faced Zoe with another drink in hand.

'Thank you, Marc. That was, um..what should I say? Very sweet but we hardly know each other.'

'I know, but I fell for you immediately. I couldn't help it.'

Zoe took his hand, knowing she needed to nip it in the bud. 'Marc you are a sweet, kind and talented individual, but I don't feel any chemistry between us.'

'Well, I tried. I guess we can stay friends?'

'Of course,' replied Zoe, relieved that he took it so well.

Talents aside, there wasn't enough to make the relationship develop.

After that, Zoe had a few casual dates but no-one special. *Will I ever find someone to love?*

Zoe's friend Pam booked a private room for her birthday party, in the pub down the street from where Zoe worked. Pam was a bubbly redhead, who liked lots of attention, hence this extravagant event. There were about thirty people, most of whom Zoe knew, lots of good food and plenty of drinks. Zoe was sitting at the bar when she met Jean Marc who had been hired as the entertainer. He sang very well and Zoe was immediately attracted to him. *Another French Canadian musician?* Each time he had a break, they would sit together at the bar and talk. They chatted long after the party finished then disappeared from everyone for three days of sheer bliss.

He was from a family of thirteen and all of them had double-barrelled French names. His English and French were both perfect. Zoe loved listening to him play the piano and each time she went to visit him at work, he would play her favourite song, "Piano Man," by Billy Joel.

However, as time went by, Zoe noticed he drank quite a bit - not enough to get drunk but spent a lot of money. Some weeks his paycheck was barely enough to pay his rent. Zoe asked him to stop drinking.

'No problem,' he said. A week went by, and Zoe walked in as he was sipping a pint. When he was on his break, she called him over.

'Jean Marc, can we talk for a minute?'

'Of course, Zoe. What's on your mind?'

'Earlier, I saw you drinking again. We talked about this. You promised me you would stop.'

'I know, I know. I'm sorry, Zoe. It was just one drink. I didn't think it would matter.'

'But it does matter. It's not just about one drink. It's about trust, your health and your finances. You promised me you would stop for two weeks and then cut back.'

'I didn't mean to break your trust. I was just feeling really stressed, and I thought one drink would help.'

'Jean Marc, stress is a part of life. There are healthier ways to cope with it. Drinking isn't the solution.'

'I know. I'm really sorry, Zoe. I need to do better.'

'I want us to be happy. Maybe you should talk to a counsellor or join a support group?'

'Well, let's not go that far.'

That was not the response Zoe was hoping for. Their relationship went downhill after that. Zoe really tried to mend things between them, but Jean Marc had no ambition and carried on drinking away his wages. Zoe put up with him a little longer, thinking he would change – but he didn't.

They broke up a year later but remained friends. They had a lot of friends in common, so she often visited him and his roommates for casual dinners or parties.

At one of these birthday parties, Zoe was introduced to a friend of theirs, called Julian. Zoe couldn't keep her eyes off him. He was intelligent, interesting and witty. She was enjoying her time, but reluctantly, after a great meal and a few drinks, she was tired.

'Well guys, it's been fun but I'm tired and gotta go.'

Julian came up and shook her hand, holding on a little longer than necessary. Zoe felt the electricity shoot through her body. *What is it with me? Love at first sight. Again? Or is it lust at first sight?* He was intriguing and Zoe was immediately drawn to him. The attraction was so strong and luckily for Zoe, it was mutual as he said, 'That's a shame, I was enjoying your company, will I see you again?'

Wild horses wouldn't stop me, thought Zoe as she picked up her coat and handbag.

Two nights later Julian and Zoe met again at Jean Marc's house. As she was leaving Zoe found herself alone with him in the hallway. For a brief instant his cologne seduced her. She wanted to kiss him. Impelled with shyness, she said something stupid, like, 'We can't keep meeting like this.' She rushed out to her car, feeling totally embarrassed but she couldn't stop thinking about him.

Three days later they met again in the local bar where Jean Marc was entertaining, with a pint in his hand. He looked a little drunk. Although deep in conversation, Zoe wasn't totally unaware of the furtive glances from Jean Marc. She looked over and he quickly looked away. *Now you see what you're missing, jerk,* she thought, moving closer to Julian.

Julian had to return home to Miami the following day, so as Zoe was not working, she offered him a ride to the airport. She felt the growing excitement of spending a couple of hours alone with him, however disappointment struck when he called to say his plans had changed and he wouldn't need the ride.

'Oh, okay.'

Maybe he heard the disappointment in her voice when he asked, 'Would you have dinner with me on Saturday?'

'Of course,' she said without hesitation.

It was over a year since her breakup with Jean Marc and this was her first date since. *What to wear?* Julian was a casual guy so designer jeans, a white turtleneck and a jacket, would work perfectly. Her long straight hair was misbehaving. *Why wasn't I born with gorgeous, thick, manageable hair,* as she fought with a couple of strands that didn't belong anywhere. Satisfied with her fashion choices she picked up Julian and drove to the restaurant. On the way, she noticed the extent of his good looks. Blond shoulder length hair, lithe body, slightly tanned face and penetrating deep blue eyes.

A dinner, a movie and a little too much wine found them back at Zoe's apartment. There was no doubt about it, their instant mutual attraction couldn't be restrained any longer. They ripped off each other's clothes and made passionate love until early dawn. This Sunday was one of the most beautiful days Zoe had spent in a long while. Lovemaking, a late brunch, a crisp walk on the beach and a visit to some friends, showing off her handsome lover. Back at her apartment they ordered Chinese food. The ending of a perfect day – well almost.

Somehow Jean Marc figured out what was going on. The phone rang and Zoe picked it up, 'Hello.'

'Hi,' replied Jean Marc.

'What do you want'

'I'm sorry Zoe. I still love you. I can't stand you being with anyone else.'

'I'm sorry Jean Marc, it's a bit late to tell me that. It's over, we are just friends. That is unless you keep making stupid phone calls like this.' She tried to whisper so Julian wouldn't hear, but her voice rose with anger. After all this time Jean Marc decided he couldn't stand seeing her with someone else.

'We'll discuss this tomorrow,' she said and hung up the phone. After two more melodramatic phone calls, Zoe realized he was drunk so she took the phone off the hook.

Julian was busy the following day due to business, so Zoe used the time to talk with Jean Marc. She used to love him very much. But too much time had passed to make amends, so their friendship would stay platonic. One thing that Zoe never did was to go back to a relationship once it had been broken. Like a piece of rope that has been cut and knotted back together, it's never the same.

Zoe decided to cook for Julian, what she thought would be their last dinner together.

But, she was wrong.

39

The yacht

Zoe slept soundly and woke up early; the gentle rocking of the boat mixed with lack of sleep got the better of her. She was still groggy when she eventually got up and groped her way down the steep three steps to the Galley to make coffee.

It took several days for her to get used to life on a sixty-five-foot yacht. It was certainly glamorous. Even though it was docked, the waves still rocked the boat, so keeping her balance as she moved about above or below deck was an endless challenge, as was such matters as remembering to dip her head when she went into the *Head*.

The good news was she had it all to herself until the rest of the crew arrived the following Friday. This was the perfect time to be in Florida, temperatures in the eighties and the magical cooling effect of the sea breeze made the place a total one-eighty degrees from Canada. She was certain she had arrived in Paradise.

That evening she sat on the deck, drank a cold beer and marvelled at the difference of just a few weeks can make in a person´s life. Only two days earlier she was trudging through three feet of snow, cursing at ruining yet another pair of expensive leather boots, due to the salt on the roads. Toronto is truly a beautiful Canadian city but has way too much snow. After so many years, she was ready for a change. The chance of being on a luxurious yacht, cruising around the Caribbean was not to be missed, even it was only as a crew member.

Julian had hired her as the cook, but in truth cooking wasn't her greatest talent. Still, she knew she could get by making average meals for the down-to-earth crew of six. Fortunately, when Julian's parents or relatives came aboard, they brought their personal chef with them. As she walked along the deck, college kids passed her and smiled. It made her feel a little old, but even though she was thirty-three, she was closer in mindset to them than to people her own age. However, she was unmarried, had no children and no real career. She was tangled in a web she could not see. *Am I running away from the promise of intimacy and long-term companionship, because I could not bear to have those precious experiences ripped apart by my own insecurities?*

As she sat with another cold beer, the smell of the salty sea and the warm sun on her skin, she thought about how she had ended up there.

That last day spent with Julian was the best ever. Out of the blue, he asked, 'Do you like working and living here?'

'Well, I love Canada, but I am so tired of the snow. My job is fun, but nothing special. Why?'

'How would you like to work on my father's yacht?'

'What!' When do we leave?' She laughed. 'But doing what?'

'As a cook for a crew of six.'

'I can't cook.'

'Well, if this meal is anything to go by, you've aced the test.

It's tough work, but the rewards are worth it.'

Zoe was stunned. Getting away from the snow to work in the sun and to be close to Julian. What more could a girl ask for?

The following days were spent finding someone to take over her lease, packing up her belongings and buying a bunch of cookbooks from charity shops.

The day she landed in Miami, she was a nervous wreck. The airport was crazy - How would Julian ever find her amongst this screaming crowd of spring breakers. As she waited in the arranged spot she thought about Jean Marc. She had been too much of a coward to tell him the truth, so told him she was returning to England for a while as her mother was not well.

That part was true, her mother, who was seventy-four had just gone through an eye operation. She wasn't feeling great, but fortunately her brother Jonathan was taking care of her. Zoe hadn't been home since her brother's wedding three years ago, as she and her mother were having problems, getting along.

'Hey lady,' chirped a skycap. Probably keen for a bit extra work and certain that the suitcase that had passed him for the third time on a lonely journey, was hers.

'Oh...er yes.'

'You OK?' he asked as he grabbed the case off the carousel onto a trolley.

'I´m good, just tired,' she mumbled.

She stepped outside. The humidity attacked her like a vicious jellyfish. This was going to take some getting used to. She waited patiently for almost 45 minutes, when a taxi driver asked her if she needed a ride.

'I'm not sure. Someone was supposed to pick me up.' She was feeling quite sweaty and nervous. She had no American coins for the phone, and she couldn't remember where her phone book was.

'Can you take me to the harbour?'

'Which one?'

'How many are there?' Zoe gasped. *Why am I so unorganised?*

The driver looked at her and rolled his eyes, 'Several but the main ones are Port Miami and Miami Beach Marina. Are you catching a cruise ship?'

'No, a private yacht.'

'Well, I think your best choice is the Miami Beach Marina.'

Let's hope so, thought Zoe as she climbed into the taxi.

'Don't you have the phone number of the person you are meeting?'

'Probably somewhere in my suitcase.'

Zoe sat back and tried to relax. *He probably thinks I'm a real idiot.*

They arrived, and after she paid him, she dragged her suitcase along, searching for any sign of Julian. She approached several people on nearby yachts, inquiring if anyone knew him, she didn't even have a photo of him, but sadly, no one did.

What if I'm at the wrong harbour? What if he forgot I was coming? I feel so stupid.

She plonked down on a bench gathering her thoughts when she heard someone call her name.

Thankfully Julian was walking towards her, smiling. He hugged her tight and gave her a passionate kiss. 'What happened,' asked Zoe.

'My fault, I got the times mixed up, I'm so sorry.'

He took hold of her hand and grabbed her suitcase and

walked her down to the end of the dock. 'Here we are,' he said proudly.

Shibumi, his father´s yacht. The boat rocked gently in the harbour, and the gentle clanging of the ropes against the mast was soothing and almost romantic. *Shibumi*, was named after Julian´s fathers' favourite novel by Trevanian. It was a 65ft yacht built in Europe about fifty years earlier.

As well as cook, one of Zoe's chores was to make sure the cabins were clean, especially the main stateroom which was only used when Julians' parents came aboard. The décor, done in rich burgundy, accented by various shades of green reflected their expensive taste.

It was a beautiful evening, so eventually after making passionate love, they took a shower and headed into town. They ordered Stone Crabs at a rather expensive restaurant. The sound of the waves gently lapped at the shore, mingled with the lively chatter of diners around them as Zoe and Julian sat at a cozy table with an ocean view.

Zoe looked at the menu. 'Wow, everything looks amazing! Have you ever tried the grilled octopus here?'

'I did last time! It's incredible. Perfectly charred with a nice lemon drizzle. You should try it.'

'I don't know. I think I'll stick to the shrimp tacos. Can't go wrong with those.'

The food arrived quite quickly. Julian dug in his fork, 'Fair enough, but you'll have to try a bite of mine. It's a Miami classic!'

'So, any plans for the weekend?' asked Zoe.

'I was thinking about hitting up that new beach club. I heard they have a great happy hour.'

'Sounds fun.' Zoe looked lovingly at him and thought, this

adventure was going to be the best ever.

Julian conducted his import/export company from his home in N. Miami. Most of his business was conducted in the evenings because of the time differences abroad, so they got to spend most afternoons together. When Zoe was on her own, she spent time acclimatising to her new lifestyle. A big part of that was socialising in the hotel bar in the evenings. She couldn't wait to start her next adventure.

Julian had told her he wanted to keep their romance a secret for now as he would prefer the rest of the crew not to know about it. The crew arrived a few days later and Zoe was glad of their company as most of the hotel patrons were older folks, so she was excited to have full-time company who were all under fifty and not overly tanned.

40

The Crew

The captain was a jolly Swede named Gudbrand, who liked to drink and make the same joke that he was a good brand. Of what, Zoe used to wonder. He was about forty, with a tummy that looked like a Michelin tyre under his shirt and a couple of tattoos in Swedish, which he never did explain the meaning to any of them. He was always cheerful and jolly. Whenever we pulled into a new port, he would grin like a conquering Viking and say, 'Vell I must go. I have an appointment vith Captain Morgan.' That man loved his rum. He had a very good command of the English language, but W was always pronounced like a V

Teresa, Rick and Bob were experienced sailors doing all the stuff Zoe knew nothing about. Les was the engineer. He kept the engine in running order and sorted out electrical stuff around the vessel. He liked to smoke a lot and Zoe didn't mean cigarettes. They allowed him that pleasure as it was beneficial to all of them - without it, he was a miserable human being. However, the captain convinced him to keep a stone in his bag of dope so it could be thrown overboard if ever the Coast Guard boarded. Apparently, it happened often in the Caribbean due to the growing drug trade.

Teresa was twenty-eight, slightly built, and medium length brown curly hair. They were the only two females aboard and quickly became best friends. She was a lot of fun and an experienced sailor as she used to work on charter boats in Belize.

Rick and Bob kept to themselves, playing poker whenever they got a chance – Zoe believed them to be life partners, but never talked about it. In fact, she really didn't know much about any of the crew. They didn't even exchange last names.

Captain Gudbrand kept them amused with his stories of his previous sea adventures, when he wasn't sleeping off his hangover.

The yacht had two fuel tanks. Once they were full, the guys checked the rigging and the sails and then they headed off for a short voyage. *Shibumi*, was a well-built vessel, it cut through the heaving waters with grace and confidence of a world class blue-water yacht. If the winds died down, the engines would be turned on. Everything was running perfectly. The following three glorious days of sailing were exciting. All crew members, including Zoe, had to do a four-hour watch each day. Zoe took the four 'til eight as when it got dark, it was hard to stay awake, especially since she had to be up by five each morning.

On the third day they pulled into the Port of Georgetown, in the Cayman Islands. As they cruised into port, Zoe lay on the bow watching the dolphins swim alongside in the clear blue sea. She could almost touch them. The sea-spray splashed her face, it was warm, salty and exotic. She was thrilled-what a life.

They docked late afternoon and while the rest of the crew reset rigging and other nautical things, Teresa and Zoe sat with a cocktail and watched the sun lower like a golden balloon towards the horizon. A huge cruise ship moored in the commercial zone and unloaded its cargo of excited tourists, all clearly from some place far away where beauty and island calm were in short supply. According to Captain Gudbrand, the Port of Georgetown could accommodate the largest cruise ships in the world. This area was famous for its sandy *Seven Mile Beach* on the west shore or the city's historic Georgian sights. Of all these attractions the shopping mall was the destination of the majority of disembarking tourists.

The next morning, after cooking eggs and bacon for the crew, Zoe set off on an island adventure with Teresa. They went to the *Cayman Turtle Centre,* a conservation facility that had been running since 1968. One of their missions was to farm turtles for meat as it was popular with the islanders, and farming turtles meant that the wild population would not be depleted by overfishing. Because of this, the Centre had developed into an important research and conservation facility. When Zoe saw all these cute little turtles, she made certain that she would never join the Islanders by eating them. It took two to three months for baby turtles to hatch and their journey back to sea was dangerous enough for their survival.

After lunch, they headed for the *Seven Mile Beach.* It was everything a beach should be. The warm water as perfect as the holiday brochures claimed it to be. It was like swimming in a crystal bowl of blue-tinted lake water, just a lot saltier. They spent over an hour snorkelling with the spectacular shoals of colourful, tropical fish. After a much- needed rest sunning on the warm sandy shore, they dined at a beach bar called the

Royal Palms. They had the best *Pina Coladas* ever.

'I certainly could get used to this,' laughed Teresa raising her glass.

'Me too,' said Zoe, knocking back her third *Pina Colada*.

With the contentment of weary travellers, a little buzzed by rum and sun, they quietly watched the orange, gold orb of warmth drift below the horizon, and splash the Caribbean sky with one last wash of glorious colour ... then staggered back to the boat and immediately fell into a deep slumber.

The following morning just as the sun rose, Shibumi set off for Jamaica, but the sun soon disappeared when they were hit by a horrendous storm. Between the boat rocking furiously against the vicious waves and Zoe's late-night drinking, she felt green in the gills and puked against the wind. This was the first time she had ever been seasick. The rain pounded them as if they deserved to be punished for reasons the sea gods considered egregious. The wind god helped out with a screeching wail as it ripped apart their main sail. The wave gods saw their chance and, in the chaos, tumbled over the bow crashing fiercely against the battened down hatch, hoping to sink their craft and be done with it. The boat felt like a toy jostling around a baby's bathtub. Zoe's stomach coiled in an inverted roller-coaster loop. Fear jammed against her chest. She made her way down to the cabin, but seawater was gushing through the hatches. She got Les to help close them, but there was already an inch of water swirling around their ankles.

Back on deck the captain assured Zoe that they were quite safe. He had managed vessels in much worse weather.

'Don't vorry, Zoe, it von't last long,'

She had full confidence in this man, so as the adrenaline shot from her brain to her hands, she hung on tight to the rail as water smashed against her, making the deck very slippery. The whole ordeal was over in about twenty minutes, but the ocean remained choppy. However, they weren't out of trouble yet. No sooner than the storm abated, the Coast Guard appeared on the horizon... heading straight for them.

'Shit, Vot do these jerks vant?' exclaimed a red faced Gudbrand.

They pulled up a few metres off starboard.

'Are you okay?' one of the coastguards called out to them with his megaphone,

'Yes,' replied the captain, with exaggerated gestures.

'Mind, if we come aboard?'

'Do ve have a choice?' the captain mumbled.

The coastguards lowered a dingy and four lads with rifles, probably no older than eighteen, motored over. The choppy waves bounced their little dinghy against the sides of the yacht as they struggled to clamber aboard, with as much dignity as their trembling little hearts could afford.

As Zoe stood by the captain, taking photos with the camera Julian had bought her, she heard Teresa fighting with Les.

'Toss it!' she screamed.

'No, they won't find it, if it's in my pocket.'

'Damn you. I can smell it from here. Give it to me.'

Zoe turned in time to see Teresa grabbing the bag from Les and throwing it overboard.

Can fish get high? she wondered.

'Your boom mast is busted. Are you okay?' asked the Coast Guard.

'Yes, ve are on our vay to Jamaica where ve vill have it repaired,' said the Captain.

'You won't mind if we have a quick look around?'

'No, Ve have nothing to hide.'

'Not now,' Teresa whispered to Zoe.

Zoe hid her smile and wondered what they could expect from Les having no "medicine" as he liked to call it, for the rest of the journey.

After fifteen minutes the Coast Guard left, wishing them a happy Thanksgiving.

They were all eager to reach their destination, especially Les who was sulking about losing his stash.

'We couldn't take any chances,' said Teresa, soothing a shell-shocked Les. 'Don't worry, I know you'll find some even better stuff in Jamaica.'

By the time they docked in Ocho Rios, there was not a single dry piece of clothing on board, so Teresa and Zoe packed everyone's gear, and with a bag full of quarters, headed to the nearest laundromat. They got the best deal as they sat and watched the clothes jostling around the machines, sipping on their rum concoctions, while the guys cleaned up the mess below deck and repaired the mast and boom. Sometimes it paid to be a female.

41

Life on the High Seas

With so much history and exciting things to see, the captain told the crew they would dock in Ocho Rios for a few days while Julian and his parents came aboard. When they arrived, Julian wanted to take them for a sail around the islands, entertain their guests and then they would fly home. Zoe didn't know why they had such an expensive yacht, unless it was just for show. Julian used it more than they did.

One of the greatest places to visit in Ocho Rios was the famous Dunns River Falls and Teresa couldn't wait to go. She said excitedly, 'It is believed to have been the site of the famous battle of "Las Chorreras", fought in 1657 between the Spanish and the English for possession of the island. The Spaniards called the area "Las Chorreras", which means "the waterfalls or the springs"

'I do know that, Teresa. Remember I used to work here.'

'Aw, come with me,' pleaded Teresa.

'Next time,' said Zoe, 'I have seen the sights many times. If you visit the Plantation Inn, you'll see photos of me with tourists scrambling up the Falls. I have an old friend in town I want to meet.'

'Okay, I'll go alone then join the boys in the bar later.'

Zoe's old friend was actually Julian. They were meeting secretly in a local hotel before he announced his arrival to the rest of the crew and before his parents arrived.

At the hotel, Julian was nowhere to be seen until he sneaked up behind Zoe and wrapped his arms around her waist. He whispered, 'Let's go. Time for some fun.'

Her cheeks were still flushed as they rode the elevator to his room. His hand roamed over the bareness of her neck then down to her breasts. No sooner than the hotel room door closed, he picked her up and threw her gently on the bed. Once again smothering her in kisses. Stripping off their clothes, her arms wound themselves around his neck as his tightened around hers, locking their bodies in heated embrace. He kissed her all over; a moan escaped from her throat as they both lay there in each other's arms.

Zoe wanted to stay the night but that would have caused too much curiosity from the rest of the crew. As they were getting ready to leave, Julian said, 'Damn, I wish my parents weren't coming tomorrow. Thankfully they only stay long enough to impress their snooty friends.'

He kissed Zoe goodnight, and she climbed into a taxi back to the boat.

On this visit Julian's parents were accompanied by a dark-haired woman and a blonde-haired child. 'Hello everyone,' said Julian's mother. 'I'd like to introduce you to my son's wife and child.'

Any conversation that followed, Zoe didn't hear. She was in shock. *The bastard! How come I got involved with a married man? He sure kept that a secret.*

While they were all on board, Zoe kept a very low profile. His parents probably thought she was just an unsociable bitch. No wonder Julian kept their little affair a secret. He remained on board for the two days while his parents and extended family joined him. He was very good with his daughter, but a little cold with his wife. He seemed relieved when they all left.

It was very hard to avoid someone on a 65ft yacht, so when Zoe bumped into him the next evening and no one else was around, he stopped her.

'Zoe, can we talk?'

'There's nothing to talk about.'

'Please.'

'Go away, I don't even want to see you.'

Zoe pushed passed him, fighting back the tears and stayed in her cabin until morning.

The following evening Julian turned to Teresa and Zoe. 'Why don't you ladies go out and enjoy yourself? I booked a table for two in Jimmy Buffet's Margaritaville resort hotel, for dinner and a show. All paid for.'

'Wow!' said Teresa. 'Let me go change. Coming, Zoe?'

'Sure, she said, and turned to Julian. 'A little guilt present?'

The resort was set on a hill overlooking the Caribbean Sea, with two huge pools and only a twelve-minute walk from a white sandy beach. Zoe and Teresa ordered a Seafood Delight, which consisted of conch, lobster and scallops. The Maitre d' suggested a bottle of his best white wine. Then another bottle with dessert. Why not, it was all paid for by Julian.

With all that wine, Teresa and Zoe were feeling a little giddy and laughed at the first act, who was a bad comedian. It was followed by acts of fire-eaters, limbo dancers and naturally Reggae music. This gave them a chance to dance with the locals. Reggae has a particular rhythm which takes a few moments to get in the stride of the music. Soon they had all the local lads dancing with them. Exhausted and quite tipsy they left before the show finished and grabbed a taxi back to the dock.

They paid the taxi driver and gave a huge tip, then walked towards the boat.

'Are we in the right dock?' said Zoe, 'I don't see the boat.'

'I think we are.' Teresa slurred.

'Well, that's too weird, I don't see it. Let's go sit in the clubhouse until those boys decide to come back from their little jaunt.'

Zoe was pissed. Teresa was too drunk to care, as she nodded off on a couch. Zoe eventually fell into a light sleep until she was awakened by Captain Gudbrand.

'Ladies, what happened? You came back early.'

'Well, I know you like to drink with the boys but didn't expect you to sail to another island to do it.'

'It wasn't planned, ve...'

Zoe interrupted him with an angry stare and narrow eyes. He steadied Teresa while she walked, as Zoe followed him back to the boat.

Julian stood, legs astride, hands on hips and a scowl on his face.

'Why did you come back so soon? I told you to have a good time.'

Zoe glared at him. 'I'm tired and I'm going to bed. We'll talk in the morning.'

As she lay on her bunk, she smelled something strange. *Was the engineer, Les smoking pot again? It was much stronger than usual.* That night the smell seeped into her strange dreams.

During breakfast an awkward silence fell over everyone. Usually, they enjoyed the camaraderie during the first meal of the day. Today both the Captain and Teresa were feeling the effects of too much alcohol. Rick and Bob sat arguing about last night's poker game and Julian gave Zoe the silent treatment. She couldn't stand it any longer.

'Okay, what the hell is wrong with everyone?'

'Stop shouting,' whispered Teresa, 'My head hurts.'

'Ya! I feel a little delicate too,' added the captain.

'What do you mean?' asked Julian, putting down his coffee cup, a little too abruptly.

'All this tension and silence. Your little jaunt last night. And the strong smell of..what? Pot?'

'I found some new medicine,' said Les, sarcastically.

The captain looked at Zoe. 'Vell, if you must know. Julian has a membership to the Royal Yacht Club so ve sailed over there to have dinner and check out the lovely ladies.'

The boys club just laughed as they left the table. Julian lingered and looked at Zoe, 'Can we talk?'.

'I really don't think there is anything to talk about. You're married.' said Zoe and stormed off. Julian yelled back, 'Well, I'm leaving today, and you guys will have to bring the yacht home. See you in Miami.'

'Not if I see you first.' mumbled Zoe under her breath.

As they sailed home, the sea was calm and there was no wind. So, on went the motors. Three hours later Zoe was down in the galley preparing a meal when the yacht lurched forward, spilling the future lunch all over the floor. It came to a grinding stop. Zoe went up on deck to see what had happened. The captain was steering so the tide wouldn't pull the vessel in the wrong direction. Les, the engineer was down in the engine room. When he emerged, his scowling face was smeared with oil, and he was rubbing his greasy hands.

'Vell?' asked the captain.

'We're out of fuel.'

'Vot? Ve just filled up before ve left.'

'Well, we have a damn leak. We'll have to sail home.'

'There is no vind.'

'So, what do we do?' asked Zoe.

Teresa had joined them. 'We'll have to tack back and forth until the wind picks up.'

'It had better work,' said Les 'We are a bit too close to Cuba for my liking.'

Except for Zoe, they all had US passports and the idea of getting too close to an enemy state was not appealing. An exhausting two hours passed and luckily the current was taking them toward the Florida coast.

'Captain!' yelled Les. 'There's a shrimp boat port side.'

They all stood on deck yelling and waving their arms. Zoe covered her nose from the stench as it pulled up alongside.

Within minutes Les was on board siphoning fuel. The captain was scrounging cigarettes while Teresa and Zoe collected bottled water.

42

Dry land at last

Shibumi docked at Miami three days later. Teresa and Zoe headed for the rented house and hit the showers. Almost finished, Zoe heard a knock on the door. 'Zoe, come out.'

'Teresa, I'm not finished.'

'It doesn't matter, grab a housecoat and come out. The DEA is here.'

'Drug Enforcement Admin, what do they want?'

'Just get your arse out here, now.'

Captain Gudbrand informed them that they had to be there to watch the agents as he didn't trust them. They had been known to plant false evidence, according to his sources.

A short, dark-haired guy dug through Zoe's personal belongings, a gun packed on his side, making her feel a little uncomfortable. As she watched, his face showed a scowl. Zoe wondered why he was so angry.

'Why are you so nervous?' he growled.

'I happen to be English, and I'm not used to being in the presence of handguns and rifles.'

'Get used to it lady and hope I don't have to use it.'

Zoe opened her mouth but decided to stay quiet.

The agents pulled the fuel tanks apart. The unpleasant agent left, and Zoe spoke to another, who was more friendly.

'What's his problem? Why is he so mean?'

'Him? He had his wheels stolen off his Corvette this morning.'

Zoe laughed. 'So, are you going to put the tanks back together as our engineer has gone home?'

'Normally, we wouldn't, but you guys seem like a good bunch.'

After that fiasco, Teresa, the captain and Zoe ate dinner at Casa D'Angelo. It was an expensive restaurant, but the captain footed the bill, if they promised to get him home safely. The restaurant owner's wife remembered the captain from several previous visits so gave them special attention. The captain had quite a few vodkas claiming it was to relieve the stress.

Back at the house Teresa and Zoe packed their bags for tomorrow's departure.

'Darn it, I left my diary on board the yacht. I'm going back for it,' said Zoe.

'Come on, Zoe. A diary? You want to go all the way back for a diary?'

'Yes, it's very important to me. I keep record of all my travels. Who knows I may want to write my memoir one day.'

'Well, I'll come with you as the docks are a little dangerous at night.'

'Thanks, Teresa, I'd appreciate that.'

They called a taxi and arrived at the dock in twenty minutes. Zoe was about to get out when she saw two Jamaican men whom she didn't know, removing boxes from the boat.

'Who are they?' she whispered to Teresa.

'Heck if I know.'

Then they spotted Julian and heard him say, 'Hurry up guys, we don't have all night.'

Zoe ran over there with Teresa on her heels. 'Julian, what's going on?'

'Zoe, Teresa... what are you guys doing here?'

'I left something on the boat,' said Zoe, 'But more importantly, what the hell are you doing? And what's in those boxes?'

Then Zoe smelled it. 'My God. Is that marijuana? We smuggled pot?'

'Shit!' said Teresa.

Julian looked mad to the point of being dangerous. 'Okay, ladies. You'd better leave right now. You saw nothing. If anyone asks and if you value your life, you will tell no one.

Wow a different side to Julian.

Zoe was furious, but Teresa pulled at her sleeve. 'Come on girlfriend, let's go.'

Back in the taxi Zoe was shaking, then felt a chill down her spine. 'Teresa, how could we have been so naive?'

'Well, I . . . er ... I.'

'Oh no! Teresa, you knew all along. Back there you sounded as surprised as I did. Bloody hell, you're a damn good actress.'

'I'm sorry. But I had to let you think I didn't know what was going on. Why do you think they paid us so well?'

'Not enough for being involved in such a dangerous scheme! I trusted you as a friend.'

'I thought if I told you, you would go to the police.'

'You're damn right I would. In fact, I will go now and report it. Driver, please take us to the police station.'

Teresa grabbed her arm, 'Please don't.'

'It's okay I won't tell them you knew.' said Zoe.

'Thanks. But Julian might incriminate me.'

'Maybe, but that's a chance we'll have to take. How did the DEA not find anything when they searched the boat?'

'It was well hidden. Between the two bunks where the guys slept. They had a metal cupboard installed, which also disguised the smell.'

The trip to the police station was silent between them. Zoe was fuming, the anger simmered in her gut. *To think I actually liked and trusted Julian. It was bad enough he cheated on his wife but this ... and Teresa, she was supposed to be my friend.*

They entered the Miami police precinct and asked to speak to a detective. The officer tried to wheedle out the information, but Zoe insisted on speaking with a detective. Teresa stayed silent as they sat nervously on a hard wooden bench. Eventually a young man in an expensive suit appeared. Pushing back his black glasses he outstretched his hand introducing himself.

'Hello, I'm detective Armitage. I hear you need to speak to me.'

'Yes,' said Zoe,' then explained the situation.

'You're telling me that you didn't know anyone's last name?'

'Yes, I didn't see the need and even if I did, they were probably false,' said Zoe.

The detective shook his head and looked at them as if they were dumb females.

'They probably didn't even use their real first names. This really is a matter for the DEA, but if we go now, we may be able to catch them in the act,' said Detective Armitage.

'They are there now, offloading the contraband,' insisted Zoe.

'Okay, you ladies can stay here or go back to your hotel, but please don't leave the state.'

Teresa and Zoe returned to the house.

'What about our flight tomorrow?' asked Teresa.

'I don't know. Let's see what happens.'

Teresa helped herself to the alcohol while Zoe lay on the bed trying to stay calm. She dozed off and jumped when the phone rang.

It was the detective. 'Sorry miss. We went there and there was no boat and no sign of any drugs.'

'Damn. I gave you the name of the yacht. Can you track it eventually?'

'These guys sound like pros. They probably have changed the name already. Anyway, it's obvious you ladies knew nothing about it, so you're free to go.'

Teresa who was already half drunk, lifted her head slowly. 'I'm sorry. I hope we can still be friends. I was petrified the police would take the money from us.'

'I'm sure they're not concerned about us. At least I know I earned it fair and square.'

'Zoe, I never told you, but I needed this money for my mother. She needs medical treatment, and we don't have insurance.'

Zoe really wanted to believe it was the truth. However, she knew they would never see each other again. 'Let's get some sleep. We have a plane to catch tomorrow.'

Zoe never did retrieve her diary.

43

Captain Brian

Back in Miami, Zoe was wandering what to do next. However, a few days later she received a letter from Captain Brian, a friend she had met on one of her trips when she worked for the travel agency. He was a Captain of an awfully expensive yacht and said he would be docking in Miami for a few months and would love her to come and help him with his boat cleaning business. She had friends there, Sofia and Carlton, who could put her up, so Zoe accepted his offer.

It was a cooler day than normal and as she went to meet her friends, she felt a little awkward as they were also friends with Julian. She wondered if they knew what his real business entailed, but they wouldn't hear it from her. They were off to Europe so offered to let her stay on their boat for an undetermined time, rent free.

Unfortunately, when Zoe saw them, it brought back sad memories. She had really fallen for Julian. *Why do I have such bad luck with men?* Just as they gave her the key, Sofia said, 'By the way there's a letter for you. We've had it for ages as we weren't sure where to send it, but here you are.'

The return address said Julian Smith. Zoe laughed at the made-up last name. She poured a glass of wine, sat on the window seat, and opened the letter.

My dearest Zoe,

I am so sorry if I hurt you. After we met in Canada and I returned to Miami, I realised the only thing keeping my wife and I together was our little girl. We had an amicable breakup, but I had no idea that they would turn up with my parents, who thought that we could reconcile the marriage. We never did. After you left, Teresa returned for another trip. She was there to console me, and you weren't, so we are now dating. I thought you should hear it from me.

Also, I do know if you had known about the drugs, you would have gone to the police before the trip ended, so I'm sorry to have deceived you. I've enclosed your bonus, and I wish you luck in your next endeavour.

Sincerely Julian.

What a jerk! Zoe felt every emotion in existence. So many thoughts swimming around her head. Now, she needed to plan for her future and try not to make the same mistakes, especially regarding men. However, the cheque enclosed was for $5000. Was this guilt money? Obviously drug money, but it didn't stop Zoe from cashing it. Now, the best therapy was a few stiff rums and a night in the casino... And she won a $1000.

A month later, she received a letter from Holly. She was still in California but needed a break. Captain Brian drove Zoe to the airport the next day. Zoe and Holly hugged each other tight. 'God, I've missed you,' said Holly.

'The feelings mutual,' replied Zoe.

Captain Brian took them for drinks and suggested a trip to the Everglades the following day.

Captain Brian had a meeting, so dropped the girls off where they rented a canoe. Their canoe glided silently through the murky waters, the only sounds, the gentle dip of their paddles and the occasional splash of a fish leaping from the water. Suddenly, a rustle in the reeds caught their attention, and they froze, eyes scanning the murky depths for any sign of movement.

'You know there are alligators around here,' said Zoe.

'No way!' said Holly, 'They wouldn't allow tourists out here if they did.'

A ripple in the water ahead sent a shiver down their spines just as a massive alligator emerged from the depths, its eyes fixed on them. Zoe and Holly paddled furiously, their hearts pounding in their chests as they tried to put distance between themselves and the formidable predator.

But the alligator was relentless, its powerful tail propelling it forward with alarming speed. Panic rising within them, Zoe and Holly dug their paddles into the water with all their might, their adrenaline pumped through their bodies. Just as the alligator closed in, its gaping jaw mere inches from their canoe, they spotted a narrow channel leading to safety. With a burst of renewed energy, they veered off course, the alligator's frustrated hiss echoing behind them as they navigated the waters to freedom.

Breathless and trembling, Zoe and Holly collapsed onto the bank, their hearts still racing.

'Jeez,' said Holly, 'I thought you said there were no alligators here,'

They looked back at the murky waters of the Everglades, and then at each other and burst out laughing. They decided to carry the canoe back to base. They recounted what happened to the manager.

'That little thing? He's like a pet and harmless. Alligators eat once a week and we feed him regularly. He was just messing with you.'

'So, what do you usually feed them?'

'Mainly lost tourists,' He banged his hand against his leg and let out a raucous laugh.

'We should ask you for a refund,' said Holly annoyed.

A couple of days later, Holly left and promised to return soon. Zoe sat with a hot cup of tea and thought about her future. She remembered what someone once told her: *We help define our path by our strength of character.* So, she showered, dressed, and took a long walk to clear her mind.

On her return there was a lot of action on the dock. She didn't take too much notice until a voice shouted, 'CUT!!'

No one warned her they were shooting a TV series. 'Excuse me,' she said sarcastically, 'This is my home.'

An overweight lady with bleached blonde hair approached her. 'Darling, my name is Beatrice, and I am the casting director for this new TV show. We are trying to finish a pilot.' She paused and looked over at the boat. 'Oh darling, would you mind terribly if I placed two lovely ladies on the bow of your boat?'

'For how much,' asked Zoe mischievously.

Zoe was half joking, but the woman hesitated, then spoke to someone on her two-way radio.

'OK darling, I can only give you $1000, but you must either

stay below or get out of the way.'

She sent Zoe to her assistant who handed her a wad of cash. Then two handsome actors walked by.

'Wow! eye candy,' said Zoe, a little too loudly. They both eyed her up and down and smiled, dazzling her with their perfect teeth. *How come Americans always have such great teeth?*

The assistant laughed. 'Yeah, they're the two main leads, Don Johnson and Philip Michael Ted. It's a new TV show called Miami Vice.'

Zoe stayed out of their way for the rest of the day and went clothes shopping. Money seemed to come to her easily these past few weeks.

44

Some Like it Hot

Zoe worked hard for Brian and thought she was due a day off, not only because she was exhausted, but Brian was coming onto her. She had explained last time she saw him that they could only be friends.

'Brian, it's Sunday. I'm taking a day off. Can I borrow your car?'

'Shall I come with you?'

'No thanks, I need some me time.'

She drove off and ended up in a small town called Lake Worth. She was hungry so entered the *Mad Hatter Lounge*. It took her a few minutes to realize it was a gay bar, just before a remark from one of the male patrons .... 'Honey, I just love those red shoes of yours.'

'Thank you.'

'Are you English?'

'Yes, I am.'

'May I,' he asked pointing to the seat next to her.

'Of course.'

He sat next to her and invited over some of his friends. His name was Terry, and he was a hairdresser. He and his friends were hilarious. There were all actors, singers and dancers and involved with the theatre next door.

'I used to be a dancer until the arthritis took over,' said Zoe.

'What size dress are you?' asked a guy called Billy.

'I am not lending you any dresses.'

They all laughed. 'No, darling, we're doing a show next door and one of the ladies dropped out, and if the dress fits, you can be her replacement.'

They finished their drinks and escorted Zoe to the theatre next door. In the dressing room, they took down a dress and Zoe tried it on. It was a long, white gown with a fitted bodice that flowed down into a flared fishtail skirt, similar to the one Marilyn Monroe wore. It was a perfect fit, except it was a tad too big around the chest, so Zoe had to stuff it with tissues. Having larger breasts felt strange, and she often misjudged space, frequently bumping into things.

The show was a musical version of the 1959 film "*Some like it Hot*" which starred Marilyn Monroe, Tony Curtis and Jack Lemmon. Zoe played a couple of small roles, quickly picking up the simple dance routines and learning a couple of songs with the chorus.

The commute from Miami to the theatre seemed to get longer every day, especially after helping Brian all day. He was disappointed when she made the decision to move to Fort Lauderdale as it was much closer to Lake Worth and rehearsals were almost every night. She found a place to live and Terry, the hairdresser, became her roommate. Her hair never looked better.

After three weeks of rehearsals, the show opened to a full house and was packed every night for the next six weeks. All the cast young and old went for drinks after a show, so they all became good friends. When it finally ended, it was a sad moment. The director organised a wrap party. This is when Zoe really got to know everyone well. Some were "Snowbirds" from New York, so only spent the harsh winters here in Florida. And others lived in Miami.

For the next couple of months Terry and Zoe enjoyed co-habiting. One major rule was neither of them would bring any dates home. He was great hairdresser and in demand, making great money especially from his tips. Zoe still had some savings, which she was trying not to use, but she was still not legal.

As time passed, Terry started disappearing for days on end. Zoe asked him if he had a committed relationship. He said sort of. She never thought him to be a promiscuous gay, but she was not always the best judge of character. However, she was shocked when she came across some drug paraphernalia in the bathroom. She didn't know much about drugs, so she asked her friend, an ex-cocaine addict. Yes, it was crack cocaine.

When Terry arrived home that evening, she brought him a glass of wine and asked him to sit down. 'Terry, I know you think you're handling this, but I see what it's doing to you. You're not yourself.'

Terry sighed, 'Zoe, I've told you... I can stop whenever I want. It's just been... a rough patch lately.'

'A rough patch is one thing, but this is taking over. You've lost weight, you're losing clients, and I barely recognize the lovely man I met a few months ago.'

'Come on, you know I'm still me. Besides, everyone has their own way of coping.'

Zoe put her hand gently on his arm, 'It might feel like it helps, but you're only pushing away the people who care,'

Terry looked away, 'Maybe I don't deserve people caring. I've messed up too many times.'

'We all mess up. But you don't have to do this alone. You can talk to me.'

'I don't know, Zoe... What if it's too late?'

Zoe gave him a big hug, 'It's never too late. One day at a time. We'll tackle this together, and you'll get through it. I believe in you.'

Unfortunately, the pep talk didn't work. Terry's absences became more often and longer. Often Zoe had blue-haired women from Miami and West Palm Beach knocking on her door asking his whereabouts, desperately needing a haircut. He was a brilliant hairdresser, shame about the drugs.

The final straw came when Zoe noticed some of her jewellery was missing. Terry claimed it must have been one of his friends as he would never steal from her. Zoe wanted to believe him, but people on drugs tend to lie. Eventually through a friend she contacted Terry's parents and unfortunately her lovely gay roommate was whisked off to rehab. Now she needed to find someone else, as the rent was too high for her alone.

A friend said he knew someone looking for a room, so Zoe met with him. His name was Jim, and he was an older man with a great sense of humour. He moved in the following week and invited Zoe to celebrate over a couple of glasses of vodka. Zoe was more of a beer drinker, so she left him after two drinks. As time went by, Zoe noticed he was drinking a lot. The clank of empty bottles rattled her nerves when he emptied his rubbish into the bin. Some days he could be quite mean. He was a classic case of Jekyll and Hyde. One night Zoe even took him to an AA meeting. It was very enlightening. There were all sorts of people there and that's when Zoe learnt that alcoholism was a disease. It brought back those horrible memories of her father. She was miles away in her thoughts when the group leader asked her to stand and introduce herself. She looked around horrified and said, 'Er hi, my name is Zoe, and I am NOT an alcoholic. I'm here with him.' pointing to Jim. They all laughed.

This situation made Zoe sit and think once more of her future. In desperation she wrote to a couple of people from the personal want ads, who were looking for personal assistants. The first man she met was a millionaire. All her problems would have been solved but he was a sleazy seventy-year-old with bad breath and awful taste in everything from clothes to furniture.

She was having coffee with Billy, and they laughed hard when she described him. Billy was off to New York in a week and asked if Zoe wanted to go with him. It was purely platonic as he was gay. It was tempting but she needed her money to buy a car. She eventually found a white 1970 VW Beetle.

Then the second letter arrived from the ads, which contained a phone card, so she was able to chat with the man who sent the letter, as he lived in California.

45

Richard

His name was Richard, and he chatted with Zoe for over an hour. He was looking for a personal assistant and seemed genuinely interested in her experience.

'I need someone organized, efficient, and able to handle a fast-paced environment,' he explained. 'Does that sound like something you'd be comfortable with?'

'Absolutely,' Zoe replied. 'I've handled demanding roles before, and I thrive on multitasking.' She lied. She'd never had any kind of job like that before, but she knew she could handle it.

Richard seemed pleased. 'Great. I'll be in Florida next week. How about we set up a time for an interview face to face?'

'That sounds perfect,' she said. 'What day works for you?'

'How about Wednesday at 10 a.m.? We can meet at the Zen bar on Las Olas Blvd.'

'Got it. I'll be there.'

'Looking forward to it,' Richard said before ending the call.

As she hung up, Zoe felt a mix of excitement and nerves. This could be the opportunity she had been waiting for. She would have to phone Billy to find out where this bar was located. Thank goodness she still had some money left on the phone card.

Meanwhile Zoe packed a few things and went to stay at Billy's house while he was in New York. Her drunken roommate was worse than ever and just impossible to live with.

As promised Richard called Zoe to confirm the time of their meeting. She dressed casually but business like and they met in the bar of an expensive restaurant. He was dressed in a pair of shorts and a T-shirt and looked like any normal guy, except for his Rolex watch. His brown hair was a bit unruly, and his dark black glasses magnified his brown eyes. He was an investor in several large companies, and a film maker.

Richard leaned back in his chair, his voice steady yet warm. 'Zoe, are you free to travel? The job will require some flexibility. I have homes in Florida, California, and Arizona, and I need someone who can move between them as needed.'

Zoe nodded, already picturing the possibilities. 'That wouldn't be a problem at all. I actually enjoy traveling.'

'Good,' he said. 'Aside from managing my schedule and handling correspondence, the biggest task will be bookkeeping. I need someone meticulous with numbers—someone I can trust to keep everything in order.'

Zoe smiled to herself. *Right up my alley.* 'I have plenty of experience with that. Spreadsheets, invoices, expense reports—you name it.'

Richard let out a low chuckle. 'Honestly, I'm very impressed. You seem like a perfect fit. But can you start immediately?'

'Absolutely,' she said without hesitation.

There was an instant, unspoken trust between them. Richard didn't even ask for references.

RICHARD

Zoe told him about the problem with the drunken roommate, but he told her not to worry and handed her an envelope. 'Here's an advance on your salary so you can pay any outstanding bills. I will need you to meet me at the airport the day after tomorrow at 11 a.m.'

Zoe left on a real high. Life was getting better already.

As the drunken roommate was a real jerk, Zoe took a friend with her to persuade him to let her back into the flat. There was no argument as her friend was over 6ft tall and very muscular. Zoe packed and told Jim that the place was his and hoped he could pay the rent, which she knew he wouldn't, but it wasn't her problem as she never signed a lease with the landlord. Her friend drove her to the airport to meet with Richard.

She left her VW bug with Billy as she wasn't sure of where all of this would take her.

Richard was waiting for her in the bar near the departure lounge, but instead of going to the check in desk, they hopped on a golf buggy and drove to a hangar.

'Here we are,' said Richard.

'Oh, you forgot to mention you had a private plane,' said Zoe, as she stared at this beautiful bird. It was an Aero Commander 680. Richard was a trained pilot, but he couldn't fly as earlier that day he had had an argument with his son Robert and went for a couple of drinks to calm down. He had called his private pilot. The journey went smoothly with a refuel in Vegas.

His other son Charles picked them up in a Cadillac and they travelled silently one and half hours to Santa Paula, a small town outside of Los Angeles. Richard's house was spectacular, with large grounds and a pool, situated at the foothills of Ventura, California. There were five bedrooms plus the *servants' quarters*, which became Zoe's private domain. The house was not decorated tastefully and his grown-up children, who were not there full time, had no idea what housework meant.

The following morning, Zoe woke at 7:30 a.m., slightly jet lagged and starving. She opened the fridge, and it was empty. She had no idea where she was, so just walked until she found a 7-11 and bought breakfast basics. The weather was much less humid than Florida, so it was an enjoyable, albeit a long walk back home.

As well as his three houses, Richard owned seven cars, an airplane, a boat and two off-road bikes. His monthly bills were horrendous, and his three children all expected to live the high life in Hollywood. His Daughter Nancy, a wannabe actress, also had a young daughter to look after, his son Robert was either quite dumb or strung out on drugs and Charles had a high maintenance girlfriend.

Zoe's first day, after making breakfast for everyone was to try and get organised. The place was in utter chaos, papers everywhere. Richard´s favourite past-time was to watch CNN and make notes on a yellow legal pad. Zoe ended up filing about ten years' worth of those notes, so she was never without something to do. He hoarded newspapers and magazines, especially porn and each time she asked him to tidy up he was too tired and claimed everything was against him. She tried to stop him taking the defeated attitude and suggested instead of drooling over girlie magazines to use his energy to go out and meet people. Most of his phone calls were business, except when he called his girlfriend Lynn, who would stay over most weekends.

Zoe did all his bookkeeping, filing and organised both his business and social diaries.

They took many trips to Beverly Hills to meet with some producer or director or just to attend an industry party. The *Beau Rivage* restaurant in Malibu was one of his favourite hangouts. A sighting of a celebrity didn't really bother Zoe too much until she saw Julie Andrews and her family sitting at the table next to theirs.

Another one of those trips they met up with Sam Fuller. He came from France and was a well-known director/actor/composer/writer with such films as Big Red One (1980) and Shark (not a big success) he was 74 and full of energy. They went out and socialised and Zoe didn't see a lot of "business" being done. *Was this guy just taking advantage and only interested in partying, which Richard paid for.*

Greg, Richard's sidekick was a scriptwriter who accompanied them one day to meet Sam at *Pregos Restaurant*, another hip Beverly Hills restaurant which entertained a very chic crowd.

Greg was good looking, although a little weather beaten. He had a good sense of humour and twinkly blue eyes. He was quite talented as a writer but relied totally on Richard for his finances.

This particular meeting did not go well as Richard drank too much and admonished Greg, a little too loudly, who was supposed to help write a script with Sam. Later, on Richard's behalf, Zoe asked Sam how the script was going, and he exploded.

Sam rolled his eyes, 'Zoe, we're all busting our asses here. You shouldn't ask "great people" stupid questions. We don't have time for distractions.'

'Distractions? "Great people." I was trying to make sure we're all on the same page.' *What an arrogant arsehole!*

'When you're working with people who know what they're doing, sometimes it's best to trust them and let them handle it,' he said.

Zoe took a deep breath and tried to stay calm. 'I do trust everyone here, Sam. But you don't get to talk down to me like that.'

Zoe concluded that he had no regard for women except for his forty-year-old wife who produced him a beautiful daughter.

Richard decided it was time to go. In the car on the way home, she told Richard what she thought, and Richard actually agreed with her, so the deal fell through, and Sam returned to France.

Greg, like every other script writer in LA thought this would have been his big break. He survived with a monthly stipend from Richard and lived illegally in a mobile home far up in the Malibu Hills, siphoning electric from neighbourhood mansions. That came to a sudden end after a big fire burnt down all the surrounding trees, exposing him. He moved in with his girlfriend until he started work on a movie where the company supplied him with a room for the duration, in Miami.

Richard was very draining, so Zoe took a few days off and flew to Mexico. She was enjoying herself so much, the few days turned into ten.

Arriving back from Mexico, Zoe was surprised to see a woman walking around the kitchen, helping herself to a drink. She was quite beautiful with her long black hair and blue eyes. Her figure complimented the skimpy bikini.

'Hello,' she said, 'You must be Zoe. My name is Maria.'

'Hello,' Zoe replied. *I wonder what happened to the last girlfriend.*

Richard appeared, also dressed for a swim in speedos, which few Americans ever wear. 'Hi, you're back. This is Maria. She'll be staying with me for a while so I thought this would be a suitable time for you to go and look after the Florida house.'

'With pleasure,' said Zoe, happy that she did not have to share a house with these two lovebirds.

'Great, I booked you a flight for tomorrow at 2 p.m. and a hotel room until all the furniture arrives.'

46

House sitting in Florida

For the first few days Zoe stayed in the Marriott Hotel in Fort Lauderdale. Richard's house was right by the beach and the famous Strip, as it was known in the US. It was a street filled with bars, clubs and restaurants. During spring break all the students from the universities would head there for about a four-week period of drunk and disorderly behaviour. They would cruise up and down the strip, trying to impress the bikini-clad females. The locals were all incredibly happy when those four weeks came to an end.

Zoe's main job in the Florida house was to take care of all the deliveries until the house was liveable. Luckily, Richard had let Zoe choose the furniture, so the place was looking very elegant.

She and Richard had discussed many times how he could help her get a green card, so a few days later he flew over alone and planned to see Alex, a friend of his, who was a lawyer. He was helping Richard to form a corporation, and Richard was willing to put in $100,000 to make it look like Zoe was an investor. However, when they met up with the immigration lawyer, he advised them that investing all that money would be risky as they would have to prove where it came from, and Richard wasn't willing to do that. *Did he acquire it illegally somehow?* The lawyer suggested marriage was another alternative. Zoe hoped neither of them saw her cringe when Richard made a joke about marrying her. Convenience marriage. Right, she didn't trust him that much, not after seeing all his girlie magazines and women's lingerie slung around his bedroom.

Richard flew back to California, so there wasn't much to do work-wise and lying on the beach every day was a little boring. Zoe took advantage of having the time and money so had some head shots done and trekked around to the various talent agencies. She enjoyed a few minor parts in commercials. It was easy work as the extras sat around all day waiting for the director to call on them. The extras were interesting individuals from all over the states, so Zoe was always entertained by their stories. Her most enjoyable time was when she got a bit part in *Police Academy 5*. The uniform was scratchy and the shoes a bit tight, but it still was fun. There wasn't a lot to do but as a special extra, she got paid much more than the other extras.

One day she went to a talent agency called *Rising Star.* Harry, the owner was a real character. He sat there eyeing her up twirling his moustache.

'Well, if you have nothing right now, here is my head shot. I must get going.'

'How would you like to work for me?'

'Doing what?' she asked suspiciously.

'The usual. Finding talent work, sending out head shots to casting agents.'

'Well.' Zoe hesitated, 'I'm not sure.'

'It pays well.'

Zoe thought, she was still getting paid from Richard, yet had plenty of spare time, so any extra money would give her a financial safety net.

He handed Zoe his business card. 'I need someone here soon as I have other stuff to do. Let me know.'

So, this is how it all started for Zoe. Show business was new to Florida and there were lots of opportunities, but Zoe was still an illegal immigrant. This was an incredible way for Zoe to dive into the world of show business, meet influential contacts, and get a firsthand look at how things really operated behind the scenes. It quickly became clear that success here wasn't always about what you knew, but who you knew. Connections were everything, and Zoe was determined to make the right ones.

Zoe took the job offer. Part of her role involved organizing auditions for the talent that were registered with Harry, setting up opportunities for actors, singers, and dancers to showcase their skills. Often, Zoe would tag along to observe the process—or even try out herself for small parts in commercials.

Eventually, business slowed down, so Harry closed the agency. Once again Zoe was at a loss. It was bad timing as Richard had decided to sell his two houses, so he could keep his sons and daughter in a lifestyle they were used to. He also had lost all his enthusiasm and ambition to be in the film business, and he started to get on Zoe's nerves. Her patience with him faded quickly. In the past they'd had many a wonderful conversation about every subject imaginable but never anything personal. He never expressed his personal thoughts with his own children, and she never saw him hug or kiss his daughter. He did soften up when his granddaughter Elise was around. However, he panicked when his daughter said she wanted to concentrate on her acting career and asked him to look after the granddaughter. She was a sweet kid but really spoilt.

Although Zoe was approaching thirty-seven, she felt a youthful energy coursing through her veins. Life had so much to offer, and she was determined to embrace every opportunity that came to her. For Zoe, staying busy and tackling challenges wasn't just a preference—it was essential to her sense of purpose. Yet, the most daunting challenge loomed ever-present: obtaining a green card. Without it, her dreams of working legally and building a secure life remained frustratingly out of reach.

Her journey with Richard had been an important chapter in her life. Together, they had navigated successes and setbacks, forming a bond that was equal parts professional and personal. But all good things eventually come to an end. When the time came, they parted ways amicably, sharing a heartfelt goodbye. Richard, ever the pragmatist, handed Zoe a generous bonus—a gesture of gratitude and respect for her contributions. With a reassuring smile, he told her, 'If you ever need help, don't hesitate to call.'

As Zoe watched him walk away, she felt a bittersweet mix of emotions. This was the end of one era, but perhaps the beginning of another. With the money order in hand, she was able to put down a deposit on a small flat.

Zoe was enjoying a drink with some friends when one of them directed her to a Cajun restaurant, where they were not too diligent about checking papers. She went for an interview and was hired immediately. Apparently, most of the staff were undocumented immigrants from all over the world. Zoe found it amusing that people assumed because she was English, she wouldn't have a problem getting a green card and would be eligible for free medical. Wrong! She laughed at this and told them she was just as illegal as the little Mexican cutting everyone's grass.

Zoe became good friends with the assistant manager Chris. He was incredibly attractive, blue eyes, blondish hair and suntanned, but was spoken for. His girlfriend Sandy would be arriving very soon.

One day Zoe came in a little early for her shift and the manager called her to his office.

His tanned face wrinkled, and he stood there looking at her.

'Well, what's up?' she asked.

'I'm sorry Zoe but there were two immigration officers in here looking for you.'

'What?' she stammered, 'How do they even know I exist.'

'Well, they seemed to know a little about you. Like having two passports.'

'Mmm. The only one who knew that, was a Canadian woman I had confided in. She was very disappointed that you didn't hire her, so she must have called Immigration for revenge.'

Zoe had to leave as she didn't want to be kicked out of the country or get the restaurant in trouble. *What do I do next?*

Zoe scoured the papers for ideas. A nanny. That's what most of the English girls do over here and it's easier to get a visa. She found a position that looked like she could manage. A ten-year-old boy and a twelve-year-old girl. She called and made an appointment for the following day.

Her appointment was for 2 p.m. and she arrived ten minutes early. She knocked on the door and a young boy answered. 'Daddy's not home but you can come in.'

'Thank you,' replied Zoe, but thought it better to wait until his father returned.

She sat outside in her white VW Bug listening to the radio. Twenty minutes passed and still no sign of the father. That's when she heard the ice cream truck. She was feeling a little hungry so went over to buy a vanilla cone. As she stood there, a bunch of children came running out from next door. Then a guy holding a young boy appeared.

'Zoe?'

'Chris, what are you doing here?'

'I live here. More like. What are you doing here?'

She explained everything, so he invited her in his house. She met his beautiful sister Andrea, her husband Barry, his brother Kevin, Kevin's daughter and four raucous children.

Barry was very upper-class English. The conversation eventually moved to the subject of immigration. He mentioned that Zoe could buy a green card, which would allow her to work legally, but that made her feel uncomfortable.

'You could get married,' said Barry.

'I tried that when I lived in West Palm Beach. I had a gay room mate who offered but drugs won him over. I don't know anyone here at the moment.'

'I'll marry you,' said Kevin.

47

Finally Legal

Zoe sat motionless above the excited chatter between Kevin and his sister Andrea. She didn't hear a thing. She felt dazed. *Did I want to go down that route. How long would I have to stay married? What if I met someone and fell in love. Right! But the way my life is going that idea seemed way out of reach.*

As the afternoon went by between the alcohol and weed Zoe felt buzzed and thought Kevin was joking. However, his sister Andrea kept insisting he wasn't and said it would keep his ex-wife off his back.

By 3 p.m., the man next door arrived home. Zoe took a deep breath and walked over for the interview, but within minutes, she knew it wasn't going well. The house was a disaster—clothes strewn across the furniture, dishes piled in the sink, and a strange, musty smell hanging in the air. She tried to focus, but her mind kept drifting back to what Kevin had said earlier.

'So, you have experience with this kind of work?' the man asked, scratching his chin.

Zoe blinked, realizing she hadn't been listening. 'Uh, yes.

Quite a bit,' she lied, as she knew she didn't want the job.

He nodded, glancing around the room as if noticing the mess for the first time. 'Well, the job's pretty simple. Just keeping things tidy, cooking now and then—'

Zoe barely heard him. She sat there like a dummy, nodding occasionally, but inside, her thoughts were elsewhere. Kevin's words echoed in her mind, making her stomach twist.

'You still interested?' the man asked, pulling her back to the moment.

'I'm sorry. I don't think this is for me. Thank you for seeing me.'

Back home she called Kevin and asked if he was serious. They met later that evening for dinner and found they had a lot in common. He was almost as handsome as his brother Chris. He was tall, also with blue eyes but he made Zoe laugh with his weird sense of humour. Back at his sister's house they had a long chat and a few drinks, so Zoe accepted his offer.

Zoe made sure that Kevin realised that this was purely a convenience marriage. Deep down she knew they would actually get along and even like each other more than friends. She thought about the Asians who often had arranged marriages, and they lasted.

Things happened quickly after that. Zoe felt she had been hit by a hurricane. They were married two weeks later, a few days before Valentine's Day. Of course, the wedding party all had a hit of weed before the ceremony. The notary who performed the ceremony made them go through all the vows...*til death do us part* etc. His voice was so loud, they all just cracked up and Zoe felt so hypocritical.

They went to the Cajun Restaurant where she used to work

and had a great dinner and were entertained by Barry's friend Tony, who happened to be a comedian from the UK. Zoe and Kevin had been given a room and a bottle of Champagne in a friend's hotel. However, they were so drunk and tired, they just crashed. The following day, Zoe was happy nothing untoward happened. They were hungover so went their separate ways but arranged to meet later.

As Kevin and Zoe got along well, they decided to live together. Unfortunately, he had no money or job, so they moved in with his sister Andrea, her four children and Chris and his girlfriend Sandy. Chaotic, to say the least. Being alone for so long, Zoe found it very strange having an instant family. Andrea was wonderful. She was beautiful and had a heart of gold. She was with the children most of the time as her husband (who was at least 20 years older) didn't have time for her or the children. Her husband, however, was an amazing artist and made enough money to keep the whole family in a decent lifestyle. When he wasn't painting, he drank wine, smoked cigarillos and played chess against a computer.

When Zoe left the house, Chris always made sure she had $5 or $10 in her pocket. The whole family looked after her and she could always depend on them, but she didn't want to lose touch with her independence.

Chris, Kevin's brother, and his girlfriend Sandy were married a few weeks later and stayed living in the same house. They were great with the children, considering what little discipline they were given.

Over time Zoe realised Kevin had fallen in love with her. She was fond of him, but he was not her soul mate, so when they parted, she hoped she could still be considered part of the family.

When it came to matters of the heart, deep down Zoe held onto an insecurity that she would get dumped. Her past relations were quite disastrous. A good friend said maybe she felt betrayed by the first man in her life, her father and that affected her from having a real relationship.

At least now she was legal. Her lawyer, Paula, had been a lifesaver guiding Zoe through the process of obtaining a green card. She even gave Zoe a generous discount after the family offered her two paintings as a gesture of gratitude.

The interview for Zoe's green card was nerve racking, yet Kevin kept his sense of humour. They were sent to separate rooms and asked all sort of questions. Later as Kevin sat with Zoe and drank a celebratory drink, they discussed the situation.

'When they asked me what drawer did I keep my socks in,' said Kevin, 'I told them I didn't know.'

'What!' said Zoe. 'That …'

'Don't fret,' he said laughing as he interrupted. 'I told them every time I get home, you have rearranged the furniture, so I never know where anything is.'

They burst out laughing. Zoe had to admit she loved rearranging the furniture, trying to find the best position. Their room in the house wasn't that big but very organized.

Zoe started work in the Holiday Inn as a cashier while Kevin unsuccessfully interviewed for several jobs. Luckily, they weren't expected to pay rent, just contribute to the groceries.

Kevin was fun and made her laugh but him not working got old, especially when Zoe was running up her credit cards buying his daughter, from his previous marriage, clothes, and shoes.

Except for this whirlwind marriage, Zoe felt her life was

boring. She just wasn't able to nail down a career, but the Green Card, she now had, would maybe solve this predicament. She could safely interview for legit jobs.

48

The Entertainment Industry

In the next year, Zoe worked many jobs, but none that excited her. The Holiday Inn, which was steady pay, the staff were all great and genuinely sad when she left. Then she was offered $7.25 an hour to work as a Captain in the private boxes, at the Miami Dolphin Stadium. It had just opened and was known as the Joe Robbie Stadium.

It was fun as she organised the runners and ordered food and drinks, which pleased her as she didn't have to do the actual running. Her rheumatic pains in various parts of her body were worsening. She worked long hours which suited her; Kevin had too many mood swings. She never knew what he would be like when she got home. She thought maybe he was bi-polar as he could be quite nasty some days.

At the end of the season, Richard called out of the blue and told her to get in touch with his sidekick, Greg. She thought Richard just kept him around as he felt sorry for him, but Greg could be very entertaining. Richard encouraged Greg to find Zoe a job as assistant bookkeeper on a low budget film. She was hired.

'She walked into the small office of a moderate priced hotel and introduced herself.

'Hi, my name is Zoe.'

'Hi, I'm Dennis and you'll be helping me. We don't have a use of a computer so it's the old-fashioned journal entry type accounting.'

'Well, that's okay. I'm not up to speed with computers and certainly not with any bookkeeping programme.'

The accountant was a stickler. His name was Dennis, and he was from Liverpool, but he did have a tremendous, sense of humour when it actually came time to socialise. His stipulations were: write all numbers the same size, slanting all the same way and finding every single penny that went missing. Zoe felt she earned every penny from the twelve-hour days and two hours travel time. The crew were great fun, and they all stuck up for each other as the producer, Maurice Smith was a real bastard.

Kevin's mood changed when the money was flowing. He was becoming very lazy and relying on Zoe to provide. The film lasted only three months with a budget of a million dollars. Zoe's bonus was $500, which was enough money to put down a deposit for a two-bedroom apartment, so she could finally leave Andrea's house. She did have a romantic notion to find a warehouse, similar to the one from Flash Dance, where she could live and run a business, but of course this was Florida, not New York. Florida homes did not even have basements. Andrea was kind enough to help her get organized along with Kevin's mother, who told her if she ever left Kevin, she should marry his brother Chip. Zoe thought one brother was enough.

Just being around Kevin had been a struggle for Zoe. Kevin could be a sweetheart, but Zoe couldn't see it lasting much longer. His moods, lack of communication and no ability to find or keep a job, drove her crazy. She also knew that she would enjoy California much better than Florida. She couldn't imagine Kevin living on his own. He couldn't even wake up in the morning without her help. However, a couple of days before and after a long conversation, he had decided to move in with his sister, 'Just until I get back on my feet.'

'Right, like that'll ever happen,' she murmured under her breath. He had no ambition, no drive—just empty words and wasted potential.

Zoe sat in her new apartment and pondered where she would get enough money to buy furniture, but as long as she had a bed and a desk, she would be fine.

At that time, Zoe also became interested in Buddhism and meditation helped a lot. There was a Buddhist temple close by and she befriended a monk called Lama Tenzin. The mantras were in Sanskrit, but the prayers had been translated to English. Lama Tenzin said a prayer for her, and from that moment, something shifted. She felt a newfound sense of calm, no longer fretting over the small things. Instead, she learned to trust the flow of life, letting the universe guide her in its own mysterious way.

When Kevin's ex-wife came by and asked for money, she found out that Kevin had an outstanding tax bill, so to prevent his ex reporting him, Zoe calmly paid the debt. In one way it helped as when she received her own tax refund, it was all hers, so she bought her first computer and opened up a consulting business. At first her main source of income came from upcoming actors who needed a puffed-out resume, which Zoe was good at.

Her first big client was a man called George Henry, who thought he was the new Hugh Heffner. He owned a couple of strip clubs but wanted some legitimate film work for his girls. Zoe had many contacts and found work for them right away. Some would be hosts at car and yacht shows, often showing off more than the products, and others worked as extras on films. Most of the girls were lovely and just trying to pay off debts. One day Starr, (obviously a stage name) who was her most reliable girl, invited her to the club to see them work. Reluctantly, Zoe went.

The neon lights bathed the strip club in a pink and blue haze, the bass of the music vibrated through Zoe's chest. She sipped her drink, perched on a bar stool at the edge of the room and looked around. *Was I the only female in the audience?* The talent on stage—one of her girls, moved with confidence, capturing the crowd's attention. Zoe admired her poise, drawn by the art in her movements more than anything else.

'Hey there,' a man drawled, sliding into her peripheral vision. His cologne was strong, a cheap mix of spice and something vaguely chemical. 'You look like you could use some company.'

Zoe turned her head slightly, her expression calm but distant. The man was older, his shirt half unbuttoned to reveal a chest that should've stayed hidden. His smirk was lopsided, a glint of sweat on his forehead.

'I'm good, thanks,' she replied, taking another sip of her drink.

He chuckled and leaned closer. 'Come on, no need to play

hard to get. You're here to have a good time, right? So why not let me make it better?'

Zoe set her glass down deliberately, her eyes locking onto his. 'Actually, I'm here to enjoy the show. Alone.'

The sleazy man raised his hands in mock surrender, his grin growing wider. 'Feisty. I like that.'

She sighed inwardly, resisting the urge to roll her eyes, she brushed past him and sat at a table closer to the stage.

But he followed, 'Look, I'm just saying, a beautiful woman like you.'

'She's not interested.' Two of her girls stood there defiantly. Behind them, a muscular black man loomed, his steely gaze unflinching and resolute.

The man stammered, his bravado crumbling 'I—uh, I was just—'

'Leaving,' Zoe finished for him, her voice calm but steely.

Muttering under his breath, the man shuffled off, casting one last glance at Zoe before he grudgingly left through the back door.

'Thanks girls,' said Zoe, 'I think it's time for me to go. I will call you tomorrow. I have another casting call for you.'

49

Human Trafficking

Zoe often hired dancers from the club, they were eager and reliable. But today, as she sifted through a stack of files, frustration bubbled over. Grabbing her phone, she dialled George at the club.

'George,' she began, exasperation evident in her tone, 'I'm trying to run a legitimate business here, but your paperwork system is a disaster. I need to come over and sort this out, at least for the girls I'm hiring today. The producer is a real stickler for paperwork.'

When Zoe arrived at the club, George gave Zoe carte blanche to sort out his files. Starr popped her head around the door, 'You busy?'

'Actually, yes. Do you need something?'

'No, I brought you a coffee.'

'Thanks. Here, file these for me,' Zoe said, handing over a stack of papers. Starr took them without hesitation and filed them quickly.

Zoe observed her, 'Starr, why do you work in a strip club?'

'It's good money and I need to pay for Uni.'

'Okay,' said a concerned Zoe. 'As long as you stop when you graduate.'

Starr looked at her good friend and said, 'I promise.'

George walked in, a cigarette dangling from his lips, the sharp smell trailing behind him. His puffy eyes and sluggish movements betrayed the telltale signs of a late night.

Zoe was going to hire a new girl called Xena. She was very beautiful, yet something about her seemed out of place—her shy, almost fearful demeanour, her reluctance to mingle with the other dancers.

'George, doesn't this strike you as strange?' Zoe asked, holding up the copy of Xena's documents.

He glanced over them with a raised brow. 'Strange how? Paperwork's messy sometimes. You know how these agencies are.'

'But look—her date of birth is different on the ID and the work permit; she's underage, and her photo...' She paused. 'I don't know. Something feels wrong.'

George waved dismissively. 'It's probably just a clerical error. I'll follow up if it's an issue. Don't lose sleep over it, Zoe.'

But Zoe couldn't let it go. Determined to find answers, Zoe approached Xena directly after her shift that night. The club had emptied out, the music silenced, leaving only the distant hum of the cleaning crew's vacuum.

'Hey, Xena,' Zoe called softly, catching the dancer on her way out. 'Do you have a minute?'

Xena hesitated, clutching her bag, 'Yes?'

Zoe offered a reassuring smile. 'I just wanted to check in. Are you doing okay? If there's anything you need, you can talk to me.'

'I'm fine,' she murmured, her voice barely above a whisper.

But Zoe pressed gently. 'Look, I know it's hard being new here. If there's something you're worried about—anything at all—I'm here to help. You can trust me. I wanted to hire you for this upcoming film, but I need to get your paperwork in order.'

'Thank you, I appreciate the offer.'

'Where are you originally from?'

Xena hesitated and whispered, 'Moldova.'

Zoe tried to make conversation about her family and what it was like living there, but Xena apologised and said, 'I'm sorry. I have to go.' She took off like a scared rabbit.

Zoe sensed the hesitation the moment she asked. Xena's expression had tightened, her gaze flickering away as if shielding something too personal to share. Moldova. That was all she had given—no details. Zoe didn't push, but curiosity gnawed at her. Was it painful memories that kept Xena silent? Or was it simply a past she had no desire to revisit? Either way, Zoe understood the need for distance. Some stories weren't meant to be told—not yet, maybe not ever.

The following evening, Zoe returned to the club, staying quietly in the office, her thoughts still on Xena. She needed to know—was there even a chance Xena would audition for the film? When she finally caught her alone and brought it up, Xena shook her head.

'I can't act,' she said simply. 'And I have to be home to look after my little sister.'

Zoe frowned, sensing there was more beneath the surface. 'Where's your mother?' she asked.

Xena's expression barely changed, but something in her

eyes flickered—pain, maybe, or just resignation. 'She's still in Moldova.'

That was all she said. No explanation, no emotion, just a quiet fact that left Zoe wondering what kind of life Xena had left behind—and why.

Zoe went to the club every night for a week, determined to get Xena to confide in her. She knew Xena wasn't an actor, but she would land a role—she was stunning, after all.

It was a quiet Tuesday, the perfect opportunity. Tonight, Zoe was determined to get Xena to open up. 'Hello Xena, how are you?'

'Good.'

'Come to the office with me.'

Once again, Zoe tried to persuade her to open up, but Xena remained guarded.

Xena turned to leave and then stopped and nervously looked around the quiet office.

'My real name is Elena,' she began, her voice trembling. 'I'm from a small town in Moldova. A man came there last year, offering me a job as a waitress in a restaurant here. He said it would change my life.' She paused, her hands shaking. 'But when I arrived, it was nothing like what he promised. His people took my passport. They said I had a debt to pay for the travel, the paperwork... everything. And if I didn't work for free...'

She trailed off, tears streaming down her face.

Zoe felt her stomach twist. 'You don't have to say more,' Zoe said gently, placing a hand on Elena's. I'll figure this out. I promise.'

Zoe knew she couldn't tackle this alone. She reached out to

Luca, a man with connections to the criminal underworld, but a code of honour. She trusted him but convincing him wasn't easy.

You're walking into dangerous territory, Zoe,' Luca warned, his arms crossed as they sat in a dimly lit café.

'I can't just look away, Luca. She's trapped. And there are probably more like her. You know these people—how they operate. I need your help.'

He sighed, rubbing the back of his neck. 'Fine. But if we do this, we do it carefully. No reckless heroics.'

Luca returned a couple of days later with a breakthrough. He had found a weak link—someone desperate to escape the organization. In exchange for money and a new passport, he had promised to gather the evidence he needed.

Their investigation uncovered forged documents, hidden ledgers, and a network of recruiters, enforcers, and corrupt officials. As the pieces fell into place, so did the risks. Threats emerged—an anonymous note was slipped under Zoe's door.

'Luca, I found this note slipped under my door. How do they know where I live?'

'They have their ways. Don't you have somewhere else to stay?'

Reluctantly, she called Kevin, and he said it would be okay to stay with him. Zoe was tired and left the club early to pick up a change of clothes from her apartment. Her eyes hurt. She couldn't look at one more piece of paper. As she walked through the courtyard, she thought she saw a shadowy figure lingering near her flat. She fumbled in her bag for her keys, the small, attached light casting a faint glow. As she approached, heart pounding, she realized the shadow had vanished. *Am I being paranoid? Am I imagining things? Or am I just tired?*

She enjoyed a peaceful night's sleep at Andrea's house. Kevin still hadn't moved out.

'You need to back off,' George warned her when she returned to the club. 'They're dangerous, Zoe. If you keep digging, they'll come for you.'

'I can't stop, George. Elena and others like her... They need us.'

Reluctantly, George joined the cause. 'Okay, I have a friend in the police force. Let me get hold of him.'

Once the police were involved, Zoe handed over all the evidence. Luca stayed out of the picture. Two weeks later there was a raid on the traffickers' main hideout.

Zoe's phone buzzed and she answered quickly.

'Hi, this is DCI Reynolds,' the voice on the other end said. 'The raid was successful. We may not have completely shut them down, but we've dismantled the local operations.'

Zoe was by Elena's side, holding her hand. 'You're safe now,' she whispered, tears in her eyes.

Zoe's determination, Luca's resourcefulness, and George's support proved that even in the face of overwhelming odds, hope and justice can be achieved.

Six months later, Xena was given a supporting role in an upcoming film.

(Today, human trafficking affects 50 million people worldwide, including 12 million children.)

50

The Oscars

Another client called Fred Smith wanted her to take over the coordination of his water products catalogue. She had a contact for a great photographer from the film shoot and hired some of the girls from the club to model in their swimsuits and produced a first-class catalogue.

Her next client was Jackson Marine, and they had an upcoming boat show, so once again she hired the girls and because the company was so pleased with her work, she received an invite to their private party on a large yacht. She made lots of new contacts and even an invitation to California. Her marriage was coming up to two years and she couldn't wait for that final interview with the immigration people. So maybe California was not that far off.

It was at that party where she met Scott. He was fun and they enjoyed each other's company. Zoe was attracted to him although he wasn't really her type. *But what is my type? The wrong type, which I have been choosing most of my life.* Scott was short, a little overweight with a thick head of black hair and piercing blue eyes.

Their relationship began to flourish although they lived 64 miles apart and it was the first time she ever cheated on Kevin. She told Scott about the situation, and he was very understanding. He paid attention to her, complimented her, kissed, and hugged her. Something she had missed for the last two years. There was something about him that was magnetic. His strong character, his sensitivity, and his passion for boats. The only thing was, at 28 he was the youngest person Zoe had ever dated, but their relationship lasted some time until Kevin became suspicious. Zoe received a card from Scott, which said, 'I'm here, you're there, one of us is in the wrong place.' This is when Zoe told him they would have to take a break until her situation changed, but deep down she knew she would be leaving to travel to California in the near future.

The next few months were exciting when Zoe started working with celebrity lookalikes. She had Bea Arthur, Hot lips and Radar from the TV show, Mash. George Burns, Jackie Collins, Burt Reynolds, Charles Bronson and even a Prince Charles.

When Zoe was out with Bea Arthur lookalike, the older generation would come and ask for autographs, so rather than disappoint them, she would tell them they were in a hurry but would return in about 30 minutes and then disappear.

On one occasion she went to see the play, "Run for your wife," starring David McCallum. She was with Roxy, another dancer from the club, and a dead ringer for Charles Bronson. Roxy claimed to know David and insisted they wait for him by the stage door. When he finally emerged, he pulled Roxy into a tight hug, whispering something in her ear that made her laugh. Then, with a playful grin, she introduced Zoe and the Bronson lookalike.

(The irony was that the real Charles Bronson had married David's ex-wife) Zoe was surprised when David suggested going to Denny's. The place was open 24 hours, and the Hollywood branch was especially lively, attracting all kinds of eccentric characters looking to indulge in a stack of pancakes drenched in maple syrup.

Zoe found it very funny when the waiter came to the table. He looked at the lookalike, who said, 'No I'm not the real Charles.' The the waiter looked at David, who said in a very posh accent, 'No, no, I'm not he. I get asked that all the time.' It was hard for Zoe and Roxy not to laugh.

Zoe loved working with the girls from the club and continued to find them gigs, but over time, the lack of a steady pay check and the endless string of empty promises from film companies wore her down.

A surprise call from Holly made her day. 'You're only a short flight away, so hop on a plane and come visit me tomorrow.'

'What's the hurry?'

'The Oscars.'

'Why? I have a friend who's having an Oscar party. He has a huge TV in his home.'

Holly laughed, 'No, we are going to the Oscars.'

'What?' said an excited Zoe.

'Well, sort of. I got a gig with a catering company. She needs two waitresses, so I signed us up.'

'Waitressing. Oh well, I just hope I don't spill a drink on anyone famous.'

Holly and Zoe stood in a bustling, sweltering kitchen backstage at the Oscars. The heat from industrial ovens and stoves created a sauna-like atmosphere, beads of sweat rolling down their faces as they juggled multiple tasks. The air was thick with the rich aroma of gourmet dishes being prepared—truffle-infused hors d'oeuvres, delicate soufflés, and perfectly seared cuts of meat; and of course, the vegetarian and vegan delights.

However, the waitressing gig was a misnomer; more like slaves in a hot kitchen.

Holly, with her blonde hair tied tightly into a bun, her chef's whites stained with smears of sauce, looked over at Zoe and whispers, 'Are you ready?'

Zoe also looking hot and frazzled whispered back, 'Yes, let's go.'

Holly and Zoe exchange a conspiratorial glance as they stepped out into a small party room. They entered the plush bathroom, their breaths quick and excited. They shoved the door closed behind them and locked it, ensuring their escape remained undetected.

Discarding their sweaty chef's whites, they tossed them into their bags with zero ceremony. Holly fumbled with the faucet, splashing cool water under her arms and across the back of her neck, her cheeks flushed from the heat of the kitchen and the thrill of rebellion. Zoe followed suit, using a paper towel to dab at her glowing skin.

Holly pulled out her dress—a midnight-blue number with tiny sequins. She grinned as she shook it out. 'I'm glad we brought the sparkly ones. They don't crease.'

Zoe chuckled softly, sliding into her own dress—a red cocktail gown that hugged her figure perfectly. 'Yeah, because nothing says, 'we totally didn't sneak in here' like showing up wrinkled,' she quipped, applying crimson lipstick to match her outfit.

A quick spritz of perfume and some hurried adjustments later, they stepped back to examine each other in the mirror. The transformation was dazzling. The two women who were sweating over stoves and dodging shouting chefs now looked like they'd been mingling with Hollywood royalty all evening.

With a final deep breath, Zoe unlocked the bathroom door and peeked out. The hum of conversation and clinking glasses welcomed them into the glamorous chaos. Holly grinned, her eyes sparkling as brightly as her dress. 'Ready to crash the Oscars?'

'Born ready,' Zoe replied, looping her arm through Holly's. Together, they slipped into the glittering crowd, seamlessly blending into the sea of elegance and champagne.

'Shhh! Don't shout,' said Holly pulling the blanket over her head.

'I brought you coffee,' said Zoe. 'I told you not to mix champagne with liquor.'

'Yeah, yeah. Right as always.' She sat up and took the coffee. 'It was fun though.'

'It sure was. I was standing right behind Michael Caine. I was really tempted to say, "Hello Mate" in my best cockney accent, but chickened out.'

'Yes, when mingling with celebs, you have to keep your cool and act if was a part of your normal life,' said Holly laughing.

Holly managed to recover and drove Zoe to the airport.

One day, while visiting George Henry's office, Zoe had an unexpected encounter. She was introduced to Fred and his wife, Maria, a dynamic duo in the film industry from California.

The couple made a lasting impression on Zoe from the start.

The conversation began casually but Zoe's intellect and charm captivated Fred and Maria, and the trio quickly hit it off, and what started as a chance meeting became an opportunity for some work.

Before long, Fred and Maria extended an invitation to join them in California to work in their film company. Encouraged and inspired, Zoe left the meeting with a sense of renewed purpose.

Zoe had had her final interview with immigration but was told that she had to stay married for the next two years. *Did they know the marriage wasn't real?* This was disappointing as she already had plans to move to California, without Kevin.

She would keep Andrea's address, so immigration would think she was still in Florida with Kevin. Fortunately, he didn't object. He actually understood when Zoe told him of her plans. 'We'll keep in touch.' she said.

Holly had finally responded to Zoe's long letter, in which she had shared details about her convenience marriage to Kevin coming to an unofficial end and the opportunity to move closer to her in California. But in an ironic twist, just as Zoe was considering the move, Holly was preparing to leave. She was heading to Phoenix, Arizona, where her lifelong dream had finally come true—she had been offered the chance to become a partner in a dance studio.

51

Hollywood

Zoe caught a taxi to Miami airport and boarded a plane for LAX airport. Unfortunately there was no first class available, but she managed to reserve a seat in row one. Almost six hours later, on arrival at the airport, a redheaded woman held up the crowd as she walked precariously down the steps in her expensive, Lucite high heeled shoes. She held onto the rail, her nails as long as tiger claws, lightly tapping as she descended. Not a strand of hair was out of place, while the rest of the passengers looked as it they had flown an international flight. Later the flight attendant at the gate informed her that it was Maureen O'Hara (70) who was known for many classic films, one being "Miracle on 34th Street"

Zoe's new friend Brooklyn, whom she had met at an industry event in Florida, came to pick her up. She had also moved there and lived in an apartment building in Hollywood and told Zoe of an available one bedroom. The move wasn't difficult – just a couple of suitcases and Richard, her ex-employer gave her some furniture. Zoe was also happy that she was only a short drive from Holly, who was living in a trendy area of West

Hollywood.

For Zoe's first evening out with Brooklyn, they headed to the local pub, the "Cat and the Fiddle". The place had a lively atmosphere, and rumour had it that it was a regular spot for people from the film industry.

This is where she met Saul, a writer. They hit it off right away. He was intelligent, talented and very witty. She was surprised when he told her he played hockey due to his slight frame.

'So, you just arrived here in sin city?' he asked.

'Yeah, I was offered a job, but it's only for a couple months.'

'Well, I'm working on a play and will need a reliable stage manager,' said Saul.

'Oh great,' said Zoe.

'I'll call you in a couple of weeks.' he said and handed her a business card.

Zoe wondered if that would happen as so far, she had experienced a lot of broken promises from people in the industry.

A few days later she arrived at a beautiful house in Laurel Canyon, where she was to begin work with Fred and Maria for the next few weeks. She walked in and there were people all over setting up lights etc. 'Over here Zoe,' called Maria.

She gave Zoe a long shopping list including many jars of Abalone cream, which is good moisturizer for the skin, and a credit card and sent her on her way. Zoe was totally new to California, so finding her way around was not easy. In fact, a trip which should have taken no more than an hour took her over two hours. She arrived back flustered, tired, and thirsty to a disgruntled Maria. 'Where the hell have you been?' she yelled at Zoe.

'I got lost.'

Maria grumbled and walked off.

In a way Zoe was glad, as when she had spoken about working on their film, they had informed her it was an adult film. Zoe was naive to think they meant PG13. No, it was a porn movie. Luckily with doing that errand, she had missed a lot of the sex scenes. She hadn't anticipated what unfolded over the next few days. The Abalone cream certainly came in handy with the actors, but the entire experience was unforgettable—for all the wrong reasons. Though she was paid well, Zoe knew she could never work with those people, or on that type of movie, ever again.

Not long after Zoe received a call from Saul. He was ready for a prop mistress and stage manager for his play. Once again, her evenings were consumed with rehearsals, but she loved it.

The play was a success, and the theatre was filled every evening for three weeks. When it finished, Saul introduced her to Giovanni and on his recommendation, Giovanni asked Zoe to work on his play, which he had written and directed.

After six weeks of intensive rehearsals, they opened to a full house. The investor of his play was his uncle who happened to be Joe Pesci. On opening night, he arrived escorting his mother and was pleased with the result. He made the effort to go backstage and thank all the actors and crew. The play made a huge profit, which was unusual for Hollywood, so Zoe received a decent pay check.

Working on the film and stage plays gave Zoe the taste of the industry, so when the play wrapped, she enrolled in Film School. Every student in class, except Justin Stills, son of Stephen Stills, wanted to be a director. Zoe was a good organizer, researcher and apt in the art of conversation which led her to believe she could be a good Producer. That never happened. The school was in trouble financially and Zoe was lucky enough to get her fee refunded.

A little later, she took another course in Script Supervising, with Shirley Ulmer, who was well known in the industry. Shirley Ulmer acted as script supervisor on nearly all of her director-husband Edgar G. Ulmers' films from 1934 on. She also wrote screenplays and a novel, "Sinners in Sight" (Empire Publishing, 1934). Her book "Script Supervisor's Role in Film and TV" was published by Hastings House. For over 20 years, she taught classes in script supervision and spoke at the many tributes and retrospective of her former husband.

After the course, Zoe did some work on student films. It wasn't a job she enjoyed following the director around like a puppy dog, so she decided to change paths and became a production assistant. She made a living from various commercials, but the entertainment industry was cut-throat and flaky. Each time she worked for someone, they complimented her, saying what a good job she had done, but never heard back from them. At the end of a student shoot, she got a call from a guy called Keith B. to be his production secretary for six weeks at $350 per week.

While working on his TV show called *Totally Hidden Video*, Zoe experienced a few hilarious and unforgettable moments. One particularly comical incident occurred during a segment involving a load of live chickens. Chaos ensued when the chickens unexpectedly escaped, scattering in every direction and causing pandemonium on set. The studio erupted into laughter as cast and crew, including Zoe, scrambled to corral the frantic birds. It was a scene straight out of a slapstick comedy. It was the best six weeks ever. But once again, time to move on.

What am I doing wrong? Why can't I be like everyone else and hold down a job that lasts longer than a few weeks or months? Is there something wrong with me? Am I just not cut out for stability, or am I simply choosing the wrong jobs?

Maybe the problem isn't me, but the fact that I haven't found the right fit yet. Maybe if I found a job that truly suited me—something I actually enjoyed, something that didn't drain me or make me feel trapped—I'd finally be able to stick with it. But what if the problem runs deeper than that? What if I'm just not meant to fit into this routine, this cycle of working, earning, and repeating the same thing every day?

I see people around me settling into careers, moving up, making progress. Meanwhile, I'm stuck in this endless loop of starting over. I tell myself, next time will be different, but it never is. What if I never find a job that feels right? What if I never feel at home anywhere?

Or maybe I'm just scared—scared of making the wrong choice, scared of getting stuck in something that doesn't make me happy. Maybe that fear is what's really holding me back.

52

East Berlin

Zoe sat quietly in a cozy café, sipping her coffee, when a loud voice with a distinct, boisterous public-school accent caught her attention. She looked up to see a rather handsome man, likely in his forties, ordering a cup of tea. With a smirk, she thought, *Good luck with that.* After all, the Americans hadn't quite mastered the art of a proper English brew, no matter how many attempts they made.

The man's confidence and charm piqued her interest, and she couldn't help but wonder what had brought him here.

As he passed by her, she smiled and said hello.

'Are you English?' he asked.

'Yes, but from the opposite end of the country to you.'

'That obvious?' he said laughing. 'May I join you?'

They settled into their seats, exchanging introductions. His name was Liam Brendan Murphy, but he definitely didn't sound Irish. He pointed out that he preferred to be called by his middle name. They chatted about all sorts of things—from the quirks of English culture to his work in the film industry. Well, *he* did most of the talking. Zoe listened, amused by his lively tales and sweeping gestures. As he carried on, Zoe found herself wondering if perhaps he didn't have anyone else to talk to, and she became a willing audience for his stories. But after an hour, she felt the need to escape the one-sided exchange. She offered a polite excuse and was ready to leave when he handed her a business card. 'Zoe, here's my card. Give me a call. We may be able to work together.'

'Okay thank you,' she said, wondering if he meant it. She glanced down at the card, "Silver Horizon Studios".

A week later, Zoe found herself at Brendan's office, a modest space in a nondescript building just off Hollywood Boulevard. It certainly didn't match the name on the business card. The card bore a different kind of promise—something bold and ambitious, maybe even pretentious. But standing here, looking at the cluttered office crammed into a small suite, she couldn't help but feel the disconnect. The room was small, with barely enough space for the essentials: a desk, two well-worn chairs, and a side table piled high with papers, scripts, and scattered notes. The place had a distinctly lived-in feel, reflecting both the busy and chaotic nature of the film industry.

Zoe took it all in, noticing the contrast between the man's charismatic demeanour and his unassuming workspace. She felt a twinge of curiosity about what brought him to such an unglamorous corner of Hollywood.

After two weeks she discovered Brendan was not an easy person to get along with, but Zoe found herself digging deep for the patience to work with him. His project—a documentary about Germany and the Holocaust—was both ambitious and emotionally heavy, demanding long hours and meticulous attention to detail. One of Zoe's major tasks involved travelling to East Berlin to review a series of films made by other filmmakers, selecting impactful excerpts to incorporate into Brendan's documentary.

Zoe arrived at Berlin Brandenburg Airport at noon to a fierce downpour. She caught a train to Potsdam, where she stayed with her Servas host, Klaus, a local photographer. Klaus also had another guest—a traveller from Mexico named Miguel.

The next day, the three of them visited Sanssouci, Potsdam's renowned historical palace and park. 'This was built as the summer retreat of Prussian King Frederick the Great,' Klaus explained, slipping into the role of tour guide. 'It's often regarded as Germany's answer to Versailles.' They enjoyed a late lunch and that evening, and before Klaus drove Zoe to meet her next hosts, they stopped at a phone shop so she could buy a phone card.

Her new hosts were kind, but noticeably traditional and conservative, seemingly uneasy with the changes brought about by the new regime. The location was far from Chronos, the archive studio where she had to look over some documentaries, so the owner of the company, a very sweet gentleman called Bengt, picked her up.

After watching just three or four films, the gravity of the footage began to weigh on her. Each story was more harrowing than the last, and the dark reality captured in those frames left her feeling emotionally drained. By the end of the day, she was barely able to shake off the sadness.

'Hi, how's it going?' Konstantin, the son of Bengt came in, holding a coffee for himself and one for Zoe.

'Phew! It's tough. I have to fight to keep back the tears.'

'Come on, take a break. I'll take you for a ride.'

A black Porsche Boxster sat waiting in the car park. 'This is it,' he said.

'Wow. It's beautiful.' Zoe walked around stroking it gently. Its low-slung body, sculpted side panels, and signature rear fenders give it an athletic stance, enhancing its sporty appearance. The interior had a luxurious yet minimalist cockpit. She slipped onto the soft, grey leather seat, just as Konstantin climbed in and revved the engine. In a flash, they were speeding down the street.

'Yikes, slow down!' she yelped, gripping the edge of her seat. 'I'd like to see the sights, not a blur of buildings!'

They passed the Berlin Wall Memorial on Bernauer Strasse, where remnants of the wall and a poignant outdoor exhibit captured the reality of the city's division. Nearby, the East Side Gallery—a long stretch of the wall transformed into an open-air gallery—displayed colourful murals by international artists, each expressing hope, resilience, and freedom. They headed to Alexanderplatz, East Berlin's bustling square, famous for its imposing TV Tower (Fernsehturm). Once a symbol of Soviet power, it now offered panoramic views of Berlin's sprawling landscape from the observation deck.

'There is so much more to see, but I have to get back to work,' said Konstantin.

'Yeah, so do I,' said Zoe, regretfully.

Zoe found herself unexpectedly off work the next day due to Germany's Unification Day holiday, commemorating seven years since the fall of the Berlin Wall. It was the perfect opportunity to join the city's spirited celebrations. Adding to the festive atmosphere, Berlin was also hosting the "Golden Lion Awards"—an event similar to the American Oscars, though with a more understated European flair. Coincidentally, Zoe came across the hotel where the festivities were being held.

Curious, Zoe slipped unseen into the hotel lobby. 'Champagne madame?' asked a smartly dressed waiter.

'Danke schön,' she replied, grabbing a glass of bubbly and continued to watch the parade of celebrities drift by. Although she didn't recognize any familiar faces, the thrill of being among the glamour was enough. She also overheard whispers that former U.S. President George H.W. Bush was in town, adding a touch of international intrigue to the evening.

Zoe's next Servas hosts were a young couple, Lukas and Petra, who lived with their daughter, Anke. They welcomed her warmly and took her to explore the local market.

'My goodness, the price of food is much higher than in the U.S., and there are not many clothing choices,' remarked Zoe.

'True, since the wall came down the cost of living has soared and our wages cannot keep up,' said Lukas.

Back at their home, Lukas and Petra prepared an elegant dinner of Duck à l'Orange, pairing it with a bottle of Châteauneuf-du-Pape. Zoe couldn't help but feel a pang of guilt; it was clear her hosts had gone out of their way—and likely spent generously—to make her feel welcome.

Back in the studio, Zoe pushed forward, determined to find the right pieces that would give depth and authenticity to Brendan's vision. Eventually, Zoe managed to pull together several clips that captured the essence of survival, resilience, and the haunting legacy of the Holocaust. Instead of the usual grim footage often portrayed in documentaries—scenes of skeletal bodies being thrown into mass graves—she discovered some lesser-known, yet deeply poignant, clips. These moments captured the resilience of survivors, the rare flashes of human connection, and the quiet strength of those who resisted in small but meaningful ways.

Through Servas, Zoe met a diverse array of people living in East Berlin, each at a different stage in life and with unique perspectives on the city's transformation. Members of the older generation often lamented the loss of the social benefits they had enjoyed before the Berlin Wall came down, while the younger crowd were happy and enthusiastic by the newfound freedom to travel and explore a world that was once off-limits.

Zoe was confident that Brendan would be pleased with her research. She had captured not only the contrasting sentiments of East Berliners but also highlighted the generational divide in how the city's history and changes were perceived—far exceeding his expectations.

Lukas kindly offered to drive Zoe to the airport, but it quickly turned into a stressful situation as part of the road had been dug up for construction, forcing them to navigate a diversion. Feeling a surge of panic, Lukas shouted to the workmen. Fortunately, when they realised they were trying to reach the airport, they allowed them to pass through, easing Zoe's anxiety.

Upon arriving at the airport, Zoe encountered another delay during check-in, and her heart raced as she feared she might miss her flight. Finally, once on the plane, a profound emptiness settled over her. She deeply missed the wonderful friends she had made during her travels and the vibrant atmosphere of Europe. The thought of flying to Los Angeles didn't feel as exciting as when she first arrived there. But, on second thoughts, while she cherished the memories of her time in Europe, she didn't miss the cold, damp weather that often accompanied it.

53

A Documentary

As soon as Zoe returned to Los Angeles, she dived into work with Brendan on their new project. Surprisingly, one of his first requests was for her to set up a DBA (Doing Business As) registration for their venture. Zoe couldn't believe he hadn't done it already, given how simple it was. But she quickly took care of it, and they got the wheels turning.

Over the next few weeks, the pace only intensified. Their network of friends—actors, voice-over artists, and musicians—were eager to contribute their skills. They joined the team without expecting upfront payment, trusting they'd be rewarded once the project was sold.

Brendan was thrilled with the footage Zoe brought from East Berlin, and the clips fit seamlessly into the documentary. Six months later, the project was complete. Now came the real challenge: Publicity.

Zoe was tapping away on the computer keyboard when a familiar voice said hello.

She swung round to see Holly standing there. 'Surprise,' said Holly.

'Oh my God, what a sight for sore eyes. Why didn't you tell me you were coming.'

'I wanted to surprise you.'

'You keep doing that.' Zoe jumped up and hugged her friend. 'Come on, I need a break. Let's get a coffee.'

Zoe asked her how the dance school was doing.

'It's closed for a couple of weeks. We are renovating it. That's good as I'm little tired. I want to relax for a while.'

'Are you not well?'

'I'm fine,' replied Holly. 'You know me, I get bored easily, and working for someone else is hard. We disagree on a lot of choices. I can't wait to own my own place.'

'So, what do you want to do now?'

'I want to help you.' said Holly.

'Great. It will give you time to think about your future. Now, let me tell you, Brendan is tough to work for, so you can give me the support I need,' said Zoe frustratingly.

They ordered more coffee and a couple of muffins. 'So, Brendan managed to pull off a cinema preview – and he didn't spend a penny,' said Zoe.

Holly's nose wrinkled, her lips pressing into a tight line as her eyebrows lifted, giving her a look that was halfway between disbelief and amusement, 'He certainly has a talent for accomplishing things without spending a dime.'

'Yeah. He got the theatre on board, free advertising, but I was the one who roped in that local restaurant for appetizers and drinks,' said Zoe.

Holly shook her head, 'Sounds like he could sell ice to an Eskimo.'

'Apparently, he convinced them it was perfect exposure for their upcoming screenings, so they loved idea.'

Holly laughed and said, 'How did he manage to get all those actors to do voice overs for free?'

'Don't ask. I have no idea. Must be his Irish roots; he's got the gift of the gab.'

'Maybe next time, he can pull off an all-expenses-paid vacation for you and me.' said Holly.

'With Brendan, that's probably not even a joke!'

Work had become so much more enjoyable now that Zoe had Holly by her side. Together, they shared little inside jokes about Brendan that kept them laughing and prevented him from getting under their skin.

Both Zoe and Holly thought the documentary dragged on, but Brendan was adamant he knew what he was doing. During the preview, they sat at the back of the theatre, watching the test audience, who seemed captivated at first. But then, as the film hit a natural pause, a few people began to clap, assuming it was the end—only to awkwardly stop once they realized it wasn't over yet. Zoe and Holly exchanged a look, stifling grins, as Brendan sat blissfully unaware of the subtle, unintended feedback. 'I knew that would happen,' Zoe whispered to Holly.

Brendan pitched his documentary to countless companies, but no one seemed interested. In Zoe's opinion, he came on too strong for a first-time filmmaker, making demands about retaining full rights that likely turned people off. And, with his posh English accent, he often sounded more arrogant than passionate.

Zoe could see the project was stalling, with no funding in sight. Eventually, Brendan was advised to transfer the film from 16mm to video to try and sell it to a company like Netflix. Once again, he somehow persuaded a company to do the work upfront, promising they'd be reimbursed once it sold. But the sale never happened, and the project lingered in limbo.

A couple of weeks later Holly met with Zoe. 'I decided to stay in Phoenix, so I bought a house and a partnership in a dance school.'

'What?' exclaimed Zoe.

'Yeah, Phoenix. It's just an hour's flight, so you can come visit anytime.'

What surprised Zoe most was that Holly buying a house meant she was, in some way, settling down. The thought of Holly—always the free spirit, constantly chasing new adventures—rooting herself somewhere felt oddly out of character. Zoe couldn't help but wonder if this meant a new chapter for Holly, one where spontaneity might take a back seat to stability. But of course owning a dance school had always been her dream.

Zoe hugged her friend goodbye, promising to visit soon. As she watched Holly drive off, reality set in—Zoe needed to find a job, as no money was coming in from the film company. Living off her savings wasn't an option; she'd worked too hard to build that safety net to let it dwindle away now. With a sigh she headed home, ready to start her search.

54

9/11 (2001)

The local newspaper featured an ad for a UK-based travel company called Gulliver's Travels, which was opening a new office in Los Angeles and looking for staff. Zoe applied and was hired as the manager of the hotel department—a perfect fit for her. She led a small team of four employees, all responsible for booking hotels in Los Angeles and Las Vegas for travellers from around the globe. One of the best perks of the job was being personally invited to visit the hotels, where she could tour the facilities and enjoy complimentary meals. It was an exciting opportunity that blended her love for travel with the chance to experience top-tier hospitality firsthand, all while leading a dynamic team.

One morning on her way to work, traffic was unusually light, so Zoe sat back to enjoy this phenomenon and listened to her classical music station, arriving at the office in record time. The car park was empty. She wondered if there was a public holiday that no one had told her about. Her boss sat in his office and was surprised to see her.

'Oh, I didn't expect anyone to come in due to the circumstances.'

'What circumstances?' she asked.

'The Twin Towers.'

'The what?' she asked.

That is the moment Zoe learnt about 9/11. Usually, Zoe only listened to classical stations while driving and never watched TV in the mornings, so she was completely in the dark. She didn't even know what the Twin Towers were but soon learnt. Her boss wanted her to stay.

'No way,' she said, 'There is a plane missing and we work right next to Los Angeles airport. I don't think it would be a wise idea,' She left and stayed home for the next three days watching the disaster on television. As a travel company it was obvious that business would no longer be continued as usual, so the office cut back on the staff.

Zoe was growing weary of Los Angeles. The glitz had long worn off, leaving behind a city that felt empty beneath its glamorous surface. People flitted in and out of her life as though on a whim, cancelling plans at the last minute or vanishing entirely when something—or someone—shinier caught their eye. The relentless gridlock only made it worse; sitting in bumper-to-bumper traffic for hours every day drained her spirit as much as her patience. And then there was Brendan, always broke, always reaching out with another story, another excuse, and yet another request for a "small loan" that she knew she'd never see again.

After one particularly frustrating day, she grabbed her phone and called Holly. 'I can't do this anymore,' she said without even a hello. 'I want out. I'm thinking of moving to Phoenix.'

Holly's response was instant, 'Oh my God, Zoe, you're going

to love it here! And guess what—there's a condo for sale in my complex. We could be neighbours!'

Holly's enthusiasm caused Zoe to smile. She had been to Phoenix a couple of times and knew how hot it could be, but warm nights, slower pace, and most of all, a fresh start—she suddenly felt this was meant to be.

Two months later, Zoe was sitting in her new house, two doors down from Holly. Zoe felt a surge of happiness; not only had she landed a job, but she'd also found the perfect place to call home. It was beautiful—polished wooden floors, two spacious bedrooms, and two bathrooms. The garden was alive with bright Bougainvillea, and a charming fountain added a gentle sound of trickling water that made everything feel peaceful. Her neighbours were warm and welcoming, and before long, she'd built a lovely social circle. Life felt brighter, more settled, and filled with possibility.

News came from Zoe's brother Jonathan that her mother wasn't doing too well. She was almost 92. It was time to make a visit. As Zoe sat on the train, memories of the day she left for London flooded back. The city she remembered had changed quite a bit. The train pulled into Newbury station early on that October afternoon. She had forgotten how cold it could be. Pulling her coat tightly around her cold body, she picked up her suitcase and called for a taxi. Although the sun was shining, the city still felt dark to her.

Zoe's long-time friend Dot offered her a place to stay. Dot would have picked Zoe up but didn't want to lose her parking spot. *What's the point of having a car*, she thought.

Shivering, Zoe climbed into the taxi while the driver put the suitcase in the boot. She gave him the address and he asked, 'Where a' ye from pet?'

Zoe laughed, 'I was born here, but have lived abroad for many years.'

'Eeh! You must be from the posh end of town. You don't sound like a local.'

Zoe smiled as she reflected on her upbringing. Despite growing up in the "not so posh end of town", she never developed a strong accent or spoke in dialect.

On arrival, Dot stood at her door to greet Zoe. She gave her a big hug and grabbed the suitcase, then climbed up the stairs to her flat.

'First things first,' said Dot, 'I'll put the kettle on for a lovely cuppa tea.'

Her mom was living in a care home and the carer's said her mother was quite frail. Zoe had arrived three days before her brother and after one night at Dot's she moved into a local B&B to be closer to her mother. The next morning, before entering her mother's room, she asked one of the staff how she was. 'Well, the last few days she has been sleeping more than usual.'

Zoe knocked on her mother's door. No answer. She opened the door slowly and saw her lying there. 'Hello mum. It's me. How are you?'

There was no answer. Zoe looked down at the frail figure lying beneath the thin sheets, watching as her mother's chest rose and fell in shallow, uneven breaths. She reached out and touched her shoulder, stirring her gently awake. Her mother's eyes fluttered open, unfocused at first, then slowly settling on Zoe's face. There was a flicker of recognition, but Zoe couldn't quite tell if it was relief or surprise. She managed a small smile, her hand still resting on her mother's shoulder, unsure if her presence was a comfort or a reminder of the time that they had argued.

Her mother sat up and they chatted. Zoe sat back and listened to a few moans about other people's children always being there for their mothers.

This is why I rarely visit you, Mum, Zoe thought, *because it always seems to end in arguments or complaints about me not being a good daughter.*

For three days Zoe was allowed to go in the kitchen and make cups of tea. She would bring her mother a cup and she'd take a sip, 'Agh it's too hot.' Her mother would take another sip of tea, only to complain a little later that it had grown too cold. So, Zoe spent much of her time making fresh cups of tea. On the third day, her mother seemed especially frail and didn't sit up as usual. She lay there with her eyes closed, motionless. Zoe sat beside the bed, gently holding her mother's hand, and softly spoke to her, telling her what a wonderful mother she had been—how she had raised Zoe and her brother all on her own. Though her mother didn't respond, Zoe knew she could hear her. Two quiet hours passed before Zoe felt her mother's hand go limp.

'Nurse come quickly,' yelled Zoe.

Zoe met her brother at the train station and they literally talked about funeral arrangements. He and Zoe would only be there a few more days. They knew mum wanted to be cremated and her ashes to be strewn across her favourite park. As most of her friends had already passed there wouldn't be too many invites to go out.

9/11 (2001)

An English funeral, no matter how grand or costly, still carries with it a sense of solemn pomp and traditional circumstance. The funeral director walked slowly in front of the hearse, top hat under his arm for a few feet and then joined the drive. Once again, a few yards from the crematorium; he exited the hearse and walked slowly in front until they reached the entrance.

Her brother recited a poem, and Zoe contributed a heartfelt piece of her own. There wasn't a dry eye in the room, and with Zoe having developed laryngitis, her voice added an unexpected touch of drama to the moment.

The *Blue Danube* played as the coffin entered the curtained off room. It was her mother's favourite music since visiting Zoe's brother Jonathan in Vienna. The curtains closed precisely as the music ended. The funeral director commended them, remarking on how well everything had come together in such a short time. The timing, he said, was flawless—something he had rarely seen executed so perfectly by any clergy.

55

Arizona

Back in Arizona, Zoe started her new job at U-Haul, a massive company that had offices in almost every state and offered many services: Customers could rent moving trucks or cargo vans for local or long-distance moves. They offered trailers and car dollies for towing vehicles or extra cargo. Secure storage spaces for rent. Boxes, packing materials, and other moving essentials, and installed hitches for towing trailers.

Holly had already been there for a year, so she could financially support her dance school. In the short time she had made a name for herself, moving up the ranks with a reputation for her sharp instincts and no-nonsense attitude.

Thankfully, having Holly there made the transition smoother for Zoe. Holly introduced her to coworkers, guided her through the endless corridors, and shared insider tips on everything from the best places to grab lunch nearby to handling the company's quirks and culture. For the first time in a long time, Zoe had solid ground beneath her feet—a fresh start, a stable job, and a friend who had her back.

Zoe felt as if she had stumbled upon a hidden gem. It wasn't just a job; it was an opportunity to reshape her career—and perhaps her life—in ways she had never expected. After years of searching for the perfect workplace, she wished she had discovered U-Haul earlier. It was a massive company, bustling with people, ideas, and—most importantly—opportunities for growth. Every six months, employees had the chance to switch departments, a concept Zoe found thrilling. No more stagnation or the dread of waking up to a job that had lost its charm. Instead, she could explore different roles without ever leaving the company. It was a dream come true for someone who craved variety but valued stability. it was also a good opportunity to improve her computer skills.

Zoe and Holly sat in the cafe one lunchtime. 'It's weird where life has taken us,' said Holly.

'I know,' said Zoe. 'Why did we get bored so easily? How many jobs have we had between us? Most people get a job and stay for forty years or more and then retire.'

Holly shook her head and laughed, 'I don't know. I guess we're just cut from a different cloth.'

But life, as it so often does, had other plans. One chilly morning, Zoe made her way to work when she noticed something was wrong. She wheezed as she walked, her chest tightening in a way that felt far from normal. With a sense of growing unease, she stopped by the emergency room. She expected a quick visit—a prescription, maybe some advice on exercise or diet—but what she got was far more serious. After a whirlwind of tests, Zoe was diagnosed with Atrial Fibrillation, (an irregular heartbeat). Her quick trip turned into a six-day hospital stay, during which the weight of the diagnosis began to sink in. Both her knees were hurting, but she decided just to deal with one problem at this time.

That wasn't the only shock. Upon leaving the hospital, Zoe realized that her health insurance hadn't yet kicked in. She was left staring down an astronomical hospital bill of sixty thousand dollars. Despite years of hard work and careful saving, her nest egg fell far short of covering the staggering bill. Like countless other Americans trapped in a flawed system, she was eventually forced into bankruptcy.

After another week of sick leave, Zoe returned to work and was offered the option to work from home. Though she knew she'd miss the daily interactions with her colleagues—even with the chat group keeping them connected—the chance to ease the pain in her knees was too important to pass up.

Six months passed, and during that time, her health insurance finally came into effect. But by then, another challenge had arisen: her knees had deteriorated to the point where surgery was unavoidable. She underwent surgery for two knee replacements in the following six months. As she lay in recovery, Zoe began to reflect on her journey.

In the span of ten years, Zoe thrived. She worked in eight different departments, mastering new skills, meeting new people, and keeping her professional life as interesting as ever. From logistics to customer service, then onto project management and marketing, she found each role brought something new to her world. U-Haul had become more than just a company; it was a playground of possibilities, for the last few years of her working life.

But now, after health battles, she started to question what she wanted from the future. The vibrant, fast-paced life at U-Haul had been thrilling, but it had also been exhausting. Maybe, she thought, it was time for a simpler life. After much reflection, Zoe decided it was time to retire. But the question remained: where to go? She toyed with the idea of Mexico, Belize, or South America, but after a long chat with her brother Jonathan, who lived in Vienna, she chose to retire in the UK.

As Zoe had become quite proficient with computers, navigating various programs and social media platforms, she found herself browsing Facebook one day when she came across her ex-husband, Kevin. Curious, she messaged him, but when he didn't respond, she reached out to his sister, Andrea, her former sister-in-law. To Zoe's surprise, Andrea replied and revealed that she had left the U.S. and was now living in a picturesque town called Fowey (pronounced Foy) in Cornwall. Intrigued, Zoe paid her a visit. On her return, she immediately put her house up for sale. She was thrilled that the price had doubled and soon had an interested party.

However, an unexpected snag was revealed: a $10,000 lien on her house. Stunned, Zoe immediately called her lawyer, who informed her that the lien was from "Silver Horizon Studios." Her heart sank as the realization hit her. Brendan. He hadn't "taken care of it" like he'd promised months ago. All those reassurances, the casual way he'd waved off her concerns—she'd been foolish to believe him.

Anger simmered beneath her embarrassment. She should have followed up, should have pressed harder, maybe even filed a claim for forgery when she first noticed the suspicious signature on that paperwork. But now it was too late. The only way forward was to pay off the lien herself—a bitter pill to swallow. She knew the money was gone, as good as if she'd handed it to Brendan directly.

She contacted him and he said he would pay her back a small

sum each month. After two months the payments stopped. 'When I sell my film, I will pay you back,' he said without embarrassment. The film was never sold!

Six months later, she packed up her life in America and moved to Cornwall. She traded the fast-paced corporate world for the rolling green hills and tranquil lifestyle she had long craved. She hoped one day, Holly would make the same decision. Maybe they both could look forward to more exciting adventures.

Zoe's journey wasn't just one of exciting adventures; it was a testament to resilience, reinvention, and the wisdom to embrace new chapters. In the end, the greatest adventure often lies not in what we accomplish, but in recognizing when it's time to rest and start anew.

56

About the Author

The Red Sea (1975)

In the past, Anna Alcott had her articles and short stories published in various magazines. But in 2023, she took a big step and published her first novel, *Mexican Interlude*, which is available on Amazon.

A few years ago, she began writing her memoir. However, she soon realised that memoirs by non-famous individuals often go unread. Instead of abandoning the project, she reimagined it as a work of fiction, bringing her story to life in a new way and "The Adventures of Zoe Hunter," was created. (Names have been changed to protect both the innocent and the guilty.)

The question is: What is truth and what is fiction?

(Cover Design: SelfPubBookCovers.com/litberry)

For more information: www.annaalcott.com

Printed by Amazon Italia Logistica S.r.l.
Torrazza Piemonte (TO), Italy